Essays on
Social Protection in India

Including Social Security, Social Protection Floor, Social Safety Net and Social Audit

Vol. I

R K A Subrahmanya

SHIPRA

₹ 1500; US$ 60
ISBN: 978-93-86262-83-7

First Published in India in 2019

Essays on Social Protection in India: Including Social Security, Social Protection Floor, Social Safety Net and Social Audit

Published by:
SHIPRA PUBLICATIONS
LG 18-19, Pankaj Central Market
I.P. Ext., Patparganj, Delhi 110092, India
Tel.: +91 11 2223 5152/6152
E-mail: info@shiprapublication.com
www.shiprapublication.com

Foreword

Social Security coverage to workers in a country that is primarily informal in nature is a basic requirement for securing a decent living condition. Such a provision not only checks the 'race to the bottom' by strengthening workers' bargaining power to demand legitimate wages as also decent workplace conditions. It was in this background that the Constitution of India, under Article 41 calls on the States to extent "…..public assistance in cases of unemployment, old age, sickness and disablement, and in other cases of undeserved want." Again in Article 42, it desires that "the State shall make provisions for securing just and humane conditions of work and maternity relief."

The Constitution of India, on placing Social Security in its Concurrent List, has empowered both the Central and State legislators to enact law. Consequently, a large number of laws have been enacted on the subject of social security. Incidentally, these include fifteen laws enacted by the Parliament, e.g. The Workmen Compensation Act, 1923; The Employees State Insurance Act, 1948; The Employees' Provident Funds and Miscellaneous Provisions Act, 1952; The Maternity Benefit Act, 1961; The Payment of Gratuity Act, 1972; The Building and Other Construction Workers Cess Act, 1996; The Unorganized Workers' Social Security Act, 2008; etc.

India, therefore, is committed to extending social security coverage to the citizens of India. Social security has, as such, occupied central position in the social policy formulation in India. Accordingly, during the seven decades of independence, Indian social policy makers have devoted a lot of energies towards securing social security for all in India. Unfortunately, till date there is no social security system that covers all in India. The existing legislations as also social security schemes/programs are primarily focused towards workers in the formal sector. However, the majority of the workers in the formal as also informal sectors remain uncovered by the existing schemes. This gaps in government's intensions and realities at the ground level has been highlighted by various studies including the one by the 2nd National Commission on Labour and National Commission on Enterprises in the unorganised sector.

Currently, the Central Ministry of Labour and Employment is engaged in bringing about reforms in labour laws so as to enhance its coverage as also effectiveness. The proposed Labour Code on Social Security is in an advance stage of making. The Government is also hoping to establish Social Protection Floors as the recommendation of the International Labour Organisation's Recommendation 202 adopted in 2012. India is also passing through a rapid period of transformation, particularly in the manufacturing, wherein the interests of workers are going to be negatively influenced.

In this background, the vast knowledge and experience of Mr. R K A Subramanya, former Additional Secretary (Labour), Government of India and founder Secretary General of the Social Security Association of India, New Delhi would prove helpful in making delivery of the social security benefits easier. We have been collaborating ever since 1992 to see how the Indian social security system is reformulated so as to bring in universal approach to the social security coverage. Mr. Subramanya's contributions to the study of Social Security system in India is unparallel. His publications and presentations during various educational programs have made contributions in enhancing understanding of the purpose of the social security system.

This volume containing chapters on various aspects of social security system in India, backed by author's vast experiences of ground level conditions. His extensive interaction with workers' representative's as also at the SSAI has given suggestions that would prove useful for an emerging market which will be highly informal in nature. The book will also prove useful towards achieving targets proposed under the UN's Sustainable Goals, ILO's Future of Work and India's aim of creating additional decent job for a very large working population.

Pravin Sinha, *Ph. D.*
Secretary General, Social Security Association of India, New Delhi; &
President, National Labour Laws Association, New Delhi

Preface

A Workshop was held on Social Security under the UNDP sponsored Research Project on Strategies and Financing of Human Development at the Indira Gandhi Institute for Development Research, Mumbai in December 1993. One of the background papers placed before the Workshop was Survey on Social Security in the Unorganized Sector in India by T. S. Sankaran. In this paper the author had suggested inter alia that the Ministry of Labour should bring out a report on the status of Social Security in India periodically in collaboration with the Ministry of Welfare. The Workshop considered this suggestion and recommended a stocktaking of the Social Security situation in India.

The Social Security Association of India took up these suggestions and submitted a proposal to the Ministry of Labour for carrying out a stocktaking of Social Protection Schemes in India. The proposal was approved and the Government agreed to fund the project. The project was started in April 1996 and it was to be completed within two years. The report was submitted to government. There is no information on what action was taken on the report.

It is nearly twenty years since that report was submitted. It is felt that it is high time to update the information contained in the report. In this book an attempt has been made to update that report.

As the resources available for updating the report were limited the scope of the report has also been limited. I hope that if the readers find it interesting and useful, they will support a further effort to enlarge it.

Contents

1
Food and Nutrition Security

Food security is one of the major components of social security. It consists of ensuring that "food is available at all times, that all persons have means of access to it, that it is nutritionally adequate in terms of quantity, quality and variety and that it is acceptable within the given culture". There are three elements in this definition: availability, access and stability. In recent years, nutrition is considered as part of food security so that it is called "Food and Nutrition Security".

According to the Human Development Report, 1994, Food Security means that all people at all times have both physical and economic access to food. This requires not just enough food to go round. It requires that people have ready access to food — that they have entitlement to food, by growing it for themselves, by buying it or by taking advantage of a public distribution system. The availability of food is thus a necessary condition of security — but not a sufficient one. People can still starve even when enough food is available — as has happened during many famines.

The overall availability of food in the world is not a problem. Even in developing countries per capita food production increased by 8 per cent on an average in the 1980s. And there is enough food to offer everyone in the world around 2,500 calories a day — 200 calories more than the basic minimum.

But this does not mean that everyone has enough to eat. The problem often is the poor distribution of food and a lack of purchasing power. In South Asia 30 per cent of babies born are underweight. This is the highest ratio for any region in the world and a sad indication of inadequate access to food, particularly for women, who are often the last to eat in the household.

Access to food comes from access to assets, work and an assured income. And unless the question of assets, employment and income security is tackled, the problem of food insecurity cannot be solved.

Starvation amidst Plenty — The Bengal Famine of 1943

Famines are commonly thought of as Nature's revenge on hapless humanity. Although Nature can certainly create local food shortages, human beings turn these shortages into widespread famines. People go hungry not because food is unavailable, but because they cannot afford it.

The Bengal Famine of 1943 shows why between two to three million lives were lost, even though there was no overall shortage of food. In fact, the per capita supply of food grains in 1943 was 9 per cent higher than in 1941.

The famine was partly a product of an economic boom. Sudden increases in war-related activities exerted powerful inflationary pressures on the economy and caused food prices to rise. In the urban areas, those with work could pay these prices. But in the rural areas, agricultural labourers and other workers found they could no longer afford to eat, and thousands headed for the cities, particularly Calcutta (now Kolkata), in the hope of survival. Prices were then driven even higher by speculation and panic buying.

The famine could probably have been averted by timely Government action. But the Colonial Government did nothing to stop hoarding by producers, traders and consumers. The general policy was "wait and see". Relief work was totally inadequate and the distribution of food grains to the rural areas was inefficient. Even in October 1943, with 100,000 sick and destitute people on the streets of Calcutta, the Government continued to deny the existence of a famine. The result was one of the largest man-made catastrophes of our time.

Public Distribution System

The Government became wiser after the event. It has since introduced a Public Distribution System, which has successfully prevented the occurrence of a large-scale famine after independence.

The Public Distribution System (PDS) is the instrument through which Government seeks to ensure food security at the household level.

Under the PDS, the Central Government has assumed responsibility for procurement and supply of essential commodities. The commodities are made available at fixed issue prices involving heavy subsidies.

The total amount of food subsidy incurred by the Central Government in 1996-97 was Rs. 6,066 crore. It has since gone up to Rs. 1,34,988 crore (2017-18). In terms of money it represents the largest outlay on social security.

India has become more or less self-sufficient in food since the seventies. But the distribution is uneven and, therefore, there are pockets of scarcity and starvation.

Several studies have been conducted into the working of the PDS in India. The general conclusion appears to be that the PDS is highly differentiated across States and that its coverage is very limited except in Kerala and a few other States. In other words, PDS is not reaching the vast majority of the population. Madura Swaminathan has taken the extreme view that "the PDS has failed in large parts of the country and that it needs to be restructured to be an effective tool of food security. Large number of poor are excluded from the PDS. The quantities supplied are generally inadequate and prices have risen rapidly in recent years. In many States there is large scale diversion of grains, wastage, low quality and unreliability of provisioning".

It is, however, acknowledged that the system of PDS is working very well in the Southern States, especially Kerala. According to Madura Swaminathan, Kerala has the most effective Public Distribution System in the country.

The National Commission on Rural Labour had recommended that the PDS should be re-oriented to target directly the poorer sections and that food items should be supplied through the PDS to hungry families only. Accordingly, a targeted PDS was introduced. But not all States have accepted this principle. While targeted populations are supplied specified quantities of food grains at specially subsidised prices, the benefit of the PDS has not been withdrawn for the other classes of people with the result the burden of food subsidy is growing.

Some States are providing additional subsidies in supplying food grains to the poor people over and above what the Central Government provides. These moves appear to be politically motivated. They are announced at the time of elections and modified thereafter.

There is an obvious need for rationalisation of the whole system of the PDS.

The government has enacted a law called National Food Security Act (NFSA), 2013 to ensure Food Security. The *Economic Survey* for 2014-15 has described it as follows:

> "As passed by the Parliament, Government has notified the National Food Security Act, 2013 on 10th September, 2013 with the objective to provide for food and nutritional security in human life cycle approach, by ensuring access to adequate quantity of quality food at affordable prices to people to live a life with dignity. The Act provides for coverage of up to 75 per cent of the rural population and up to 50 per cent of the urban population for receiving subsidized foodgrains under Targeted Public Distribution System (TPDS), thus covering about two-thirds of the population. The eligible persons will be entitled to receive 5 Kgs of foodgrains per person per month at subsidised prices of Rs. 3/2/1 per Kg for rice/wheat/coarse grains. The existing Antyodaya Anna Yojana (AAY) households, which constitute the poorest of the poor, will continue to receive 35 Kgs of foodgrains per household per month."

> "The Act also has a special focus on the nutritional support to women and children. Besides meal to pregnant women and lactating mothers during pregnancy and six months after the child birth, such women will also be entitled to receive maternity benefit of not less than Rs. 6,000. Children up to 14 years of age will be entitled to nutritious meals as per the prescribed nutritional standards. In case of non-supply of entitled foodgrains or meals, the beneficiaries will receive food security allowance. The Act also contains provisions for setting up of grievance redressal mechanism at the District and State levels. Separate provisions have also been made in the Act for ensuring transparency and accountability."

Food Subsidy

Provision of minimum nutritional support to the poor through subsidised foodgrains and ensuring price stability in different States are the twin objectives of the food security system. In fulfilling its obligation towards distributive justice, the government incurs food subsidy. The programme covers over 65 million BPL households serviced through 4,50,000 fair price shops. While the economic cost of wheat and rice has continuously gone up, the issue price has been kept unchanged since 1 July 2002. On account of implementation of the NFSA, the CIP has further gone down for the APL and BPL categories. The government, therefore, continues to provide large and growing amounts of subsidy on foodgrains for distribution under the TPDS/NFSA and other nutrition-based welfare schemes and open market operations. The food subsidy bill has increased substantially in the past few years putting severe strain on the public exchequer (Table 1.1).

Table 1.1: Quantum of Subsidy

Year	*Amount (In crore)*
2010-11	62929
2012-13	84554
2013-14	89740
2014-15	113171
2015-16	134919
2016-17	105672
2017-18	134988

(Source: *Economic Survey 2017-18*)

Per capita Calorie Intake

Per capita calorie intake in India grew marginally for the first time in 30 years i.e. from 1980 to 2010, new official data shows, and protein intake grew for the first time in over a decade.

The National Sample Survey Office's (NSSO) 2011-12 data on Nutritional Intake was released which shows that per capita calorie consumption rose to 2099 kilocalories per day in rural areas and 2058 kilo calories per day in urban areas. Both numbers are still below a Planning Commission benchmark of 2,400 kilo calories per day.

But the proportion of acutely under-nourished people seems to be declining; the proportion of Indians who get less than 80 per cent of the recommended nutritional intake has declined to under one in five in rural areas.

The implications of this change are, however, unclear. For one, India's most developed States have the lowest average calorie consumption, pointing to the fact that higher calorie intake may not be a direct predictor of well-being. While Kerala, Tamil Nadu and Maharashtra saw slight increases in their per capita calorie consumption between 2009-10 and 2011-12, the number fell in rural Gujarat.

Karnataka's per capita income is nearly twice that of Jharkhand, but both have nearly the same average calorie consumption in rural areas. Calorie consumption does rise steadily with family incomes, however, in both rural and urban India. The top five per cent of rural Indians consume double the calories as the bottom five per cent.

Economists Angus Deaton and Jean Dreze noted in a 2009 *Economic and Political Weekly* article that calorie intake had declined in a period of rising incomes, and a possible explanation could be lower levels of physical activity.

These possible explanations apart, the Indian population undoubtedly suffered from severe nutritional deficits, they said, of this "puzzle".

The share of cereals in total calorie intake has steadily declined, the data shows, and is down to just over 60 per cent in rural Indian and 50 per cent in rural India. The share of meats and dairy has grown only slightly, while the share of oils and fats has grown sharply.

While protein intake has grown on average, there are mixed trends among States. Protein intake fell in Bihar, Gujarat, Haryana and Rajasthan, but rose in Kerala, Andhra Pradesh and Tamil Nadu.[1] *The Hindu* 28 Dec 2014

Social Floor for Food Security

Concept of Social Floor

A social floor, also called a social minimum, is the concept that there is baseline level of social services and human rights to which every human being should have access. A social floor encompasses a system of social protection, or a social safety net, that would create a minimum "bundle of resources that a person needs in order to lead a minimally decent life in their society". The purpose of a social floor is to "prevent people from falling into destitution".

Components of a Social Floor

A social floor is the resources and services that every member of a society should have access to. Varying points of view exist on which services and resources should be included in the social minimum. The widely-accepted definition of a Social Protection Floor, as defined by the International Labour Organization (ILO) and the United Nations (UN), includes the following four guarantees:

1. Universal access to basic healthcare
2. Child/family benefits: guaranteed income security for children
3. Social assistance for the poor and unemployed
4. Guaranteed income security for the elderly and disabled

Recommendation of ILO

The ILO has recently adopted a recommendation concerning social floor to provide guidance to Member States. The recommendation lays down inter alia that the social protection floors should comprise certain basic social security guarantees including access to a nationally defined set of goods and services.

Food Security

The World Food Summit of 1996 defined food security as existing "when all people at all times have access to sufficient, safe, nutritious food to maintain a healthy and active life". Commonly, the concept of food security is defined as including both physical and economic access to food that meets people's dietary needs as well as their food preferences.

So defined food security may be construed as falling under basic income security required to be provided under the ILO recommendation concerning social floors.

Food Security in India: Public Distribution System

The objective of the Government Food Security Policy is to ensure availability of food grains to the public at an affordable price. The Public Distribution System (PDS) has over the years become an important instrument of Government Policy for regulating the open market prices of essential commodities and for ensuring food security at the household level.

Under the PDS, the Central Government has assumed responsibility for procurement and supply of essential commodities, viz. wheat, rice, levy sugar, imported edible oils, kerosene and soft coke to the State Governments and the Union Territories for distribution at almost uniform and affordable prices to the public. These commodities are made available to the States/ UTs at fixed Central Issue Prices which are determined by the Central Government and generally involve subsidies borne by the Central Government. Some States/ UTs also distribute additional items of main consumption through the PDS outlets.

The implementation of the PDS is the joint responsibility of the Central and the State Governments/ UT Administrations. The Central Government is responsible for procuring the commodities, storing and transporting the PDS items up to the Central godowns and making them available to the States. The responsibility for actual distribution to consumers and administration of the PDS is entirely that of the State Governments/ UT Administrations.

The allocation of PDS commodities among the States/ UTs is decided on by a Committee headed by the Secretary of the Ministry of Food and Civil Supplies.

The total number of fair price shops in the country as reported by States and Union Territories as on 30.06.2011 was 505,879. Each FPS is expected to serve a population of about 2000.

Different States have issued different types of cards like white cards, green cards, saffron cards, etc., to provide concessional food grains. Increased emphasis has been laid in the past few years on improving the reach of the PDS to remote, far flung and inaccessible areas. Mobile fair price shops/ vans are pressed into service in these areas.

Central Issue Prices

PDS commodities are issued to all States/ UTs at uniform Central Issue Prices which generally involve subsidies borne by the Central Government. These prices are fixed after taking into account the Minimum Support Prices and interest charges at the prescribed rates of interest. The Central issue prices of food grains for Revamped Public Distribution System (RPDS) area is Rs. 50 per quintal lower than the Central Issue Prices of food grains for normal public distribution system areas. In the case of other items like sugar, kerosene, soft coke and imported edible oils, the cost of procurement/ production, margins to dealers, transportation, incidentals, etc., are included while working out the Central Issue Prices.

The Central Government supplies PDS items in bulk. The State Governments/ UT Administrations fix the retail prices after taking into account margins for wholesalers/ retailers, transportation charges, levies, local taxes, etc., which may vary from item to item and State to State. The States/ UTs have been advised not to add more than 25 paise per kg over the CIP for RPDS areas while fixing the retail prices. However, in the case of sugar, the retail prices are fixed by the Ministry of Food, Consumer Affairs and Public Distribution.

Revamped Public Distribution System

A programme of Revamped PDS was launched in January 1992 to improve the reach of the PDS to far-flung, hilly, remote and inaccessible areas where a substantial section of the people live. This programme covers about 1700 blocks including the areas covered by Drought-prone Area Programme, Integrated Tribal Development Projects, Desert Development Programmes and certain Designated Hill Areas. These areas are identified in consultation with the State Governments/UT Administrations. Under this scheme, additional items like tea, soap, pulses and iodised salt are also supplied to the households located in the selected areas.

Targeted Public Distribution System

The Public Distribution System (PDS) is the major instrument of government's economic policy for enhancing food security to the poor. Under the PDS the Central Government bears the responsibility for the procurement and supply of five commodities, viz., rice, wheat, sugar, imported edible oils and kerosene to the States and Union Territories. Some States add a few more commodities for distribution under PDS. The States/ UTs arrange distribution of PDS commodities to the consumers through a network of about 4.5 lakh retail outlets or Fair Price Shops

PDS is operated under the joint responsibility of the Central and State governments, with the former responsible for procurement, storage, transportation (up to the district headquarters) and bulk allocation of foodgrains. The State governments are responsible for distributing these foodgrains to consumers through a network of Fair Price Shops. This responsibility includes identification of families below poverty line (BPL), issue of BPL cards, and supervision and monitoring of the functioning of the Fair Price Shops. States are also responsible for movement of foodgrains from the district headquarters to the PDS shop, which requires storage at the sub-district level. As food was always a non-plan subject, such an infrastructure is often weak in the northern States.

Until 1992, the PDS had universal targeting, being available to all consumers. GoI introduced a revamped PDS (RPDS) in 1992 in limited areas, primarily drought prone, tribal and hilly, and remotely located. The RPDS was a purely location targeted scheme, being available to all in the selected area. This has been substituted in 1997 by the Targeted PDS (TPDS), specifically aimed at BPL people in all parts of the country. State-wise BPL quota is fixed on the basis of the adjusted poverty share determined by the Planning Commission based on official poverty lines in 1993-94, adjusted for growth in population in the interim. There would have been two implications, if the 1999-00 survey was used as the basis for determining the number of eligible households in each State. First, poorer States would have got higher allocation (but these States have poor capacity for lifting), and a very large number of poor people would have lost their status as BPL in States where poverty has sharply declined (Andhra, Tamil Nadu, etc.).

Under TPDS each poor family was entitled to 10 kg of foodgrains per month at specially subsidised prices. The allocation of foodgrains for the BPL families was increased to 20 kg w.e.f. April, 2000, and to 25 kg per family per month with effect from July, 2001. It was further increased to 35 kg in 2003-04, which corresponds to 84 kg per annum per unit, taking the average size of family as five. The central issue price for wheat and rice has remained unchanged since April 2000.

In accordance with the provisions of TPDS guidelines, any requirement from States over and above TPDS quotas, can be met subject to availability of foodgrains in the Central Pool and at the rates commercially viable to FCI. The additional allocation of rice and wheat were at economic cost from June 1997 to November 1997.

Antyodaya

According to the National Sample Survey, about 5 per cent of the total population in the country sleeps without two square meals a day. This section of the population can be called as “hungry”. In order to make TPDS more focused and targeted towards this category of population, the “Antyodaya Anna Yojana” (AAY) was launched in December, 2000 for one crore poorest of the poor families. AAY contemplates providing them foodgrains at a highly subsidised rate of Rs. 2 per kg for wheat and Rs. 3 per kg for rice. The States/ UTs are required to bear the distribution cost, including margin to dealers and retailers as well as the transportation cost. Thus, the entire food subsidy is being passed on to the consumers under the scheme. The scale of issue that was initially 25 kg per family per month has been increased to 35 kg per family per month with effect from 1 April 2002. The AAY Scheme has been expanded in stages each time by 50 lakh households; in 2003-2004, August, 2004 and the third in May, 2005, thus bringing the total number of beneficiaries to 2.5 crore households, which is about 38 per cent of the BPL households.

Procurement of Foodgrains

Procurement of foodgrains is one of the essential aspects of the food security policy of the government. It serves the objective of providing price security to the farmers which induces them to sustain production levels besides meeting the government's objective of PDS as an instrument to protect the vulnerable sections against price volatility. Procurement prices are based on support prices announced by the government. The Central government maintains food stocks commensurate with the requirements of: (i) the prescribed minimum buffer stock for food security, (ii) operational stock for monthly releases of foodgrains for supply through the PDS, and (iii) market intervention stock for release in the open market to help moderate the open market prices.

The procurement operations of wheat, paddy and coarse grains are totally voluntary. The producers have the option to sell their produce to FCI/ State agencies at support prices or in the open market whichever is advantageous to them. Rice is collected by way of statutory levy on rice millers and rice dealers. The percentage of levy is fixed by the State governments with the approval of Central Government. Procurement of rice depends on the quantum of paddy milled by the rice millers/ dealers. Therefore, no targets for procurement of foodgrains can be fixed

Food Subsidies

The Central Issue Prices for the PDS are lower than the procurement prices. These prices were not revised for three years from February 1994 to February 1997 although the procurement prices were revised annually. Under the RPDS food grains are supplied at prices lower than the Central Issue Prices by Rs. 50 per quintal. People below the poverty line are supplied 10 kg of rice per month at half the normal issue prices. The difference between the procurement prices and the issue prices constitutes the food subsidy which is borne by the Central Government.

Subsidy on foodgrains borne by the Central Government has been rising progressively over the years. Food subsidy was Rs. 2,850 crore in 1991-92. It rose to Rs. 9,000 crore (BE) in 1998-99. It was nearly Rs. 65,000 crore in 2012-13.

The widening gap between economic cost of FCI (for procurement, storage, distribution, storage, etc.) and the FCI's average realisation based on the issue prices of PDS is bridged by the Central Government through consumer subsidy. It has been a regular practice in the past to adjust the PDS issue price of rice and wheat consequent on the increase in the MSP. However, the issue price was not changed after February 1994. In fact, from June, 1997 the issue prices were actually lowered for the BPL population thus widening the gap between the MSP (and consequent economic cost of FCI) and the issue price. The issue prices have remained unchanged since 2002.

State Schemes

Some of the States have their own more liberal schemes of food supply. For instance, Karnataka has recently introduced a scheme under which rice is supplied at highly subsidised prices of Re. 1 per kg to persons below the poverty line. There are similar schemes in AP, Kerala and Tamil Nadu

Working of Public Distribution System in Kerala

The establishment of an effective PDS was the outcome of a strong people's movement for food. Rationing was first introduced during the Second World War. The government action came in response to the food crisis of 1942-43 and public demand for action. Large sections of the population, including women, joined the struggle for food. Kerala was the first State where rural rationing was established.

Although begun in the 1940s the expansion of the PDS took place in the mid-1960s. In 1964, there was an acute shortage of food in Kerala; prices rose sharply and there was a statewide people's protest movement. The Central Government agreed to supply Kerala with an adequate quantity of food for the PDS. The demand for food and, specifically, for distribution of cheap foodgrains through ration shops was an important political demand raised by the Left in Kerala and even the Congress Government at the Centre agreed to support the policies and demands of the Government of Kerala. The political demand for food reflected in mass protests and struggles was thus critical in establishing and strengthening the PDS.

In Kerala, the rationing system is almost universal. All the families that do not produce foodgrains adequate to meet their consumption requirement are eligible for a ration card. In practice, about 90 per cent of households possessed ration cards in 1991. The network of ration shops is well developed with one shop for every 389 households. The Kerala Government has an additional chain of stores that sell a wide range of consumer goods at regulated prices.

The new ration subsidy scheme for those falling under the poverty line was implemented in the State with effect from 1 June 1997. They would get 10 kg of rice at half the Central issue price. The Central issue price was raised for those who are above the poverty line but the State Government decided to continue with the subsidy scheme for those sections also.

After the introduction of the Targeted PDS Scheme, the Central subsidy would be available only for 25 per cent of 60 lakh ration card holders. The State

Government extended the benefit to an additional 15 per cent families as per the IRDP and Urban Poverty Alleviation Programme lists thus raising the limit to 40 per cent. The task of identifying the actual beneficiaries has been handed over to the Panchayat Raj institutions.

Each family under the poverty line would get a subsidy of Rs. 36 for the 10 kg of rice while those not falling under this category would get a benefit of Rs. 16 because of the Re. 1 State subsidy. 42 per cent of the ration card holders get 16 kg of rice at a subsidy of Re. 1 per kg Each kg would then cost Rs. 6.50 only. This would be in addition to the 10 kg of rice being provided under the Central subsidy at a price of Rs. 3.90 a kg.

Card holders with incomes above the poverty line would get 16 kg of rice at a subsidised price of Rs. 6.50. They have to pay Rs. 7.50 a kg for additional quantities.

Tamil Nadu—Public Distribution System

The Public Distribution System in Tamil Nadu is a success story, in its coverage as well as its pricing. Each family, whether below the poverty line or not, is entitled to 20 kg of rice at Re. 1 a kg. The State Government opted for universal coverage for both practical and good political reasons. Effective targeting of Below Poverty Line (BPL) families was felt to be an administratively difficult task and there was a genuine risk of the people most in need of food security being left out. The State is now deservedly held up as a model for effective implementation of a comprehensive food security system.

When the DMK Government took office in 2006, one of its first steps was to supply rice through the PDS for Rs. 2 a kg. This was a key election promise of the party. In September, 2008, the PDS price was reduced to Re.1 a kg of rice.

From May, 2007, in addition to rice, kerosene, and sugar, Tamil Nadu has been issuing wheat, wheat products, pulses and palmolive oil to cardholders — under the Special Public Distribution System. It is the only State to do so.

At present, the monthly offtake of rice under the PDS is 317,000 tonnes, though the Central allotment is only 296,000 tonnes (supplied at Rs. 5.65 a kg). The additional quantity of rice needed is being met from the open market sales scheme (OMSS) allotment by the Food Corporation of India and also from other State Civil Supplies Corporations (the price ranges from Rs. 11.50 to Rs. 15.70 a kg). In the case of sugar, the requirement is of the order of 33,055 tonnes as against the Central allotment of 10,832 tonnes. As the Central allotment is not sufficient to meet the demand from cardholders, the State is purchasing sugar from the open market at the prevailing rates. By streamlining the distribution, Tamil Nadu is able to meet the demand of kerosene to a certain extent. Moreover, distribution of free LPG connections has helped bring down the offtake of kerosene in the PDS.

By selling rice and other commodities at prices much lower than the price fixed by the Central Government, the State Government has been incurring substantial expenditure by way of food subsidy. From Rs. 734.85 crore during 2003-04, the subsidy increased to Rs. 1,017.78 crore in 2004-05, Rs. 1,559.64 crore in 2005-06, Rs. 1,833.02 crore in 2006-07, Rs. 1,961.06 crore in 2007-08, and Rs. 2,795.85 crore in 2008-09. During 2009-10, Tamil Nadu had to enhance the subsidy to Rs. 4,000 crore. This was because it had to provide for an increased offtake of rice over and above the Central pool allocation, and also for the purchase of sugar and pulses from the open market. The allocation for 2000-11 is pegged at Rs. 3,750 crore as there is an expectation that the market prices of sugar and pulses will come down.

The success of the scheme in Tamil Nadu relies heavily on groundwork. The mammoth task of minimising diversion and reaching 317,000 tonnes of rice to more than 1.97 crore cardholders who draw ration from about 31,439 outlets in 32 districts (including the newly formed Ariyalur and Tiruppur) involves technological interventions, drawing up innovative fool-proof delivery mechanisms, old-fashioned policing, surprise checks and constant reviews, and fixing responsibility at each level.

The movement of stock from the 310 warehouses across the State to the PDS outlets begin from the 20th of the preceding month (August 20 for September, for instance). By the end of the month, 60 per cent of stocks for the next month reach the PDS outlets. By the 5th of the month of issue, the whole quota reaches the shops. At any given point of time, Tamil Nadu maintains six months' supply of rice, wheat, and other commodities in its warehouses. The movement from the warehouses to the PDS outlets is through trucks — which are tightly controlled by route charts. The charts display the route the truck has to adhere to, details of commodities it carries, and the shop to which the goods are to be delivered. Any elected representative or government official who notices any deviation from the route is authorised to check the vehicle and report to the nearest police station.

Control rooms have been opened in all districts, including in Chennai, to receive information on diversion of PDS commodities. As a trial measure, a GPS-based vehicle movement monitoring system has been implemented in Thiruvallur and Krishnagiri districts to track the movement of vehicles carrying PDS goods. Similarly, the State Government has introduced an online godown monitoring system for enabling online capture of all transactions in warehouses in a phased manner. To prevent mass diversion of goods by lorry drivers, every vehicle is accompanied by a department assistant who is provided with a special SIM card attached to a BSNL tower and through this the movement of the vehicle can be tracked from the control room in the Civil Supplies Corporation.

Further, SMS-based fair price shop stock monitoring has been set up by the Cooperative Department to track the stock of every commodity at each fair price shop on a daily basis. This enables officials to identify stock levels at each shop every day and move stocks swiftly as needed. Under the present network, it is possible to identify a shop that may be involved in diversion of stocks by keeping tabs on sudden increases in rice offtake in a month. When there is an abnormal increase in the offtake, vigilance teams swing into action to find out whether the increased offtake is genuine or bogus.

Handheld billing machines with a GPRS connection have been installed in all fair price shops in Chennai to enable real time monitoring of sales and stocks. A usual complaint of cardholders is short measurement and to avoid this fair price shops are being supplied electronic weighing machines. In the present setup, cardholders can register their complaints against the shopkeeper through an online service.

A majority of fair price shops in the State are run by the Cooperative Department. In fact, Tamil Nadu is the only State where fair price outlets are run either by the Government or by its agencies. This system has proved to be advantageous since the wholesaler is a government corporation and all the retail shops are either Government-run cooperatives or under the control of the Civil Supplies Department. Most shops run on a loss. The Government routinely provides about Rs. 300 crore as subsidy to run the Cooperative shops (to cover establishment costs, wages, etc.).

Despite these measures, some shop keepers indulge in malpractices; and where these are discovered, criminal prosecution is launched against them. Similarly, vehicle permits and driving licences are cancelled if the vehicles and drivers are found indulging in the diversion of commodities.

For the universal PDS across the State, the going has been good so far. The concern is that with the United Progressive Alliance Government set to prescribe 35 kg of rice or wheat a month at BPL prices for each Below Poverty Line family and also set to bar Above Poverty Line families from accessing rice or wheat at subsidised rates at PDS outlets, Tamil Nadu's subsidy burden will rise hugely.[1]

Chhattisgarh's Food for Thought

The nation should note that over the past few years, the State of Chhattisgarh has scripted a remarkable, but largely unnoticed, PDS turn-around. Thanks to its governance reforms, this "Chhattisgarh model" of PDS reforms continues to win admiration among policymakers.

The reform was initiated in 2003 after the Supreme Court Commissioners' office and the Right to Food Campaign reported, through detailed surveys, the wide-ranging corruption in foodgrain distribution. One key reason for this leakage was the privatisation of the FPS network. In 2001, the government had added almost 5,000 private traders as FPS dealers, ostensibly to increase the outreach of the PDS. In reality, this was a cynical move to extend political patronage — local elite invariably ran the FPSs. The first reform, then, was to cancel all private FPS dealers in a single stroke and hand them over to cooperative societies, *panchayats*, women's self-help groups and other public bodies.

After the initial euphoria of de-privatisation, it became apparent that more drastic changes were required. FPSs depended on private transporters to get grains into the shops. The State food and civil supplies corporation undertook the doorstep delivery of foodgrains to each of the shops. Chhattisgarh also used its own finances to increase FPS commissions fourfold, allocating Rs. 40 crore to recapitalise all the shops — their working capital needs could then be met without their having to pilfer foodgrains to make up the deficit.

In 2007, grass-roots surveys by the Right to Food Campaign brought out a startling fact. Though rice was now reaching the shops, the poor's access to the subsidised rice remained limited. Only 1.9 million families were listed as being below the poverty line (BPL): The Union government released foodgrains only for these households. The state government decided to double the number of households which were receiving foodgrains, also reducing the rate at which rice was sold to the BPL households to Rs. 3 per kg. Chief minister Raman Singh launched the Chief Minister's Food Security Scheme and made it his government's flagship programme.

Simultaneously, state-wide drives were undertaken to eliminate nearly 300,000 bogus ration cards. All the 3.7 million ration cards were reprinted centrally through the creation of a database, which allowed both photo identifications and bar codes. As an additional measure of transparency, each BPL household had its details painted on the house, the entire list of card-holders prominently painted on the *panchayat* building too.

To curb leakages during transportation, all the trucks carrying PDS commodities were painted in bright yellow colour: consumers could alert the food department in case this truck was found unloading foodgrains at any location other than FPSs. Global positioning systems were installed in the trucks as well. That was not the only good use of technology: the government used SMSes to alert those who registered for this service to the quantity of foodgrains and the registration number of the truck carrying it. A toll-free helpline was set up to receive and, more importantly, redress complaints.

Chhattisgarh made an annual fiscal commitment of close to Rs. 1,800 crore for this programme and enforced a zero-tolerance policy on corruption. A number of senior officials from the State food and civil supplies corporation were booked under the Essential Commodities Act, with arrest warrants issued against them. This had a salutary effect in reducing corruption: the latest survey by the Right to Food Campaign in a sample of 650 villages (excluding the Naxal-affected pockets in south Bastar and Dantewada) showed that 92 per cent of respondents received their full quota of foodgrains; 96 per cent had their ration cards in their possession (compared with 58 per cent in 2004); 97 per cent of the respondents were satisfied with the food quality.

Many States have subsidised rice schemes for the BPL households. The only difference Chhattisgarh made was to add the highest level of political commitment.

If politics is all about numbers, the evidence from this State is clinching. In Parliamentary and Assembly elections, in which the Bharatiya Janata Party won, many a seasoned political commentator felt that it was paddy rather than the lotus that seemed to have bloomed here. First, an expanded PDS, with universal or near-universal coverage, stands a much better chance of succeeding rather than one driven by minimalist BPL quotas. A scheme only for the very poor will always remain a very poor scheme. Second, privatisation that just strengthens the local elite should be done away with; instead, it is government machinery that should be strengthened. Third, a majority of leakages occur much before the foodgrains reach FPSs: An excessive focus on the "last mile", with solutions such as smart cards and unique IDs, will change little on the ground.

Fourth, political will and good governance need to translate into specific reform steps. You know you have it when you are willing to prosecute offenders without fear or favour and you commit your best human resources to strengthen a programme. As the last general election showed, the States (Odisha, Chhattisgarh, Tamil Nadu and Andhra Pradesh) where political parties successfully managed to break the anti-incumbency factor, had expanded their PDS. What greater incentive can there be for reforms than success at the polls?[2]

The National Food Security Act, 2013

The Indian National Food Security Act, 2013 (also Right to Food Act), was signed into law on September 12, 2013, retroactive to July 5, 2013. This law aims to provide subsidised food grains to approximately two thirds of India's 1.2 billion people. Under the provisions of the bill, beneficiaries are to be able to purchase five kilograms per eligible person per month of cereals at the following prices:

- rice at Rs. 3 per kg
- wheat at Rs. 2 per kg
- coarse grains (millet) at Re. 1 per kg

Pregnant women, lactating mothers, and certain categories of children are eligible for daily free meals. The bill has been highly controversial. It was introduced into India's Parliament in December 2012, promulgated as a Presidential Ordinance on July 5, 2013, and enacted into law in August 2013

Salient Features

1. 75 per cent rural and 50 per cent of the urban population are entitled for three years from enactment to five kg food grains per month at Rs. 3, Rs. 2, Re. 1 per kg for rice, wheat and coarse grains (millet), respectively;
2. The states are responsible for determining eligibility;
3. Pregnant women and lactating mothers are entitled to a nutritious "take home ration" of 600 calories and a maternity benefit of at least Rs. 6,000 for six months;

4. Children who are 6 months to 14 years of age are to receive free hot meals or "take home rations";
5. The central government will provide funds to States in case of short supplies of food grains;
6. The current food grain allocation of the States will be protected by the central government for at least six months;
7. The State government will provide a food security allowance to the beneficiaries in case of non-supply of food grains;
8. The Public Distribution System is to be reformed;
9. The eldest woman in the household, 18 years or above, is the head of the household for the issuance of the ration card;
10. There will be state- and district-level redress mechanisms;
11. State Food Commissions will be formed for implementation and monitoring of the provisions of the Act;
12. The cost of the implementation is estimated to be Rs. 1.25 lakh crore, approximately 1.5 per cent of GDP; and
13. The poorest who are covered under the Antyodaya yojna will remain entitled to the 35 kg of grains allotted to them under the mentioned scheme.

Intent

The intent of the National Food Security Bill is spelled out in the Lok Sabha committee report, *The National Food Security Bill, 2011, Twenty Seventh Report*, which states, "Food security means availability of sufficient foodgrains to meet the domestic demand as well as access, at the individual level, to adequate quantities of food at affordable prices." The report adds, "The proposed legislation marks a paradigm shift in addressing the problem of food security — from the current welfare approach to a right based approach. About two thirds (approx 67 per cent) of the population will be entitled to receive subsidised foodgrains under Targeted Public Distribution System. In a country where almost 40 per cent of children are undernourished the importance of the scheme increases significantly."

Scope

The Indian Ministry of Agriculture's Commission on Agricultural Costs and Prices (CACP) has referred to the Bill as the "biggest ever experiment in the world for distributing highly subsidised food by any government through a 'rights based' approach." The Bill extends coverage of the Targeted Public Distribution System, India's principal domestic food aid programme, to two thirds of the population, or approximately 820 million people. Initially, the Lok Sabha Standing Committee on Food, Consumer Affairs and Public Distribution estimated a "total requirement of foodgrains, as per the Bill would be 61.55 million [metric] tons in 2012-13." The CACP calculated in May 2013, "... the requirement for average monthly PDS offtake is calculated as 2.3 mt for wheat (27.6 mt annually) and 2.8 mt for rice (33.6 mt annually)...." When volumes needed for the Public Distribution System and "Other Welfare Schemes" were aggregated, the CACP estimated rice and wheat requirements to total an "annual requirement of 61.2 million metric tons." However, the final version of the Bill signed into law includes on page 18 an annex, "Schedule IV", which estimates the total food grain allocation as 54.926 million metric tons.

The Standing Committee estimated that the value of additional food subsidies (i.e., on top of the existing Public Distribution System) "during 2012-13 works out to be . . . Rs. 2,409 crores," that is, 24.09 billion rupees, for a total expenditure of 1.122 trillion rupees. However, the Commission on Agricultural Costs and Prices (CACP) calculated, "Currently, the economic cost of FCI for acquiring, storing and distributing foodgrains is about 40 per cent more than the procurement price," the Commission added,

The stated expenditure of Rs. 1,20,000 crore annually in NFSB is merely the tip of the iceberg. To support the system and the welfare schemes, additional expenditure is needed for the envisaged administrative set up, scaling up of operations, enhancement of production, investments for storage, movement, processing and market infrastructure, etc. The existing Food Security Complex of Procurement, Stocking and Distribution — which NFSB perpetuates — would increase the operational expenditure of the Scheme given its creaking infrastructure, leakages and inefficient governance.

The Commission concluded that the total bill for implementation of the Bill ".... may touch an expenditure of anywhere between Rs. 125,000 to 150,000 crore," i.e., 1.25 to 1.5 trillion rupees.

Critics

Criticism of the National Food Security Bill includes accusations of both political motivation and fiscal irresponsibility. One senior opposition politician, Murli Manohar Joshi, went so far as to describe the bill as a measure for "vote security" (for the ruling government coalition) rather than food security. Another political figure, Mulayam Singh Yadav, declared, "It is clearly being brought for elections... Why didn't you bring this bill earlier when poor people were dying because of hunger?...Every election, you bring up a measure. There is nothing for the poor."

The report of the 33rd meeting of the Technical Advisory Committee on Monetary Policy stated, "...Food prices are still elevated and the food security bill will aggravate food price inflation as it will tilt supply towards cereals and away from other farm produce (proteins), which will raise food prices further... Members desired that the Reserve Bank impress on the government the need to address supply side constraints which are causing inflationary pressure, especially on the food front."

Dr. Surjit S. Bhalla warned, "The food security bill...if implemented honestly, will cost three per cent of the GDP in its very first year."

The writer Vivek Kaul noted, the government's estimated cost of food security comes at 11.10 per cent...of the total receipts. The CACP's estimated cost of food security comes at 21.5 per cent...of the total receipts. Bhalla's cost of food security comes at around 28 per cent of the total receipts...Once we express the cost of food security as a percentage of the total estimated receipts of the government, during the current financial year, we see how huge the cost of food security really is. The Indian Ministry of Agriculture's Commission on Agricultural Costs and Prices warned that enactment of the Bill could be expected to "induce severe imbalance in the production of oilseeds and pulses," and "...will create demand pressures, which will inevitably spill over to market prices of food grains. Furthermore, the higher food subsidy burden on the budget will raise the fiscal deficit, exacerbating macro level inflationary pressures." The Commission argued further that the Bill would restrict private initiative in agriculture, reduce competition in the marketplace due to government domination of the grain market, shift money from investments in agriculture to subsidies, and continue focus on cereals production when shifts in consumer demand patterns indicate a need to focus more on protein, fruits and vegetables.

Advocates

The bill was widely viewed as a "pet project" of Indian National Congress President Sonia Gandhi. Gandhi addressed Parliament on the night of the August, 2013 Lok Sabha to vote on the bill, saying its passage would be a "chance to make history".

Former National Advisory Council member and development economist Professor Jean Drèze, reputedly one of the architects of the original, 2011 version of the bill, wrote, "...the Bill is a form of investment in human capital. It will bring some security in people's lives and make it easier for them to meet their basic needs, protect their health, educate their children, and take risks." Professor Drèze dismissed opposition from business interests, saying, "Corporate hostility does not tell us anything except that the Food Bill does not serve corporate interests. Nobody is claiming that it does, nor is that the purpose of the Bill."

Minister of Consumer Affairs, Food, and Public Distribution K.V. Thomas stated in an interview,

> "This is no mean task, a task being accomplished in the second most populated country in the world. All the while, it has been a satisfying journey. The responsibility is not just of the Central Government but equally of the States/ Union Territories. I am sure together we can fulfill this dream. The day is not far off, when India will be known the world over for this important step towards eradication of hunger, malnutrition and resultant poverty.... By providing food security to 75 per cent of the rural and 50 per cent of the urban population with focus on nutritional needs of children, pregnant and lactating women, the National Food Security Bill will revolutionise food distribution system."

In a rebuttal to Dr. Surjit S. Bhalla, three economists responded, "... the food subsidy bill should roughly double and come to around 1.35 per cent of GDP, which is still way less than the numbers he put out."

Identifying the Problems

Sri N.C. Saxena has listed the following problems in the implementation of the PDS.

TPDS, targeting around 400 million people and budgeted around for Rs. 25,000 crore annually, is affected by targeting errors (both inclusion and exclusion errors), spurious beneficiaries, diversion and pilferage and even location specific availability. The problems associated with PDS are summarised below.

1. Large errors of exclusion of BPL families and inclusion of above poverty line (APL) families.
2. Prevalence of ghost BPL/AAY cards.
3. Diversion of subsidised grains to unintended beneficiaries.
4. Section of the APL households not lifting their ration quota and thus a part of the entitlement of these households leaking out of the PDS supply chain.
5. The present procedure for selection of BPL beneficiaries is opaque, bureaucratic, and does not involve gram sabhas. The basis on which village-wise cap on the maximum number of entitled beneficiaries is fixed, is not clear and not well defined.
6. Some states, such as Bihar, Jharkhand and UP are not being released the APL quota on the ground that they did not lift it in the past when the market price was low. This policy favours the southern states which have been subsidising the APL quota out of state funds, and punishes the poorer states.
7. Selection procedure of FPS dealers is not transparent, and often based on patronage or bribes.
8. Some poor states such as Bihar and Orissa are not able to lift their entire quota.
9. Inadequate storage capacity with FCI in some districts.
10. Poor financial condition of many State Food Corporations.
11. Allocations from GoI are valid only for a month, and if the State government is not able to lift within that time, its quota lapses.
12. The poor do not have cash to buy 35 kg at a time, and often they are not permitted to buy in instalments.
13. Low quality of foodgrains.
14. Weak monitoring, lack of transparency and inadequate accountability of officials implementing the scheme.
15. Price charged exceeds the official price by 10 to 14 per cent.
16. The shop does not open for more than 2-3 days in a month, and the card holders are not allowed to lift their quota of previous months, or in instalments during a month.

17. Ration cards are mortgaged to ration shop owners.
18. No grievance redressal mechanism.
19. A large number of homeless and poor living in unauthorised colonies in urban areas have been denied ration cards, and are thus not able to avail of PDS, despite being Indian citizens.
20. Seasonal and temporary migrants face problems in receiving their entitlements during the period they are out from the village.

Issues to be Addressed

There are, however, certain major issues which need to be addressed

Universalisation or Targeting

Since the Congress (UPA) government proposed the Food Security legislation in its manifesto in 2009, there have been two broad factions of the universal versus targeted debate. The National Advisory Council and Food Security legislation supporters want food to be universally available as a right and everybody to have access to massive amounts of food for as little amount as possible. This group claims their support from two things. One is the exemplary success of the Tamil Nadu experience in ensuring food security and minimising leakages, where universal food access is available at low or nearly free prices (20 kg of rice @Re.1/kg, regardless of entitlement status); and Second, the fact that despite APL (Above Poverty Line) subsidy available to all nationally, not everyone claims it.

The Food and Civil Supplies bureaucracy, however, believes "universalisation" of the BPL (Below Poverty Line) subsidy as per Tamil Nadu model as unsustainable given the exorbitant cost of food subsidy to the nation the universalisation would imply (more than double the current amount of $10bn). Instead, they support the current system of Targeted PDS or TPDS (which has been around since 1997 in its current avatar). This current TPDS system looks something like the diagram alongside.

In a rare departure from form, Abhijit Sen, Member, Planning Commission, has challenged the view voiced by a high-level government appointed committee and made out a strong case for universalisation of the public distribution system (PDS) as the most feasible way to ensure food security.

Sachin Jain is a social researcher, development journalist, honorary state advisor (Madhya Pradesh) to the commissioners of the Supreme Court in the Right to Food Case, and heads Vikas Samvad has made a case for universalisation of the PDS. He asks:

> "Should food security legislation take the targeted approach or one aimed at universalisation of food security? If food security is considered an integral part of the fundamental right to life, how can the targeted approach even be considered? When exclusion and caste/ class/ gender discrimination have been key to social, political and economic structures, how can any targeted approach address the hunger and food insecurity situation in our country today?"

> "It is ironical that the Tendulkar Committee tried to give a rationale for empty stomachs. Accordingly, rural folk can survive on an intake of 1,999 calories, while their urban counterparts need 1,770 calories. These conclusions do not match those of ICMR, which stipulates 2,400 and 2,100 calories respectively for our rural and urban populace. In fact, hard and intensive labour requires a minimum intake of 3,400-3,800 calories."
>
> "Keeping this in mind, there is an urgent need for universalisation of the Food Security Act. Only then can we begin to think about solving the daunting problem of hunger."

In a letter to the Prime Minister some research scholars and student volunteers have urged the government to consider the importance of a 'near-universal PDS.' They have said:

> "We are a group of research scholars and student volunteers who have just spent three weeks surveying the Public Distribution System (PDS) around the country. We are writing to share a few thoughts on the National Food Security Act in the light of this experience.
>
> "Our survey covered more than 100 randomly-selected villages spread over nine States (Andhra Pradesh, Bihar, Chhattisgarh, Himachal Pradesh, Jharkhand, Orissa, Rajasthan, Tamil Nadu, and Uttar Pradesh). We inspected the local Fair Price Shops and interviewed more than a thousand "BPL" households. Oblivious of the heat or rain, we reached the country's remotest nooks and corners and spared no effort to understand people's situations and views.
>
> "This survey points to an impressive revival of the PDS across the country. In all the sample States, with the notable exception of Bihar, there have been major initiatives in the recent past to improve the PDS and these efforts are showing results. Most of the sample households were getting the bulk if not the whole of their foodgrain entitlements under the PDS (up to 35 kg per month, at a nominal price). The days when up to half of the PDS grain was "diverted" to the open market are gone.
>
> "We also found that the PDS had become a lifeline for millions of rural households. A well-functioning PDS virtually guarantees that there is always food in the house. This is an enormous relief for people who live on the margin of subsistence, and a welcome support for everyone. It is a big step towards the end of hunger, which has blighted this country for centuries.
>
> "The bad news is that the BPL list is very defective. In many States, entire communities have been left out, and almost everywhere, there are enormous exclusion errors. This has severely reduced the effectiveness of the PDS as a tool of food security. *Therefore, we support the case made recently by a group of academic economists for a 'near-universal PDS', whereby all households are entitled to food subsidies unless they meet well-defined exclusion criteria.*
>
> "The said economists also believe that there is a strong (though unspecified) 'theoretical case' for cash transfers as an alternative to the PDS. We discussed

this proposal with the respondents, and found that a majority opposed it. The reluctance was particularly strong in areas with a well-functioning PDS, and among poorer households. Further, we felt that the reasons they gave for opposing cash transfers were generally quite thoughtful and convincing.

"In most cases, the reasons pertained in one way or another to food security — an overwhelming concern for poor households. For instance, many respondents were worried that money might be misused or frittered away. Where markets are distant, they wondered where they would buy grain, and how they would cope if there is a sudden increase in local food prices. Even where markets are accessible, there were apprehensions, such as a fear that traders might raise prices if the PDS is closed. Similarly, the local bank was often said to be too far, overcrowded, or difficult to handle. Many respondents had a bitter experience of the banking system in the context of Mahatma Gandhi National Rural Employment Guarantee Act (MGNREGA) wage payments. In contrast, the familiarity and convenience of the local Fair Price Shop were widely valued. It is only in areas where the PDS was not working, notably Bihar and parts of Uttar Pradesh, that we found substantial interest in cash transfers as a possible alternative.

"Accordingly, we urge you to ensure that the National Food Security Act includes the strongest possible safeguards against a hasty transition from food entitlements to cash transfers.

"We do recognise, of course, that there is enormous scope — and urgent need — for further improvements in the PDS. We have some suggestions on this too, and would be glad to discuss them with you at your convenience."[3]

Leakages

In most debates around the Public Distribution System, the large-scale "diversion" of grain has been a major cause of concern. Diversion (or, "leakage") from the PDS has been estimated periodically (Government of India 2002 and 2005a, Jha and Ramaswami 2010, Khera 2011, Himanshu and Sen 2011, among others). In these estimates, diversion refers to the proportion of grain that does not reach beneficiary households.

While there could be several causes for these losses (e.g., during transportation or due to poor storage), the general practice has been to attribute all such losses to the illegal sale of PDS grain, meant for ration card holders, on the open market. In this paper, the conventional interpretation of diversion is adhered to, as there are no reliable estimates of losses due to other reasons.

Diversion of Food Grains

In a paper on Diversion of Food Grains, Prof Jean Dreze and Reetika Khera commented on the diversion of grains from the Public Distribution System. They said:

It is well understood that a substantial proportion of the grain, mainly wheat and rice, that is meant to be distributed to eligible families under the Public

Distribution System (PDS) ends up being sold in the open market by corrupt intermediaries, including some dealers who manage PDS outlets. The extent of this "diversion" of PDS grain has been a matter of speculation for some time. Two recent surveys shed further light on the matter.

The diversion ratio (proportion of PDS grain "diverted" to the open market) has been estimated by several researchers in the past by matching National Sample Survey (NSS) data on household purchases with Food Corporation of India (FCI) data on "offtake". The former tell us how much grain people are buying from the PDS. The latter tell us how much grain has been lifted by State governments from FCI godowns under the PDS quota. The difference is a rough estimate of the extent of diversion.

Based on this method, the estimated diversion ratio was around 54 per cent in 2004-05, the last year for which detailed data are available from a "thick round" of the NSS. Needless to say, this is an alarming figure. Tamil Nadu had the lowest diversion rate (around seven per cent); the rate was well below the national average in the other southern States also (around 25 per cent in each case). By contrast, the estimated diversion rates ranged between 85 and 95 per cent in Bihar, Jharkhand, Assam, and Rajasthan. These estimates, if proved correct, suggest a comprehensive breakdown of the PDS in these States at that time.

Having said this, the reliability of NSS figures with respect to PDS purchases is not clear. There are two reasons to assume that they are not wildly off the mark. First, the State-wise averages for 2004-05 are broadly consistent with corresponding figures from the India Human Development Survey (IHDS) for the same year. Second, the inter-State patterns are more or less as one would expect, with, for instance, very little diversion in Tamil Nadu and a huge amount of it in Bihar. Nevertheless, this approach requires independent corroboration, not just because of the uncertain accuracy of NSS data, but also because of other difficulties in this method. Incidentally, among these difficulties is the utter lack of transparency in data on "offtake": both the FCI and the Food Ministry seem to be doing their best to divulge as little as possible of it — they would do well to read Section 4 of the Right to Information Act.

Further evidence on these matters is available from a recent survey, conducted in June 2011 by student volunteers under our guidance (hereafter "PDS Survey"). The survey covered about 1,200 randomly-selected BPL households in nine sample States (Andhra Pradesh, Bihar, Chhattisgarh, Himachal Pradesh, Jharkhand, Odisha, Rajasthan, Tamil Nadu and Uttar Pradesh). The investigators were carefully trained to record the respondents' PDS purchases, in three different ways. The purchases were then compared with "entitlements" — what BPL households are supposed to get from the PDS in different States. For instance, BPL households are entitled to 25 kg of grain a month in Odisha and Rajasthan, and 35 kg a month in Chhattisgarh and Jharkhand. It turned out that in most States (with the notable exception of

Bihar), BPL households were getting the bulk of their entitlements. The ratio of purchases to entitlements was 84 per cent in the sample as a whole. Here again, there were significant inter-State variations: this ratio was above 90 per cent in Andhra Pradesh, Chhattisgarh, Himachal Pradesh, Odisha and Tamil Nadu, but as low as 45 per cent in Bihar. The sample average of 84 per cent, however, suggests much lower rates of diversion (even in Bihar) than emerged from the earlier method — at least under the BPL quota.

The findings of this survey confirm other recent evidence of substantial improvements in the PDS around the country. In most of the sample States, there have been major initiatives in the recent past to improve the PDS, and it seems these efforts are showing results.

Also of interest are provisional figures on PDS purchases for 2009-10 (the latest "thick round" of the NSS) computed by the National Sample Survey Organisation. Starting with the good news, these figures suggest that on average PDS purchases of wheat and rice have more or less doubled between 2004-05 and 2009-10. This, again, is consistent with independent evidence of a revival of the PDS in recent years.

NSS-based estimates of diversion rates, however, remain high. Applying the method described earlier to these provisional figures, the diversion rate for 2009-10 seems to be around 41 per cent. This is 13 percentage points lower than in 2004-05, but still very high. The diversion rates improved (that is, declined) in almost every State, with big improvements in some States: down from 23 per cent to 8 per cent in Andhra Pradesh, from 85 to 47 per cent in Jharkhand, from 76 to 30 per cent in Odisha, and from 52 to 11 per cent in Chhattisgarh. Interestingly, these are four States where the PDS Survey also found evidence of major improvements. In 2009-10, none of India's major States had an estimated diversion rate higher than 75 per cent (the top rate, found in Bihar), in contrast with 2004-05 when as many as eight major States had that distinction.

This broad-based improvement is good news, but needless to say diversion rates remain unacceptably high. The question remains how these high diversion rates (41 per cent at the national level) square with the fact that BPL households in the PDS Survey were able to secure 84 per cent of their PDS entitlements. Even if the comparison is restricted to the nine sample States, a similar contrast applies.

There are at least two possible explanations. First, the PDS Survey is more recent: it took place two years after the NSS survey. And as mentioned earlier, there is consistent evidence of steady improvement in the PDS in recent years in many States. However, it is difficult to believe that progress has been so rapid as to explain, on its own, the full contrast between the two surveys. Second, the PDS Survey is restricted to BPL households in rural areas.

Diversion rates may be higher (possibly much higher) under the APL quota, and perhaps also in urban areas. Indeed, the APL component of the PDS, which has expanded steadily since 2004-05 (with a big upward jump in 2009-10), is devoid of any transparency. There are no specific entitlements for APL households, and no clear allocation norms. This segment of the PDS remains highly vulnerable to corruption, as it is possible for large quantities of grain to disappear without anyone feeling the pinch.

If this tentative line of explanation is correct, two conclusions can be drawn. First, both surveys (the PDS Survey, and the 66th Round of the NSS) add to growing evidence of steady improvements in the PDS in recent years. There is still a long way to go in achieving anything like acceptable levels of functionality, especially under the APL quota, but recent progress shows that the PDS is not a "lost cause" — far from it. Second, one thing that really helps to prevent corruption is to give people a strong stake in the system (large quantities, low prices), and make sure that they are clear about their entitlements. That has already happened, to a large extent, with the BPL quota: it has become much harder to cheat the recipients, because they know their due and clamour for it if need be. As Bhukhan Singh, a resident of Kope gram panchayat in Jharkhand, put it, when the price of PDS rice for BPL households in Jharkhand was slashed to Re. 1 a kg, awareness of the new entitlements spread quickly and people made up their mind that they "would not let this go".

The recent turnaround of the PDS in Chhattisgarh (or, for that matter, Odisha) also built largely on this simple insight, as well as on the related fact that broad coverage strengthens public pressure for a functional PDS. There is an important lesson here for the proposed National Food Security Act.[4]

Wastage of Food Grains

Some years back, the Supreme Court of India had asked the Indian government to distribute food grains to the hungry and poor of the country instead of letting them to rot in the Food Corporation of India (FCI) warehouses. That the apex court had to intervene in this matter should give you an idea of how bad the food grains storage system in our country might be!

> The theme for this year's World Environment Day campaign is 'Think. Eat. Save'. It is an anti-food waste and food loss campaign that pleads all to reduce their 'foodprint'. India immediately needs to take a strong stand on this glaring issue of lack of food storage facilities and proper infrastructure. A new study says that 21 million tons of wheat goes waste in the country every year. Note here that when we waste food, we are also wasting the natural resources and the human labour that goes along with that. Take into account the time and money wasted into growing that food. For example, it takes about 1,000 litres of water to produce one litre of milk.
>
> Media reports say that this year's production leaves the government with 75 million ton of grain on its hands. With amenities to store only 63 million ton in the State-run warehouses, millions of tons of crops could be left out in the open,

> exposed to rain and rodents, or stored in makeshift spaces with only waterproof sheets to cover them. The problem is that while food grain production has increased in the last two years, new warehouses are coming up more slowly. The Food Corporation of India — which stores the grains — is reported to have told the Food Ministry last year that it has neither the warehouse capacity nor the manpower to manage the increase! How inefficient can anyone be?
>
> Indian culture and many religious sects have advocated taking only as much food as you can eat and not wasting a single morsel. It is the norm in most of the Indian families. However, wastage of huge amounts of food in hotels and at weddings is also a common and dismaying sight. With every bite you and I throw away, someone somewhere in the world goes hungry. Take these figures into account: a report by the Institution of Mechanical Engineers on global food wastage states that 50 per cent of all food produced around the world never reaches a human mouth. According to the UN's Food and Agriculture Organization, every year 1.3 billion tons of food are wasted. In the year 2012-13, the Centre spent Rs. 75,366 crore on food subsidies. Wastage of food grain is a serious concern in a country where more than 40 per cent of children are underweight or malnourished.*
>
> (**Source*: An Introduction on Food Waste, http://louelle.me/)

It's not about agriculture really. India produces enough food crops for its 1.2 billion populace. A study reveals that around 40 per cent of all fruits and vegetables get wasted in India when they move from grower to consumer. This is mainly due to lack of refrigerated transport, poor roads, harsh weather conditions, and the omnipresent corruption. We need to understand, however, that controlling the level of wastage is beyond the capability of individual farmers or even consumers. It mostly depends on market schemes, availability of power supply, quality of roads and the presence or absence of good transport hubs.

The Indian government continues to say that the recent developments like allowing 51 per cent Foreign Direct Investment (FDI) in multi-brand retail and 100 per cent FDI in the single-brand segment will lead to increased investments in infrastructure and improve the food logistics chain. There are arguments and counter-arguments on that matter.

When a country is on its way to become a superpower, it cannot afford to deny its population of their basics right. No person should go hungry simply because of an inefficient system that is unable to store or distribute food grains correctly. Think and make an informed decision this World Environment Day. Play your part, and contribute towards saving food.

The Minister of Agriculture told the Rajya Sabha that the annual wastage of fruits and vegetables was estimated at Rs. 13,309 crore. If wastage of rice, wheat, cereals and others was taken into account, it would increase to Rs. 44,000 crore, he added.

Quoting a report of the Saumitra Chaudhuri Committee in 2012, he said that the country needed 61.3 million tonnes of cold storage against the present capacity of around 29 million tonnes. He also said FDI in retail was expected to help in developing cold storage infrastructure.

Findings of the CAG

The report of the Comptroller and Auditor General of India (CAG) on "Performance Audit of Storage Management and Movement of Food Grains in Food Corporation of India (FCI)" covering the period from 2006-07 to 2011-12 was laid on the table of the Lok Sabha.

This report highlighted some of the major systemic deficiencies in the operations of the public distribution system.

A significant observation made in the CAG report pertains to the allocations made from the Central foodgrain pool for the targeted PDS and various welfare schemes during 2006-12. These stood way above what actually got lifted by the States. It points to a lack of real demand and also overestimation by the Centre while making allocations.

Equally interesting is the fact that in most years, even procurement of grain by FCI and State agencies has been lower than the allocated quantities, while more than the actual off-take. Clearly, it means a limited capacity of the system to distribute whatever grain is procured.

In the event of the NFSB becoming an Act, one can expect a further step-up in grain allocations by the Centre. That would, then, require procurement to go up even more to match the proposed allocations. Where is this extra grain going to come from — when the Commission for Agricultural Costs and Prices (CACP) has noted that up to 98 per cent of the market arrivals in major States are already being mopped up by FCI/ agencies? And even if more grain gets procured, what is the guarantee of it getting lifted? Also, what would be the impact of such large-scale procurement by government agencies on open market prices? It all raised questions on the very feasibility and sustainability of the proposed NFSB.

Storage, Accountability

The CAG report has also made pertinent points about the status of storage capacity available with FCI. The latter's 'storage gap', corresponding with the peak space requirement on June 1 after the wheat crop's procurement, was estimated at 332 lakh tonnes (lt) in 2012. That amounted to 40 per cent of the total Central pool stock of 824 tons for that date (June 1, 2012).

From this observation, it is natural to ask: If FCI does not have storage capacity for 332 tons of grain (worth Rs. 66,000 crore or $12 billion), how is it going to handle the additional quantities that will have to be procured for the NFSB? It is quite possible that in this case, the Centre would pass on the onus for creating the matching storage infrastructure to the States!

Related to this is the involvement of multiple agencies — including State corporations and even private millers — in storing foodgrains constituting the so-called Central pool. The CAG is right in observing that having so many agencies, without any "single point accountability" that should mandatorily lie with FCI, is conducive to a situation where the indicated stock in the Central pool may not actually be available for distribution at a given point of time.

That, in turn, raises strong possibilities of mismanagement, theft and pilferage of the stocks supposedly held in the Central pool. Needless to add, the chances of these would go up even more with grains selling at Re. 1 (coarse cereals), Rs. 2 (wheat) and Rs. 3 (rice) under the NFSB. At these rates, large-scale diversion and 'round-tripping' of the same grain back to the Government procurement agencies are inevitable. In the process, a new 'grain mafia' class could well emerge.

Minimum Support Price (MSP) Vagueness

Another observation by the CAG is about minimum support price (MSP) of paddy and wheat being fixed in an ad hoc manner. The MSP of wheat alone during 2006-12 was fixed anywhere between 30 and 66 per cent over the 'C2' cost. The latter, determined by the CACP, takes into account all input costs — including the imputed value of family labour and rental income foregone. While there are set procedures for computing C2 costs, there are no such established norms, though, for arriving at the margins (over the C2 costs) while fixing the MSP.

By hiking MSPs without following any norms, the impact on the quantum of the Government's food subsidy bill has been predictable. The fiscal costs will go up further when this arbitrariness in fixing MSPs gets combined with the fixed Rs. 1-3/kg retail pricing formula under the NFSB.

In 2011-12, the Government incurred over Rs. 88,000 crore ($16 billion) as the economic cost of the grains handled by it, while realising slightly over Rs. 26,000 crore ($4.7 billion) through their disposal. The FCI's economic cost for wheat alone is now about Rs. 20/kg, against a realisation of Rs. 6 or so. Under NFSB, the latter will be Rs. 2. And who knows, with progressive reductions in the coming years, it could be virtually free!

The conclusion from all this is as follows: Off-take under the PDS is currently less than allocations as well as procurement. The FCI's storage gap, at around 40 per cent, will only increase with higher procurement sought under the NFSB — unless the States oblige by augmenting warehousing capacities (which is unlikely). On top of it, there is no single-point accountability on quality or quantity of grains stored, just as the system of MSP fixation follows no norms whatsoever. The nation needs to seriously consider whether the above monolithic mechanism needs to be promoted further under the proposed NFSB law.

Findings of the Supreme Court panel on PDS. The Supreme Court-appointed vigilance committee has slammed the public distribution system (PDS) in the country for "rampant corruption, black marketing and diversion involving a vicious cartel of bureaucrats, fair price shop owners and middlemen".

The central vigilance committee headed by former Supreme Court judge Justice D.P. Wadhwa in its report to the apex court said that the Rs. 28,000 crore subsidy annually spent by the Centre was being pocketed by vested interests and suggested drastic action to stem the rot.

> "Corruption is all pervasive in the entire chain involved in PDS. It continues to remain a formidable problem. It is true that most of the functionaries under them in the department are typically callous and resort to corrupt practices.
>
> "It (corruption) is in fact a cancerous growth and has to be chopped off. Patchwork methods will not do. Central Government gives a whooping sum of Rs. 28,000 crore to subsidise food for the poor. But till the recommendations given by the committee are put in place, the poor will go on suffering at the hands of corrupt officials, dishonest FPS owners, transporters and possibly to a large extent by unscrupulous millers as well," the report said.

The committee recommended breaking the strong nexus between the forces by setting up an effective vigilant mechanism but did not elaborate.

A bench of Justices Dalveer Bhandari and K.S. Radhakrishnan took on record the report for passing appropriate orders.

Findings of the Independent Evaluator Appointed by the Government

The first task of the government's newly constituted independent evaluator was to study the effectiveness of the public distribution system. The evaluator has reported that the government spends Rs. 3.65 to deliver Re. 1 on food while 57 per cent of subsidised foodgrains do not reach the intended beneficiaries. These startling findings by the Independent Evaluation Office point to massive corruption and pilferages in the existing public distribution system.

The agency's initial findings reveal that close to 36 per cent of foodgrains are siphoned off in the supply chain, raising a serious question mark over effective implementation of UPA government's "game-changer" food security scheme which heavily depends on existing PDS network.

The agency has also found that corruption is less in the states such as Tamil Nadu where the PDS has been made universal.

The agency's first director general Ajay Chhibber said, "India can be a great economic power but must fix its Achilles Heel — which is better delivery of quality public services."

During his job as evaluator so far, Chhibber had told TOI that he has found that bureaucracy is a big problem with lack of coordination between ministries.

The former UN official claimed India could bounce back at 6.5 per cent economic growth if bureaucratic bottlenecks are removed, adding that "administrative reasons" account for 1.5 percentage point dip in country's growth trajectory.

He argued that ineffective spending on government big-ticket social sector schemes had its bad impact on the economy.

Chhibber found that the incentive structure of social sector schemes, including PDS, needs to be looked at as it is ill-thought-out.

He has said in the existing PDS, it has been seen that as the ration shop owners fail to make enough money by selling grains to beneficiaries they are tempted to sell outside.

Apart from PDS, the agency is looking at the whole issue of movement of grain from the purchase centre to the consumer. "Eventually, we will also look at the Food Corporation of India and its operations, as well as the open-ended grain procurement policy," he said.

The independent evaluator would also focus on outcomes to ensure government schemes become more effective and accountable. Today, the government schemes are more target-oriented and not outcome-oriented, Chhibber said.

The role of the agency assumes significance as the UPA government had budgeted around Rs. 2 lakh crore on its flagship programmes in 2013-14.

The evaluator will submit its final report on the public distribution system and maternal mortality in the next 3-4 months, Chhibber said after the formal launch of the IEO.

Malnutrition

According to Prof. M.S. Swaminathan "Nutrition security involving physical, economic and social access to balanced diet, clean drinking water, sanitation and primary healthcare for every child, woman and man is fundamental to providing all our citizens an opportunity for a healthy and productive life, "But the nutritional status of the people in

India is poor and the incidence of malnutrition is very high in India.

The WHO Report for 2005 puts India in the list of 51 slow progressing countries as far as infant and child mortality and maternal mortality is concerned with an estimated 1,36,000 maternal and one million newborn deaths and newborns suffering from pregnancy birth related mortality and where morbidity continued to take a toll on the lives of Indian women and their newborns.

One in every three world's malnourished children lives in India and about 50 per cent of all childhood deaths in India are attributable to malnutrition. The proportion of low birth weight babies remains high at one third of all births.

According to the latest report on the state of food insecurity in rural India brought out by the UN World Food Programme nearly 230 million people are undernourished — the highest for any country in the world. Malnutrition accounts for nearly 50 per cent of child deaths in India as every third adult (aged 15-49 years) is reported to be thin with a BMI less than 18.5.

More than 27 per cent of the world's undernourished population lives in India while 43 per cent of children (under 5 years) in the country are underweight. The figure is among the highest in the world and is much higher than the global average of 25 per cent and also higher than sub-Saharan Africa's figure of 28 per cent.

More than 70 per cent of children (under-5) suffer from anaemia and 80 per cent of them don't get vitamin supplements. According to the report, the proportion of anaemic children has actually increased by 6 per cent in the past six years with 11 out of 19 States having more than 80 per cent of its children suffering from anaemia.

Percentage of women with chronic energy deficiency is stagnant at 40 per cent over six years with the proportion in fact increasing in Assam, Bihar, Madhya Pradesh and Haryana during the same period.

According to *the National Family Health Survey III (2005-06)*, "the infant mortality rate continues to remain higher than it should be. It is as high as 71 per 1000 live births in Chhattisgarh. Although Punjab has an IMR of 42 and Maharashtra 38 both below the national average of 66, they are still below the target set by the National Population Policy of achieving an IMR of 30 by 2010

Similarly, the percentage of children below three who are underweight is disturbing. In Gujarat, the percentage has actually increased from 45 per cent to 47 per cent while in the other four states it has declined. In Punjab it is 27 per cent while in Chhattisgarh it is 52 per cent

The percentage of children between six and 35 months who are anaemic has also increased in Gujarat from 75 per cent to 80 per cent and in Orissa from 72 to 78 per cent. In Punjab it is 80 per cent and remains unchanged. It is the highest in Chhattisgarh at 81 per cent.

The number of women who are anaemic, particularly pregnant women, in all five States is also unacceptably high. This is despite targeted intervention to deal with anemia in pregnant women. Clearly, this is an area that will need to be investigated more closely as it reflects on other forms of economic deprivation in a large percentage of population. One of the direct outcomes of this is the impact on women's health, particularly during pregnancy when they deny themselves food in preference to feeding the rest of the family. Thus the cycle of anaemic mothers giving birth to underweight children who die before they complete one year remains unbroken.

The Economic Survey 2008-09 has admitted that while poverty rates have declined significantly, malnutrition has remained stubbornly high. It says:

> "Malnutrition, as measured by underweight children below three years, constituting 45.9 per cent in children under three years of age as per the National Family Health Survey 2005-06 (NFHS 3) has still remained much higher. It has also not significantly declined from its level of 47 per cent in 1998-99 (NFHS 2). Malnutrition reflects an imbalance of both macro and micro-nutrients that may be due to inappropriate intake and/ or inefficient biological utilisation due

to the internal/ external environment. Poor feeding practices in infancy and early childhood, resulting in malnutrition contribute to impaired cognitive and social development, poor school performance, and reduced productivity in later life. Malnutrition, therefore, is a major threat to social and economic development as it is among the most serious obstacles to attaining and maintaining health of this important age group. It is evident that existing policies and programmes are not making a significant dent on malnutrition and need to be modified. While per capita consumption of cereals has declined, the share of non-cereals in food consumption has not grown to compensate for the decline in cereal availability."

The *Economic Survey* suggests the following measures for improvement in the nutritional status of the people:

(i) Improvement of public health education and public health facilities have an important and positive link with nutrition outcomes.
(ii) Social welfare, while giving additional weight to the income/ consumption of the poor, must also give importance to the access of the poor to public goods. This is due to the fact that individual welfare depends not only on the private consumption but also on public goods and services supplied by the state.
(iii) Public health and literacy are interlinked, higher literacy levels lead to quality public health.
(iv) Longevity and mortality reduction are more related to public health than to treatment of individual diseases. Public health includes better drainage and sewerage system (sewage treatment plants) that provides solid waste disposal management and drinking water system that delivers disease-free water. The current position is illustrated by the low proportion of the population with access to improved sanitation facilities across many States especially Bihar, M.P., Orissa, Rajasthan, Uttar Pradesh, Chhattisgarh and Jharkhand.
(v) Public health also includes public education about nutrition, hygiene and disease to reduce the problem of asymmetric information. Literacy and primary education aids in this process and contributes to the general well-being. Together these can contribute immensely to the quality of life of all citizens, particularly the poor.
(vi) Hence, quasi public goods are of critical importance to the poor. The Government must ensure that every citizen has access to education and also making it more relevant by providing information on matters that will improve their lives (health, hygiene, nutrition).
(vii) Public health initiatives such as clean drinking water, sanitation, sewerage, control of communicable and epidemic diseases and public health education play an important role in reducing mortality rates at every age and across the gender. These should be the focus of the Government as part of its strategy to promote inclusive growth.

The emphasis in the Economic Survey on improvement in public health is unexceptionable but it is not enough. There is a social security dimension to the problem of malnutrition. Poverty may not be the sole cause of malnutrition but it cannot be denied that it is a major cause. Malnutrition is a byproduct of poverty and hunger.

It is, therefore, necessary to ensure that all the people especially those in the vulnerable sections have a basic income which enables them to have adequate nutrition especially the women when they are pregnant.

There is also a gender dimension to the problem of malnutrition.

The author of the Global Hunger Index, Ms Wiesman, said in an interview to the *Indian Express:*

> "Mothers, who are usually children's primary caretakers, and their education, nutritional knowledge, well-being and status in families and communities are particularly important in this respect. The results (of the Index) are a direct fallout of the low status of women in Indian society. In India, women eat the last and the least, increasing the chances of anaemia".

This practice partly explain why 83 per cent of women in India suffer from iron deficiency anaemia, as opposed to about 40 per cent in sub-Saharan Africa.

Not surprisingly, one-third of the babies born in India are born with low birth weight, compared to one-sixth in sub-Saharan Africa.

Lisa Smith, a IFPRI research fellow, and Usha Ramakrishnan, Associate Professor at Emory University, identified three factors contributing to the nutritional status gap between South Asia and sub-Saharan Africa in a recent study.

The first, making by far the greatest contribution among the three, is women's status, followed by sanitation and urbanisation

The implication for policy is clear in the interests of improving child nutrition, women's status should be raised.

The study also concluded that in regions where women's status is low, programmes to improve child nutritional status would have more lasting impact when combined with efforts to improve women's status.

Suggestions with regard to nutrition for Women: The National Commission on Self Employed Women and Women in the Informal Sector had made the following suggestions with regard to nutrition for women:

> "Nutrition and sufficient food is a crying need of the women workers in the informal sector. Specific nutritional programmes which include calcium, protein, iron and vitamin D could be initiated through the government health care system. A nationwide programme for the distribution of nutritious subsidised food supplements which includes calcium for women should be organised, on the lines of a similar programme for distribution of milk and egg powder in the 1950s. Coarse grains like ragi as well as milk must be made widely available at subsidised rates."

A very high level of malnutrition not only reduces physical and cognitive growth, it also hampers the productivity and earnings of individuals and leads to a negative impact on the country's economic growth — a four per cent loss of GDP in the case of India.

According to Veena S. Rao, Secretary in the Ministry for the Development of the North Eastern Region, author of the book: "Malnutrition, an Emergency: What it costs the Nation". Malnutrition in India has led to an economic loss of US $29 billion to the country. Rao has pointed out that it is an inter-generational, inter-sectoral problem that needs multi-sectoral solutions and should cover the entire life cycle of women and children. She has suggested that besides a sustained awareness generation campaign, there is a need to revise schemes like the Integrated Child Development Programme (ICDP) to provide them with a definite mandate and adequate monitoring machinery. She has called for making high energy-low cost food available to the poor. She has recommended that the problem of malnutrition could be addressed at the highest level through a revitalised National Nutrition Council and a High Powered Committee.

UNICEF in its *State of the Children Report* 1998 says:

> "Since the roots of malnutrition have long been well known, so are its solutions. Pregnant and lactating women need to work less, rest and eat well. Babies need to be breastfed — exclusively until the age of six months, and with appropriate supplements until the age of two. Families need to have access to adequate preventive and curative health care. They also need access to safe water and sanitation to prevent infection and disease.
>
> Supplements of nutrients such as vitamin A and iron can easily be made available, at minimal cost. In addition, the simple act of iodising salt can save millions from brain damage. And new techniques have been developed for easy detection of vitamin and mineral deficiencies.
>
> Cost-effective, easy-to-implement programmes, with educational and practical follow-up components, can be put in place at the grassroots level, allowing communities to take the matter of nutrition into their own hands, monitor their children's growth and organise to secure what they require to meet their children's needs. The report cites numerous such community programmes implemented throughout the world with impressively successful results, at minimal financial cost. In Tanzania, for example, such programmes have improved the nutrition of half the country's children.
>
> Tackling the problem requires the active involvement of families and communities, as well as political will at the national and international levels. Governments have to build widespread awareness of the roots and consequences of malnutrition, along with the ways of reducing it; they have to spend more on clinics, clean water supply and sanitation. Women must also have greater access to education and economic resources."

UNICEF presents the policy options in stark terms. "Governments ... may choose to allow children to be intellectually disabled, physically stunted and vulnerable to illness in childhood and later in life," or they could "resolve to consolidate lessons already learned about reducing malnutrition ... and mount massive actions that can clearly succeed."

Endnotes

1 *Behind the success story of universal PDS in Tamil Nadu* by S.Vaidianthan and R.K. Radhakrishnan

2 Biraj Patnaik is principal adviser to the commissioners of the Supreme Court in the Right to Food case and has been involved with PDS reforms in Chhattisgarh since 2003.

3 Signatories: Anindita Adhikari (independent researcher, Patna); Ankita Aggarwal (independent researcher, Delhi); Megha Bahl (Delhi School of Economics, Delhi); Pooja

4 'Diversion of Food Grains,' Jean Dreze and Reetika Khera

2
Housing

Shelter is one of the three basic needs of man. There are millions of people without shelter in India. The National Commission on Rural Labour pointed out that according to NSS data for 1997-98, only 31 per thousand rural households owned a plot of homestead land. At the beginning of the Seventh Plan, house shortage was estimated at 24.7 million units of which 18.8 million was in rural areas.

According to the Annual Report of the Ministry of Rural Areas and Employment for the year 1998-99, the rural housing shortage at the time of 1991 Census was 13.72 million consisting of 3.41 million households without houses and 10.31 million living in unserviceable *kutcha* houses. It was estimated that another 10.75 million houses would be needed to cover the population growth during 1991-2002 at the rate of an annual growth of 0.89 million. Thus, a total of 24.47 million houses would need to be constructed or upgraded to achieve the target of providing shelter to all in the rural areas by 2002 A.D. Of this 5.7 million houses had been added by various agencies until 31.3.1997 and it was anticipated that around 6.17 million houses would be added by different agencies by 2002 A.D. Thus, the housing shortage to be tackled would be 12.60 million houses of which 10.31 million houses would need upgradation and 2.29 million new houses would need to be constructed.

On the other hand, the National Building Organisation is reported to have estimated the housing shortage in 1991 at 8.23 million and in 1997 at 7.57 million. It is projected to be 6.44 million in 2001.

The Technical Group on the Estimation of Housing, constituted by the Union Ministry of Housing and Urban Poverty Alleviation has said that India was facing a shortage of 18.78 million fresh supply of houses in its urban pockets in 2012. The estimated slum population in India is 94.98 million in 2012. As against this, the number of dwelling units sanctioned under JNNURM during a seven-year mission period was 1.6 million.

The report further said, by 2031, about 600 million Indians will reside in urban areas, an increase of over 200 million in just 20 years. This change in the socio-economic landscape will have a bearing on several things, housing being the foremost. With the industry facing continued pressure in terms of raising funds for investment, the research report suggests that India must have a Real Estate Investment Trust (REIT).

A REIT is a company that directly owns income producing real estate assets and provides a trading mechanism to investors. On the one hand, an institutional market of REITs can ensure a steady supply of capital to real estate development which shall aid in increasing the supply of houses and on the other it shall serve as an investment vehicle for individuals.

The depth of the REIT investment vehicle in developed markets can be assessed from the amount of capital raised over the years. For instance, in the US market, REITs have raised $66.8 billion in 2012 (until November) alone and the momentum of fund-raising through this investment vehicle has steadily increased since the global financial crisis of 2008.

The shortage will mainly be on the back of demand-supply gap and rising levels of income among the working class seeking to purchase houses.

The shortage of urban houses stood at 18.8 million units in 2012 and it is expected to grow at a compound annual growth rate of 6.6 per cent for 10 years till 2022.

According to the "White Paper — Indian Housing Industry" by research and consultancy firm RNCOS, it is expected that the urban shortage will reach 34.1 million units by 2022.

The shortage of urban houses stood at 18.8 million units in 2012 and it is expected to grow at a compound annual growth rate of 6.6 per cent for 10 years till 2022. "The increasing urban population is leading to wide demand-supply gap, which in turn leads to increase in housing shortage. The rising income level of the working class is one of the other factors that is further driving the demand for affordable housing particularly in Tier I and Tier II cities.

"Besides, migration of working class people from rural to urban areas is also generating the demand for affordable housing further," the report said. RNCOS said the total urban housing shortage is mostly exhibited by the economically weaker sections (EWS) and lower income group (LIG) segments.

"In year 2012, around 95 per cent of total urban housing shortage was for EWS and LIG segments, which is expected to decrease in coming years backed by supportive government policies and more investment in this sector," it added.

Talking about available housing stock, the survey pointed out that with big and medium-level players launching various residential projects in various cities and for different income groups, the housing stock is expected to cross 128 million units by 2022 from 78.5 million units in 2011.

In the past several schemes were tried out for meeting the shortage in rural areas. They were later merged in the umbrella type of scheme called Indira Awas Yojana. According to the Annual Report of the Ministry of Rural Areas for 1998-99, nearly five million houses were constructed under the Yojana up to November, 1998. It should be assumed that the Ninth Plan estimate of housing shortage has taken this achievement into account. It was planned to construct about one million houses under the scheme during 1999-2000.

As far as urban areas are concerned the Government has concentrated on providing houses to economically weaker sections, slum and pavement dwellers.

The total number of houses constructed under the EWS and L.I.G. housing schemes during the year 1995-96 was less than two lakhs. Under the scheme of Night Shelters to Footpath Dwellers about 18,000 beds were provided. According to the new Housing Policy, seven lakh houses are to be constructed each year. Evidently these programmes have not had much impact on the housing situation in urban areas.

In this connection the following recommendations of the National Commission on Rural Labour are relevant.

> "The basic problems of housing for rural labour seem to be that house sites are not owned by them. Public housing agencies are not able to cater to their needs since they do not own land and the rural labour cannot afford cost of the building according to their norms. The first requirement is, therefore, to give rural labour house sites by locating suitable vested lands or other means and to make the cost of building affordable by them.
>
> If the labourer gets a site, he would, in most cases, be able to erect a shelter for himself through local materials. The provisions of homestead land, therefore, assumes the great importance.
>
> Several States have enacted measures for giving homestead lands to agricultural labourers by conferring ownership rights on the plots that they may already be occupying. The West Bengal Acquisition of Homestead Land for Agricultural Labourers, Artisans and Fishermen Act, 1975, is an example. It provides that where an occupier has been in possession of any land to the extent of 0.0334 hectares (8units), that land will stand acquired by the State Government and transferred and vested absolutely in favour of such occupier. A small compensation is paid to the owner. There is a ban on transfer of such land by the occupier and penalty for eviction of the occupier of such land. Civil Court jurisdiction is barred.
>
> Analogous provisions have been made by some of the States for conferment of homestead rights up to 10 cents of land and it has been implemented in a substantial measure in Kerala."

The Commission has recommended that other States should also make suitable legislative provision for conferment of rights to homestead and on the existing occupiers as well as future occupiers. Information is not available as to what extent this recommendation has been implemented.

Housing is a basic industry which provides not only employment but also creates the demand for other basic industries such as cement and steel and boosts the economy. Thus, it not only fulfills one of the basic needs of the people but it also contributes in a big way to the growth of the economy. Considering the difficulties involved in locating land and credit for construction activity, the matter cannot be entirely left to private ventures. The State would have to undertake a massive housing programme to supplement private construction. In doing so, the recommendations of the National Commission on Rural Labour should not be overlooked. We could learn from the experience of Singapore in this regard.

Housing Schemes of NDA Government Led by Sri Narendra Modi

Pradhan Mantri Awas Yojana (PMAY)

Launched on 25 June 2015, the PMAY is a Housing for All scheme which focuses on enabling better living. The NDA government identified 305 cities and towns across nine states for implementation of this scheme.

Housing for All 2022 | PM Awas Yojana

The PM Awas Yojana would start in the year 2015 and would be spread over for implementation till the year 2022 and would be carried out in three sustainable phases:

Pradhan Mantri Awas Yojana Phase 1: The Phase 1 of PM Awas Yojana would span from April 2015 to March 2017 and a total of 100 cities would see the developmental work started and completed during this phase.

Pradhan Mantri Awas Yojana Phase 2: The Phase 2 of Pradhan Mantri Awas Yojana would span from April 2017 to March 2019 and during this phase, a total of 200 more cities would be covered and developed.

Pradhan Mantri Awas Yojana Phase 3: The Phase 3 of PMAY would span from April 2019 to March 2022 and during this phase the left over cities would be covered and developed.

The Beneficiaries of Pradhan Mantri Awas Yojana

Pradhan Mantri Awas Yojana would target specific groups from the society, which are:

1. Women, irrespective of caste and religion
2. Economically Weaker Section of Society (EWS)
3. Scheduled Tribes (STs)
4. Scheduled Castes (SCs)

The Government of India would be granting a subsidy to people from these categories so that they buy a home for themselves and their families. The subsidy amount may range from Rs. 1 lakh to Rs. 2.30 lakh.

Features of Pradhan Mantri Awas Yojana aka Housing for All 2022

The features of Pradhan Mantri Awas Yojana are as following:

- The government would provide an interest subsidy of 6.5 per cent on housing loans availed by the beneficiaries for a period of 15 years from the start of loan.
- The houses under Pradhan Mantri Awas Yojana would be allotted to preferably the female member of the family. Along with this, preference

would be given to the female applicants, in general. This scheme could well be termed as a pro-women scheme.

- While allotting ground floors in any housing scheme under the PMAY, preference would be given to differently-abled and older people.
- The construction of houses under PMAY would be carried out through technology that is eco-friendly.

Interest Rates, EMI Calculation and Subsidy in PM Awas Yojana

The niche of the scheme lies in the fact that the EMI paid by the home owners under the scheme would be reduced significantly. The current rate of housing loan in India is at 10.50 per cent. If someone buys a property currently on a loan of Rs. 6 lakh for a tenure of 15 years today, he/ she would have to pay an EMI of Rs. 6,632 per month currently. However, with 6.5 per cent subsidy under the scheme, the beneficiary would have to pay just Rs. 4,050 per month as EMI. Thus, there is a significant reduction of Rs. 2,000 in the EMI itself.

Pradhan Mantri Awas Yojana Components (Housing for All 2022)

1. An average of Rs. 1 lakh would be granted by the Government of India to all the beneficiaries under the scheme.
2. Through Credit Lined Subsidy Scheme, a subsidy of 6.5 per cent would be given to each beneficiary belonging to EWS and Lower Income Group categories.
3. A central government assistance of Rs. 1.5 lakh would go to every beneficiary for promoting housing stock and thus 35 per cent of the units under the project would be earmarked for the Economically Weaker Section category.
4. In addition to the above, a sum of Rs. 1.5 lakh would be provided to all eligible urban poor who want to construct their own house in urban areas or wish to make necessary renovations in their existing houses.

3
Supply of Other Essential Commodities

All India

Central Government - Supply of LPG to BPL House Holds

Need

In India, the poor have limited access to cooking gas (LPG). The spread of LPG cylinders has been predominantly in the urban and semi-urban areas with the coverage mostly in middle class and affluent households. But there are serious health hazards associated with cooking based on fossil fuels. According to WHO estimates, about 5 lakh deaths in India alone are due to unclean cooking fuels. Most of these premature deaths were due to non-communicable diseases such as heart disease, stroke, chronic obstructive pulmonary disease and lung cancer. Indoor air pollution is also responsible for a significant number of acute respiratory illnesses in young children. According to experts, having an open fire in the kitchen is like burning 400 cigarettes an hour.

Providing LPG connections to BPL households will ensure universal coverage of cooking gas in the country. This measure will empower women and protect their health. It will reduce drudgery and the time spent on cooking. It will also provide employment for rural youth in the supply chain of cooking gas.

Target Beneficiaries

Under the scheme, five crore LPG connections are to be provided to BPL households. The identification of eligible BPL families will be made in consultation with the State Governments and the Union Territories.

BPL is a person/ household who suffers from at least one form of deprivation under the Socio-Economic Caste census (SECC) - 2011 Database.

While the selection of beneficiaries would be from the BPL families only, preference would be given to SC/ST and weaker sections of society. While providing the new connections to BPL households, priority would be given to the States which have lower LPG coverage (compared to the national average) as on 1st Jan, 2016.

Release of LPG connection under this Scheme shall be in the name of the women belonging to the BPL family.

The Government has also decided to cover the following categories under the Scheme:

1. All SCs/ STs households beneficiaries of Pradhan Mantri Awas Yojana(PMAY) (Gramin)

2. Antyoday Anna Yojana (AAY)
3. Forest dwellers
4. Most Backward Classes (MBC)
5. Tea & Ex-Tea Garden Tribes
6. People residing in Islands
7. People residing in river islands.

Duration of the Scheme

The Scheme would be implemented over three years, namely, the FY 2016-17, 2017-18 and 2018-19 across the country.

Benefits to the Citizens

Under the scheme, five crore LPG connections are to be provided to BPL households. The Scheme provides a financial support of Rs 1600 for each LPG connection to the BPL households. The administrative cost of Rs. 1600 per connection, which includes a cylinder, pressure regulator, booklet, safety hose, etc. would be borne by the Government.

Implementation Modalities of the Scheme

- A woman of the BPL household, which does not have access to LPG connection may apply for a new LPG connection (in the prescribed format) to the LPG distributor.
- While submitting the application form, the woman will submit details, like Address, Jandhan/ Bank Account and Aadhar number (if the Aadhar number is not available, steps would be taken in coordination with UIDAI for issue of Aadhar number to the woman of BPL household)
- The LPG Field officials will match the application against SECC - 2011 database and, after ascertaining their BPL status, enter the details (name, address etc) into a dedicated OMC Web portal through a login/ password given by the OMCs
- OMCs will undertake electronically the de-duplication exercise and other measures for due diligence for a new LPG connection
- The connection shall be issued by the OMC to the eligible beneficiaries (after completion of various stages above).
- While the connection charges would be borne by the Government, the OMCs would provide an option for the new consumer to opt for EMIs, if she so desires, to cover the cost of a cooking stove and first refill. The EMI amount may be recovered by the OMCs from the subsidy amount due to the consumer on each refill; In case the State Government or a voluntary organization or an individual wishes to contribute the cost of a stove and/or first refill, they would be free to do so in coordination with the OMCs. However, this would be under the overall umbrella of PMUY

and no other Scheme name/ tagline would be allowed without express approval of the Ministry of Petroleum and Natural Gas (MoP&NG)

- OMCs will also organize Melas' at various locations for release of connections to BPL families. This will be done in the presence of public representatives and distinguished personalities of the area.
- The scheme will cover BPL families under all forms of distributorship and for various sizes of cylinders (like 14.2 kg, 5 kg, etc.) depending on the field situation.
- Benefits under Pradhan Mantri Ujjwala Yojana has been extended to people of all hill States including NE States by treating them as 'Priority States'. This step will effectively address the difficulty faced by poor people residing in the States of Jammu and Kashmir, Himachal Pradesh, Uttarakhand, Sikkim, Assam, Nagaland, Manipur, Mizoram, Arunachal Pradesh, Meghalaya and Tripura in accessing LPG for cooking purposes.

Source: Pradhan Mantri Ujjwala Yojana website

Distribution of Cloth

In India, food, clothing and shelter are regarded as the most basic of the human needs. While there are programmes for providing food security and shelter, there are few schemes to provide clothing to the needy people except when calamities occur.

There are not many cases where Governments undertake to distribute clothes to poor people except uniforms to children and blankets etc. in the event of a calamity such as cyclone. Tamil Nadu and Andhra Pradesh governments have some such schemes for distribution of clothes. There are also many voluntary agencies who come forward and provide help whenever a calamity takes place.

According to a report, (J. Venkatesan), every year, the Tamil Nadu Government distributes free dhotis and sarees to the poor people during the Pongal festival under the scheme being implemented by the Social Welfare Department. To ensure that all the identified beneficiaries get these dhotis and sarees in time, the distribution is done by the Tamil Nadu Civil Supplies Corporation through its fair price shops. The beneficiaries receive these dhotis and sarees after making necessary entries in their ration cards.

Recently the Chief Minister of Telangana announced that the government had decided to distribute clothes worth Rs. 500 to each of 1.95 lakh poor families free of cost and to provide free meals for 1,000 people in every mosque identified in the city and districts on 8 July 8.The Government had also decided to distribute a saree, five metres cloth for kurta and pyjama, a skull cap (Topi) to the head of the family and one kg of vermicelli to each family.

The Government of Bihar also has some schemes for distribution of dhotis and sarees free of cost or at subsidised prices to poor people.

There is a strong case for introducing a national scheme for supply of clothes to the poor people free or at subsidised prices for the same reason for which schemes have been introduced for supply of food grains and for provision of housing facilities.

Other Commodities

Many States have introduced schemes for supply of other essential commodities to the poor people. Some of these schemes are mentioned below:

Andhra Pradesh

Recently the Government of Andhra Pradesh introduced a scheme to distribute LPG connections to rural women members of DWCRA groups on a subsidy of Rs. 1000 per connection. 45,000 connections were already given when the Election Commission imposed a ban on the scheme as violative of the code of conduct.

The Government of Andhra Pradesh has introduced another Scheme called Adarana under which rural artisans are supplied improved tools. Under this Scheme four lakh artisans are reported to have received the tools out of a target of 10 lakh artisans. This Scheme was also stopped by the Election Commission.

Protesting against the action of the Election Commission, the Chief Minister of Andhra Pradesh is reported to have stated that certain other States also introduced similar schemes, namely Madhya Pradesh and Maharashtra. Indeed, many states have introduced similar schemes some of which are mentioned below:

Bihar

Among several welfare initiatives taken by the Government of Bihar the 'Mukhyamantri Balika Cycle Yojna' was one of the most notable. It has changed the face of Bihar with lakhs of schoolgirls riding bicycles to their schools every day with a purpose. Prior to the launch of this project more than three years ago it was rare to find a schoolgirl riding a bicycle even on the streets of Patna. But now, you can watch scores of confident-looking

School girls pedalling away with gusto everywhere – from the narrow lanes of a remote village to the bustling roads of the cities across the State. Under this scheme, a schoolgirl gets a cheque of Rs. 2,000 upon passing class VIII to buy a bicycle so that she can go to school every day. It would be no exaggeration to say that the scheme has been an unqualified success. It has given lot of satisfaction since it has helped check the dropout rate of schoolgirls to a great extent across the State.

Take a look at the figures of the past three financial years to measure the success of this scheme. In 2007-08, the government of Bihar spent Rs. 32.60 crore to enable 1.63 lakh schoolgirls to buy bicycles; in 2008-09, it allocated Rs. 54.43 crore towards this project facilitating purchase of the same by 2.72 lakh schoolgirls and in the year 2009-10, the number of beneficiaries rose to 4.36

lakh who bought bicycles worth Rs. 87.33 crore. To sum up, government spent Rs. 174.36 crore in the past three years to make 8.71 lakh schoolgirls proud owners of bicycles which they are all using to educate themselves now.

These are not mere statistics. This is, in fact, an affirmation of the fact that a small initiative can really go a long way in bringing about a big change. In Bihar, bicycles have now become a veritable instrument for social change which can be felt in any part of the State. The dropout rate among the schoolgirls has been very high in Bihar over the years. The girls, particularly those from rural areas, often discontinue their studies beyond the primary or middle schools. Most of them are often married at an early age, which leave them with fewer opportunities to contribute their mite towards economic development of society.

After introduction of the scheme the dropout rate of students in general and the schoolgirls in particular has been reduced. It was in 2006 that the decision taken to give away bicycles to all the schoolgirls of classes VIII, IX and X studying in government schools. This has gone a long way not only in arresting the dropout rate of schoolgirls in the high schools but also be a significant step towards woman empowerment._

Karnataka

Karnataka Government has introduced several Bhagya schemes known as:

- Anna Bhagya Scheme
- Ksheera Bhagya Scheme
- Bhagya Jyothi Scheme
- Shaadi Bhagya Scheme
- Thayi Bhagya Scheme
- Krishi Bhagya scheme, etc.

Anna Bhagya Scheme: The Government launched an ambitious programme called Anna Bhagya Yojana to supply foodgrains free of cost to priority household (AAY+BPL) families across the State. A total of 108.98 lakh priority households are eligible to receive free foodgrains through a network of 20,778 fair price shops across the State since May 2015.

Ksheera Bhagya Scheme: Karnataka Government is distributing 150 ml of milk, three days a week, free of cost to students studying in Class I to X in 51000 schools of the state and also 39 lakh chilldren in 64000 Anganwadi centres, through 13 milk unions of KMF, with a daily sale of five lakh liters, at the cost of Rs. 384 crore (Up to 31.03.2014)

This scheme is benefiting approximately one crore school children out of approximately six crore population of Karnataka State by providing good quality, highly nutritious Nandini milk in the form of Milk powder.

This scheme is benefiting dairy farmers by providing a market for five lakh litres surplus milk per day.

For successful implementation of the scheme, Karnataka Government made budgetary provisions in 2013-14 budget for infrastructural development of Milk Unions.

Shadi Bhagya Scheme: Shaadi Bhagya scheme of providing financial assistance of Rs. 50,000 to brides of minority communities, has been appreciated by the Modi government.

Ex-Union minister for minority affairs Najma A Hepthullah is said to have evinced interest in the scheme commending that Karnataka should become a role model for other States. Close on the heels of earning this accolade from the Centre, Andhra Pradesh Chief Minister N Chandrababu Naidu, has decided to implement the Shaadi Bhagya programme.

Bhagyalakshmi: Scheme was launched during 2006-07 with an objective to promote the birth of girl children in below poverty line families and to raise the status of the girl child in the family in particular and society in general. Financial assistance is provided to the girl child through her mother/ father or natural guardian subject to the fulfillment of certain conditions.

Pashu Bhagya: Presenting his state budget for 2015-16, Chief Minister Siddaramaiah has announced Pashu Bhagya scheme to provide subsidies to farmers to set up cattle, sheep, goat, pig and poultry units.

Krishi Bhagya: This is the Government's flagship scheme to achieve revolutionary change in Karnataka's farm sector. Government is supporting farmers to make a farm pond with polythene lining (to prevent percolation), install pump and sprinkler irrigation system (for efficient water utilisation). This intervention helps farmers to harvest surplus rain water, store effectively and irrigate crops with stored water efficiently. If farmers take proper advantage of this programme they can save their crops or enhance yield by about 30 per cent. By delivering that much more income, this programme hopes to bring sustainability into rain fed farming. One time intervention that can potentially help farmers stand on their own feet.

Bhagya Jyoti Scheme: Bhagya Jyothi is a scheme sponsored by the Government for providing electricity to the economically weaker sections of society. In this scheme, only one bulb is allowed to be used by the consumer.

Arogya Bhagya and Jyothi Sanjeevini: Karnataka Government has launched two health insurance schemes — Rajiv Arogya Bhagya for above poverty line (APL) households and Jyothi Sanjeevini for all government employees — in Bengaluru. Government employees will get cashless treatment in 124 empanelled private hospitals under Jyothi Sanjeevini scheme without any cap while APL families will get subsidised treatment under Rajiv Arogya Bhagya (RAB) up to Rs 1.5 lakh in 110 empanelled hospitals.

Telangana

Kalyana Lakshmi/ Shaadi Mubarak: To alleviate financial distress of SC/ ST and minority families, Government decided to sanction a one-time financial assistance of Rs. 51,000 at the time of marriage for brides who are residents of Telangana State. Accordingly, Kalyana Lakshmi and Shaadi Mubaarak Schemes have been introduced with effect from 2 October 2014 for unmarried girls, who have completed 18 years of age at the time of marriage and whose parental income does not exceed Rs. 2 lakh per annum. Rs. 47 crore and Rs. 32 crore disbursed to 9,368 SC and 6,483 ST brides respectively. Another Rs. 50 crore was distributed to 10,533 brides from Minority sections.

Arogya Lakshmi: Telangana government provides one nutritious meal every day to pregnant and lactating women and children below the age of six through Anganwadi centres. The scheme was launched officially on 1 January 2015 by Honourable Chief Minister Sri K. Chandrashekar Rao. For the women, 200 ml of milk for 25 days a month and one egg each day is being given with meal. Children, aged between seven months and three years are provided with 16 eggs a month in addition to a 2.5 kg food packet. For children aged between three and six years, one egg a day in addition to rice, dal, vegetables and snacks is supplied.

A total 18,96,844 lactating mothers, 5,18,215 infants and 21,58,479 pregnant women were covered under the scheme expending Rs. 627.96 crore in the past year. The quantity of food items supplied under the scheme has also been increased across all the categories.

Aasara Pensions: As a part of its welfare measures and social safety net strategy, the Telangana government has introduced the "Aasara" pensions, with a view to ensure secured life with dignity for all the poor.

'Aasara' pension scheme is meant to protect the most vulnerable sections of society in particular the old and infirm, people with HIV-AIDS, widows, incapacitated weavers and toddy tappers, who have lost their means of livelihood with growing age, in order to support their day to day minimum needs required to lead a life of dignity and social security.

Under the sheme, the Telangana Government has enhanced the monthly pension from Rs. 200 to Rs. 1000 for the old aged, widows, weavers, toddy tappers and AIDS patients and Rs. 500 to Rs. 1500 for disabled persons.

The government has spent Rs. 4,700 crore on pensions benefitting nearly four million people including senior citizens, widows, physically handicapped, poor and old-aged artists and beedi workers, an increase of 478 per cent over the previous such schemes.

Housing for the Poor: This hallmark initiative of the Telangana government is intended to provide quality and respectable housing to the poor. The 'housing for the poor' plan provides for two and three storied buildings with the 2 BHK flats in Hyderabad and other urban areas while they are to be built as independent houses in rural areas. A pilot has been taken up at IDH Colony in Bhoidguda, Secunderabad. As many as 396 units — with each comprising of two bedrooms, hall and kitchen — are being constructed in 32 blocks of G+2 on 580 square yards at a cost of Rs. 37 crore at 7.9 lakh per flat.

Land Distribution to Dalits: Another significant welfare scheme of the government that provides three acres of agricultural land to landless SC women, along with the provision for creation of irrigation facilities, land development and other agricultural inputs for their sustained livelihood. Government distributed 2,524 acres of land to 959 Dalits spending Rs. 94 crore in the first year.

Rice Distribution: A whopping 87.57 lakh eligible families, approximately 2,86,00,000 (two crore eighty six lakh) beneficiaries, are being supplied rice from 1 January 2015 at six kgs per person at Re. 1 per kg without any ceiling on the number of members in the family. More than 1.80 lakh MT of rice per month would be required for this purpose.

To arrive at the eligibility of the BPL families, the family income limit in rural areas has been increased to Rs. 1.50 lakh and in urban areas to Rs. 2 lakh. The land ceiling has also been increased to 3.5 acres of wet land and 7.5 acres of dry land.

Government started supplying superfine rice, or Sanna Biyyam, to schools and hostels benefiting 56 lakh students annually with an additional outlay of Rs. 120 crore. More than 12,500 MT of rice is being distributed for the purpose

Strengthening security apparatus: To safeguard and secure the lives of its citizens, the Telangana Government sanctioned an amount of Rs. 271 crore for the purchase of 4,433 vehicles for Hyderabad and Cyberabad Police. Out of these, 3,883 vehicles equipped with modern technology have already been purchased. The number of new vehicles provided to the remaining nine districts in the State is 550. Additionally, 1500 motor cycles have been provided to Cyberabad Police to respond within 10 minutes of receiving a complaint or call. State government has allocated a monthly amount of Rs. 75,000, Rs. 50,000 and Rs. 25,000 to each police station in the city, district headquarters and villages, respectively.

The Government has taken up CCTV project under which one lakh CCTV cameras were to be installed in 2015-16 in Hyderabad city. All these cameras were to be connected to the proposed Command and Control Centre.

Tamil Nadu

According to the report which appeared in the *Business Standard* on 16 May 2012:

Tamil Nadu Government had allocated Rs. 18,777 crore for a variety of social welfare schemes in the State, including promises made during the AIADMK'S election campaign. The money to be spent in 2012-13 and the major beneficiaries would be students, women and the elderly.

For students Rs. 1500 crore had been allocated for procuring and distributing 784,000 laptops. The free laptop scheme was part of the Chief Minister's promise to distribute 680,000 laptops to students in government-aided higher secondary school and colleges. The total amount spent on purchase of laptops would be Rs. 10,200 crore over the next five years. The previous year, the government had spent Rs. 912 crore on the purchase of 907,790 laptops.

Other schemes for students include Rs. 330 crore to be spent on free uniforms, Rs. 324 crore on concessional student bus passes, Rs. 188 crore on free bicycle scheme, and Rs. 150 crore for free notebooks. The total spending on student welfare would be Rs. 2,492 crore

For the welfare of women the Chief Minister had budgeted Rs. 2,000 crore for purchase of mixies, grinders and table fans. The beneficiaries would belong to families who were holding family ration cards. According to one estimate 3.5 million women would benefit from the scheme during the year 2012-13.

The previous year Government had issued orders allocating a sum of Rs. 1.250 crore for free distribution of 2.5 million packages of electric fans, mixies and grinders during the year 2011-12.

The other social schemes included the food scheme (with an allocation of Rs. 4,900 crore in 2012-13), Social pension scheme Rs. 3,820 crore, Nutrition scheme (Rs. 1423 crore), Integrated Child Development Services Rs. 1,217 crore, Marriage assistance scheme including four grams of gold (Rs. 750 crore), Muthulakshmi Reddy Maternity Benefit scheme (Rs. 720 crore), The Chief Minister's Comprehensive Health Insurance Scheme (Rs. 750 crore), Free dhoti and saree distribution scheme (Rs. 269 crore), free distribution of goats/ sheep an milch cows (Rs. 244 crore) and free sanitary napkin distribution scheme (Rs. 55 crore).

West Bengal

West Bengal has introduced a scheme called Muktidhara with the object of ensuring economic self dependence, more family income, higher standard of living of the people and self help groups especially those formed by women of weaker sections of the society.

While every such scheme makes the life of the beneficiaries easier and should be welcomed it is desirable that all such schemes should be built into a grand strategy for providing public assistance to the people in need after identifying such people and their priority needs instead of sanctioning schemes in an unplanned and unbudgeted manner for select groups of people which smacks of politicalisation of peoples' needs.

4
Health Security

Health is one of the most important aspects of social security for the workers in the unorganised sector because they are prone to various kinds of illness due to the environment in which they work and live, as also their working conditions which contribute a few specific occupational diseases. Owing to poverty and under/mal-nourishment, their health problems are compounded. They lack medical attention due to their poverty and lack on means as also partly due to inadequate and unsatisfactory facilities available. The existing health insurance schemes are out of their reach. A separate health insurance scheme for the unorganised sector would not be feasible.

Augmentation of the public services is the best means by which the workers in the unorganised sector can enjoy health security. The impediments to this solution should be addressed.

One of the difficulties in providing satisfactory medical attention in rural areas is the unwillingness of the medical personnel to serve there. The National Commission on Rural Labour has, therefore, suggested as follows:

> "Besides providing necessary infrastructure of housing, education, transport, etc. as well as adequate provision of drugs and equipments to make the living and working conditions for the medical and para-medical personnel better, it may also be worthwhile to think in terms of paying a special allowance to such personnel who opt to work in rural areas. This incentive should be sufficiently attractive."

The National Commission on Rural Labour had also suggested:

> "Given the inadequate medical facilities for the general public at large, there must be a system by which the spare capacity of ESI hospitals . . , etc. may be made available to the public." In one important respect, namely: "free supply of drugs in government hospitals, PHCs and dispensaries — a greater measure of relief — is both necessary and possible."

The ILO has recommended that there is a clear case for extension of health insurance, both for raising additional finances so as to increase the access to medical services, and for enhancing their quality. On the other hand, the National Commission on Rural Labour has discounted the idea of health insurance for rural workers. It has said: "A health insurance scheme for the rural areas may not be feasible, both for operational and for financial reasons. It will be unrealistic, if not cruel, to expect the villagers to contribute towards a health insurance scheme."

Several N.G.O.s are experimenting with a variety of health insurance schemes. The ILO has described these experiments with the following words:

> "There has been a number of initiatives taken by groups of people, voluntary agencies, doctors and other medical staff, etc., to provide health services through organised community activity, often using elements of insurance. Some have ventured to provide the services to the target groups themselves, some have concentrated only on the financing of primary health services, while others have acted as intermediaries to make available insurance under the schemes of the G.I.C."

These initiatives are highly commendable but it is doubtful if they can be replicated on a large scale and whether they can be a substitute for the public medical services or a regular health insurance scheme. They can certainly be supplementary to public schemes.

Two experts called Hsino and Sen have developed a scheme called Co-operative Health Care Scheme (CHC). Under this scheme, the provision and financing of health care will be undertaken by communities characterised by strong social bonds and mutual trust. The CHC would provide preventive services, immunisation, health promotion, family planning, maternal and child care and outpatient services to all its members, including drugs for which a co-payment is levied. Each community of about 1000 people would have a health-post serviced by one health worker paid by CHC and with a stock of generic drugs specified in the essential drugs list. The CHC would also establish a primary health centre for a population of about 15,000 people, staffed by one doctor, one midwife, one clinical nurse, one primary care practitioner, one pharmacist and one assistant. These centres would refer patients to the regional centres for tertiary care possibly on the basis of a packaged fee for a captivation payment. Patients have the choice of free services at the posts and primary health centres or from private practitioners. When the service is obtained from a private practitioner, the CHC will only reimburse the patient 50 per cent of its costs. It is claimed that this new organisation would mean a significant improvement over services currently provided by the government. But the difficulty involved in organising a community to undertake such a scheme seems to have been underestimated.

It is, however, significant that a study conducted by Mathiyazhagan has revealed that insurance/ savings schemes are popular in rural areas and most of the people interviewed expressed willingness to join and pay for a rural health insurance scheme provided the health services provided under the scheme is of good quality.

The problem of health and disability is common to all.

Health Security consists of programmes designed for protection against morbidity and death. According to the *Human Development Report, 1994*:

> "In developing countries, the major causes of death are infectious and parasitic diseases which kill 17 million people annually — including 6.5 million from diarrhea and 3.5 million from tuberculosis. Most of these deaths are linked with

> poor nutrition and an unsafe environment, particularly polluted water, which contributes to the nearly one billion cases of diarrhea a year."
>
> "In industrial countries, the major killers are diseases of the circulatory system (5.5 million deaths a year) often linked with diet and life style. Next comes cancer, which in many cases has environmental causes . . ."
>
> "In both developing and industrial countries, the threats to health security are usually greater for the poorest people in the rural areas and particularly children. In the developing countries in 1990, safe water was available to 85 per cent of urban people but only 62 per cent of rural people. . .."
>
> "The disparities between rich and poor are similar for access to health services. In the industrial countries on an average, there is one doctor for every 400 people but for the developing countries there is one doctor for every 7000 people.... There are also marked disparities in health spending among developing countries...."
>
> "While poor people in general have low health security, the situation for women is particularly difficult. One of the most serious hazards they face is childbirth: more than three million women die each year from causes related to childbirth. Most of these deaths could be prevented by ensuring access to safe and affordable family planning and offering the most basic support at home during pregnancy and delivery, with the option of referrals to clinics or hospitals for women with evident complications."
>
> "The widest gap between the North and the South in any human indicator is in maternal mortality — which is about 18 times greater in the South. Thus, a miracle of life often turns into a nightmare of death just because a society cannot spare the loose change to provide a birth attendant at the time of the greatest vulnerability and anxiety in a woman's life."
>
> "Another increasing source of health insecurity for both sexes is the spread of HIV/AIDS. Around 15 million people are believed to be HIV positive — 80 per cent of them in developing countries. In 2000 this figure may rise to 40 million (13 million of these would be women)."

India has many achievements to show on the health front. There has been a long-term decline in mortality that has led to a near doubling of life expectancy between 1951 and 1996. In fact, mortality rates have been halved between 1975 and 1996. Many of the major communicable diseases have been controlled. India has also put in place a vast network of healthcare services backed by trained personnel. Between 1951 and 1997, the number of hospitals increased from 2,694 to 16,000; the number of hospital beds went up from 61,840 to 484,401; and the number of nurses grew from 16,550 to over 565,000. By 1997, there were 2,628 community health centres, 22,446 primary healthcare centres and 136,379 sub-centres spread throughout the country. The country has also acquired a reputation for high quality research and medical teaching, as well as for its super-specialty institutions.

Public expenditure on health was 1.3 per cent of GDP in 1990. This was less than what China (2.1 per cent of GDP) and Sri Lanka (1.8 per cent) spent but it was more than the proportion spent by Thailand (1.1 per cent) and Malaysia (1.5 per cent). If both public and private spending are considered, then India spends more on health than many other developing countries.

Despite the expansion in the physical provisioning of health facilities and the high levels of spending, India is far from reaching the Health for All goals which were to have been attained by the year 2000. Ill health remains one of the most prevalent causes of human deprivation. Close to two million children die every year, almost the same number as in 1960; and most of these deaths are avoidable. Almost 55 per cent of children under five — some 75 million of them — are malnourished. Iodine deficiency affects the normal development of some 250 million Indians and accounts for an estimated 90,000 stillbirths and neonatal deaths every year. It has led to 2.2 million Indian children being afflicted with cretinosis and another 6.5 million becoming mildly retarded. Close to 85 per cent of Indian women are anaemic on account of iron deficiency. An estimated 110,000 women die every year from causes related to pregnancy and childbirth.

Health Plans

The focus of the Eighth Plan on the Health Sector has been to improve access to health care for the underprivileged segments of the population. This is being achieved through:

(a) Consolidation and operationalisation of the primary, secondary and tertiary healthcare infrastructure for optimal performance and building up appropriate referral services with emphasis on primary care.

(b) Effective implementation of national programmes for combating major public health problems.

These efforts have resulted in a discernible impact on mortality with CDR declining to nine in 1995. However, the morbidity due to communicable and nutrition-related diseases has not shown parallel decline; in addition, there is now an increase in morbidity due to non-communicable diseases and newly emerging infections such as HIV infection, re-emergence of some infections such as *Kala Azar* leading to communicable diseases being high.

There are national programmes for control of vector-borne diseases, tuberculosis, leprosy and HIV infection. The performance of many of these has been sub-optimal, an important factor being the lack of key personnel such as lab technicians and multipurpose workers. Many of these programmes were initiated at a time when primary health care infrastructure was not fully operational and hence had their own vertical infrastructure. In the Ninth Plan it is proposed to make a major effort towards horizontal integration of these programmes.

There is an increasing incidence of hospital-acquired infections and accidental infections in health care providers and waste disposers. It is imperative that programmes are initiated to improve infection control and waste management through utilisation of appropriate affordable technology at all levels of health care.

Until poor sanitation, contaminated water supply and lack of adequate facilities for solid and liquid waste management, both in urban and rural areas are corrected, it may not be possible to completely prevent periodic outbreaks of infectious diseases. Nevertheless, if outbreaks are detected early enough, it will be possible to control the epidemic, reduce morbidity and ease fatality rates. According to the draft Ninth Plan, the strategy during the period would, therefore, be to strengthen health surveillance, early alert and rapid response mechanisms at district and below district level.

Changing lifestyles, longevity and dietary habits have resulted in increased prevalence and earlier age of onset of diabetes, cerebral and cardio-vascular diseases over the last decade and a concomitant rise in disease burden and DALY (Disability Adjusted Life Years) due to non-communicable diseases. The overall cancer incidence in the country is low. Even though the two cancers of the oropharynx and uterine cervix are easy to diagnose and treat, the available data indicate that majority of cases are detected at a late stage when palliative rather than curative treatment remains the only possible therapeutic modality. There is thus a need to improve facilities for early detection of cancers so that effective treatment could be improved.

Urban migration over the last decade has resulted in rapid growth of urban slums. There has not been any well-planned and organised effort to provide primary, secondary and tertiary care services in geographically delineated urban areas. In some cities the health status of urban slum dwellers is stated to be worse than that of rural population.

Health Care Schemes

There are two major programmes for health care in India: The programme to provide basic minimum services and the health programme under the Five Year Plan. The Basic Minimum Services include three health related programmes, namely: (a) primary health care services; (b) provision of safe drinking water; and (c) nutrition support. The Plan programme relating to health focuses on providing integrated, preventive, promotive curative and rehabilitative services for communicable and non-communicable diseases through appropriate strengthening of existing Primary Health Care infrastructure by filling in the existing gaps in physical infrastructure and manpower and ensuring their optimum utilisation both in urban and in rural areas. In so far as the overall objective of the two programmes is common, they tend to overlap.

National Rural Health Mission

The Government of India set up the National Rural Health Mission in the year 2005. It is operational throughout the county with special focus on certain States. The main aim of the Mission is to provide accessible, affordable, accountable, effective and reliable primary health care facilities, especially, to the poor and vulnerable sections of the population. It also aims at bridging the gap in rural health care services through creation of a cadre of Accredited Social Health Activists (ASHA) and improved hospital care, decentralisation of programme to district level to improve intra and inter sectoral convergence and effective utilisation of resources. The NRHM further aims to provide over arching umbrella to the existing programmes of Health and Family Welfare including RCH II, Malaria, Blindness, Iodine Deficiency, Filaria, *Kala Azar*, T.B, Leprosy, and Integrate Disease Surveillance. Further it addresses the issue of health in the context of sector wise approach to sanitation, hygiene, nutrition and safe drinking water as basic determinants of good health in order to have greater convergence among the related social sector programmes. At the district and village level, the institutional framework of the total sanitation campaign will be integrated with the district Health Mission and village Health and Sanitation Committee.

The Mission further seeks to build greater ownership of the programme among the community through involvement of Panchayat Raj Institutions, NGOs, and other stakeholders at National, State, District, and sub-district levels to achieve the goals of National Population Policy, 2000 and the National Health Policy.

There is a proposal to set up a similar Mission for urban areas, the National Urban Health Mission. The Union Health Minister announced recently (*The Hindu*, 23 February 2008) that the Central Government would launch a National Urban Health Mission at a cost of Rs. 8000 crore in about three months. The Mission would cover all cities and towns with more than one lakh population. To begin with, it would be launched in about 450 cities and towns focusing on 5.5 crore slum dwellers. Under the Mission the government will pay the health insurance premium for slum dwellers.

An Urban Social Health Activist would be appointed for every 200 population. An urban health centre would also be set up for every 50000 population

Self help groups of women, Mahila Arogya Samitis would be formed for every 100 households to monitor health issues at the grassroots level. The Centre would give them seed money of Rs. 2500.

The private sector as well as NGOs would be involved in reaching out to the masses. It would work in synergy with the Rural Health Mission. Urban local bodies will monitor implementation in their jurisdiction.

National Health Insurance Scheme: Rashtriya Swasthya BimaYojana (RSBY)

Rashtriya Swasthya Bima Yojana (RSBY, or National Health Insurance Programme), health insurance scheme for the poor. It provides cashless insurance for hospitalisation in public as well as private hospitals. The scheme started enrolling on 1 April 2008 and has been implemented in 25 States of India. A total of 36 million families have been enrolled as of February, 2014. In the starting RSBY is a project under the Ministry of Labour and Employment. Now it is transferred to Ministry of Health and Family Welfare from 1 April 2015 (Active smart Cards 40,430,279, Hospitalisation cases 10,630, 269 as on 31,8,2015)

Every Below Poverty Line (BPL) family holding a yellow ration card pays Rs. 30 as registration fee to get a biometric-enabled smart card containing their fingerprints and photographs. This enables him to receive inpatient medical care of up to Rs. 30,000 per family per year in any of the empanelled hospitals. Pre-existing illnesses are covered from day one, for head of household, spouse and up to three dependent children or parents.

In the Union Budget for 2012-13, the government made a total allocation of Rs. 1096.7 crore towards RSBY. Although meant to cover the entire BPL population, (about 37.2 per cent of the total Indian population according to the Tendulkar committee estimates) it had enrolled only around 10 per cent of the Indian population by 31 March 2011. Also, it is expected to cost the exchequer at least Rs. 3,350 crore a year to cover the entire BPL population.

The scheme has won laurels from the World Bank, the UN and the ILO as one of the world's best health insurance schemes. Germany has shown interest in adopting the smart card based model for revamping its own social security system, the oldest in the world, by replacing its current, expensive system of voucher based benefits for 2.5 million children. The Indo-German Social Security Programme, created as part of a co-operation pact between the two countries is guiding this collaboration.

One of the big changes that this scheme entails is bringing investment to unserved areas. Most private investments in healthcare in India have been focused on tertiary or specialised care in urban areas. However, with RSBY coming in, the scenario is changing. New age companies like Global Healthcare Systems, a company based out of Kolkata and funded by Tier I Capital Funds like Sequoia Capital and Elevar Equity are setting up State of the Art Hospitals in Semi Urban-rural settings. This trend can create the infrastructure that India's healthcare system desperately needs.

As per report from Council for Social Development, it was found that this scheme has not been very effective. Increase in outpatient expenditure, hospitalisation and medicines have compelled insurance companies to exclude several diseases out of their policies and thus making it not affordable for BPL families. Report has also found that most of the beneficiaries are from higher classes and not targeted beneficiaries.

Health Insurance Initiatives by State Governments

In the recent past, various state governments have begun health insurance initiatives. *Aarogyasri* is a programme of the Government of Andhra Pradesh. It covers those who are below the poverty line. The government issues an Aarogyasri card and the beneficiary can use it at government and private hospitals to obtain services free of cost. There are similar schemes in most of the other States.

Social Health Insurance Schemes in India

There is only one Social Health Insurance Scheme in India which satisfies the three main criteria for defining a Social Health Insurance (SHI); it is mandatory, contributory and it is administered by an autonomous body, namely, the Employees State Insurance Corporation.

The other scheme that is often mentioned along with the ESIS as a SHI Scheme in India is the CGHS. It is also contributory and employment based However, neither does it have a separate autonomous fund manager, nor is it compulsory. Further, the contributions are almost flat, and nominal enough to not warrant the definition of a contributory scheme.

The ESIS and the CGHS together cover about three per cent of the population, including beneficiaries and their families. However, some other sectors of the government are also covered by non contributory schemes, which are in the nature of social welfare scheme and are essentially benefits given to the various categories of employees in the government sector.

Certain ministries like Railways, Defence and Coal give health coverage to their employees as a benefit, while there are some government sponsored schemes that provide health coverage to specific employment based target populations. This includes schemes for handloom workers and handicrafts artisans sponsored by the Ministry of Textiles.

Employees State Insurance Scheme

The Employees' State Insurance (ESI) Scheme is a statutory scheme governed by the Employees State Insurance Act, 1948. The Scheme was started in 1952 in two centres with a coverage of 120,000 persons and has been expanded significantly across the country with the active involvement of State governments. Today it covers nearly 9.3 million workers in the country (as on 31.3.2007). The scheme is compulsory and contributory and provides medical care and cash benefits in the contingencies of sickness, maternity, employment injury and death.

The scheme provides a full range of medical benefits (out-patient services, specialist treatment and hospitalisation), through a network of dispensaries, specialist centres and ESI hospitals. It also provides for cash benefits in the nature of sickness benefit; maternity benefit; employment injury benefit; temporary disability benefit; permanent disability benefit; dependants' benefit and funeral expenses. Recently it has introduced an unemployment allowance scheme called the Rajiv Gandhi Shrama Kalyan Yojana, Ministry of Labour is the administrative and co-ordinating Ministry for the Scheme.

At the national level, the ESI scheme is administered by a statutory body called the Employees' State Insurance Corporation, which consists of representatives of employees, employers, the Central Government, State governments, the medical profession and the Parliament. A standing Committee constituted from amongst the members of the Corporation acts as the executive body. There is also a Medical Benefit Council to advise the Corporation on matters connected with the provision of medical care. At the regional level, Regional Boards have been constituted in each state and at the local level, local committees have been formed which function as advisory bodies.

For the day-to-day administration, the Corporation has set up a Regional Office in each State and for the disbursement of cash benefits, which is the direct responsibility of the Corporation; there is a network of local offices all over the country. The administration of medical care is the statutory responsibility of the State Governments. The Corporation may assume responsibility for providing the medical care in any State, subject to the condition that the State Governments will have to continue to contribute a one-eighth share towards the cost of medical care. The Corporation has, however, so far taken over the responsibilities for administration of medical care in the Union Territory of Delhi, from the Delhi Administration; it has approved the taking over of the medical scheme in other States subject to the consent of the State governments concerned.

In-patient treatment is given through ESI hospitals and annexes and reservation beds in other government hospitals. Out-patient medical care is rendered through a network of full-time ESI scheme dispensaries, part-time, mobile and employers' utilisation dispensaries and clinics of insurance medical practitioners.

The extension of the social security scheme to the areas which have not so far been brought under the purview of the ESI scheme depends upon the Corporation and the State Governments, who are mainly responsible under Section 58(3) of the Act to create the necessary establishments and their families. After these infrastructures are created, the extension of the scheme to other areas and new types of establishment become possible.

The Act applies in the first instance to non-seasonal factories using power and employing 20 or more persons. It is being extended area-wise by stages. The Act contains an enabling provision under which the "appropriate government" is empowered to extend the provisions of the Act to other classes of establishments, industrial, commercial, agricultural or otherwise. Under these provisions, most of the state governments have extended the provisions of the Act to the following new classes of establishments:

(a) small power-using factories employing ten to ninteen persons and non-power-using factories employing twenty or more persons;
(b) shops, hotels, restaurants, cinemas, including preview theatres, road motor transport and newspaper establishments employing 20 or more persons;
(c) beedi manufacturing establishments employing ten or more persons in the implemented areas;
(d) Slate-pencil manufacturing establishments employing one or more persons.

The employees of the foregoing establishments in receipt of wages not exceeding Rs. 10,000 per month are covered under the Act. The wage ceiling for coverage under the ESI Act which was initially Rs. 200 per month is being raised from time to time. The current ceiling is Rs. 15,000.

The rate of contributions from employees and employers is fixed at 1.75 per cent and 4.75 per cent respectively of the wages payable to the employees. Employees in receipt of average daily wages below a specified amount which is revised from time to time (currently Rs. 70) are exempted from payment of the employees' contribution.

The State governments bear one eighth of expenditure on medical benefit within a per capita ceiling which is revised from time to time

The ESI scheme now covers workers in organised industry mostly in urban and semi-urban areas, all over the country with the exception of the States of Jammu and Kashmir, Sikkim, Nagaland, Tripura, Arunachal, Pradesh, Mizoram and Manipur and the Union Territories of Daman and Diu.

Retired as well as permanently disabled insured persons (who cease to be in insurable employment due to an employment injury) and their spouses are eligible for full medical care on payment of a nominal contribution of Rs. 10 per month, payable in a lump sum for one year in advance, subject to fulfillment of certain conditions

It was in force in 737 industrial centres in the country covering about 9.2 million employees as on 31 March 2007. The total number of beneficiaries including insured persons entitled to medical care, as on 31 March 2007 was 39 million.

The Employees' State Insurance scheme provides comprehensive medical care in the form of medical attendance, treatment, drugs and injections, specialist consultation and hospitalisation to insured persons and also to members of their families where the facility for specialist consultation and hospitalisation has been extended to the families.

Apart from the curative services provided through hospitals and dispensaries, the Corporation also provides certain other services such as immunisation, family welfare, etc.

Central Government Health Scheme (CGHS)

The CGHS was introduced as a contributory plan in 1954 to provide medical coverage to central government employees (both working and retired) and their families, without involving the system of medical reimbursement.

The scheme was initially started in Delhi and extended over the years to other cities; currently it covers 23 cities. The beneficiaries residing outside these coverage areas are being reimbursed for their medical expenditure as per the Central Services Medical Attendance Rules and All India Services (Medical Attendance) Rules.

The CGHS is being operated departmentally with the Director General as the head of the organisation. Under the Ministry of Health. There are currently one million card holders and the total number of beneficiaries is 4.3 million. The Scheme offers a range of services through allopathic dispensaries and also through the units of alternative medicine like homeopathy. The facilities like outpatient care, emergency/ inpatient care, free drug supply laboratory and radiological investigations, etc. are being provided through such dispensaries and the network of polyclinics laboratories, and dental units. The beneficiaries are referred to the designated hospitals for the services that are not available at the dispensary level, and the expenses are reimbursed. About 500 such hospitals are recognised across 17 cities.

The employee contribution ranges from Rs. 15 to Rs. 150 per month depending on the salary. The pensioners can avail of a whole life card by paying 10 years contribution at the time of retirement. This almost flat structure and the almost negligible amount make a very different scheme from the ESIS.

The funds of the CGHS are allocated by the Ministry of Health and Family Welfare and are shown under the budget of the Department of Health. Thus, there is no separate autonomous fund manager for CGHS, which is a key feature of a SHI Scheme. Unfortunately, the detailed description of inflow and outflow of funds is not available and raises questions about planning process of the department in the absence of such basic data which constitute the tool of planning.

Railways Health Services

Railway working employees and their families can avail the railways managed health facilities without paying any contribution; the retired employees can opt for continued health benefits by contributing the last month's basic pay. The employee coverage includes 1.6 million current employees and 0.25 million retired employees. Currently, about eight million beneficiaries avail the health services through a network of 584 health units, 124 hospitals including five super-speciality hospitals, and nine apex referral hospitals. The improved quality of healthcare is ensured with exceptionally high degree of accountability, mainly because of very alert labour unions and well informed and aware employees. Out of the total railway budget of Rs. 3,20,000 million, less than two per cent is being spent on health. The budgetary allocation for railway health service is about Rs. 6,111million; about Rs. 4,750 million is spent on health related expenditure, while the rest is used for hygiene and sanitation. The perception is that the railways provide a model case of provision of quality health benefits through a network of self run and self funded health facility network.

Defence Medical Services

Similarly Ministry of Defence, through an Inter Service Organisation called Armed Forces Medical Services (AFMS), provides a comprehensive health coverage to the serving armed forces personnel and their families of all three wings, Army, Navy and the Air Force The total number of beneficiaries add up to 6.6 million. Previously the ex-servicemen also used to get limited coverage under this scheme, but with the introduction of a new scheme in the recent past, AFMS is restricted to serving personnel only. There is no contribution from the beneficiaries and the entire expenditure comes from the budget of the Ministry of Defence.

Ex-servicemen's Contributory Health Scheme

The other newly introduced scheme i.e. Ex-Servicemen's Contributory Health Service Scheme provides medical care to ex-servicemen, war widows, and their dependents. This scheme covers all diseases and provides cashless medical facilities to the ex-servicemen pensioners settled in far flung areas of the country. The out-patient services are provided through poly-clinics and in-patient treatment through service hospitals and empanelled civil hospitals and facilities. In the year 2003-04, 95 such clinics were established and the rest will be constructed in a phased manner by 2008.

It is a onetime contributory scheme: on retirement, each pensioner (w.e.f. April, 2003) will compulsorily become a member of ECHS by contributing his/ her one time contribution to avail of the life time benefits. Similarly, pensioners who have already retired prior to 31 March 2003, can voluntarily become members, either by paying a onetime contribution or in three -yearly instalments. The contribution varies between Rs. 1800 and 18,000 depending on the basic pension. The total coverage under this scheme is 76,000 including 60,000 employees who retired in 2003-04. The scheme is voluntary for the already retired pensioners and the turnout is still low with only one per cent of the estimated 1.6 million ex-servicemen enrolled in the scheme. The figure is expected to increase once it is scaled up and as more health facilities are set up.

Schemes under the Ministry of Textiles

The Ministry of Textiles offers schemes to provide social security to the handloom weavers and handicraft artisans, which involve health coverage.

Health package of handloom weavers

This scheme mainly focuses on the health problems related to the profession of handloom weaving. The scheme is a centrally sponsored one and is being operated by the State governments. The medical components of the Scheme include medical reimbursement up to a maximum of Rs. 1,500 per weaver per annum, and the eye camps including provision of spectacles. The reimbursement is applicable for the treatment of TB, asthma and inflammation of alimentary system only, and thus, the health cover is limited. There is no contribution from the beneficiaries and the total budget of the package was a substantial amount of rupees 146 million during the ninth five year plan.

The coverage in this scheme depends on the efficiency of State governments as they have to submit the proposal for such coverage and expenditure details annually. Among the estimated 6.5 million weavers, only about four per cent were covered during the Ninth Plan. From the Tenth Plan the Scheme has been opened to the self-help groups of weavers, in addition to the cooperative societies of handloom weavers. Thus, it is expected that the coverage may improve in the near future.

Health package for handicraft artisans

This contributory social security scheme is being offered in collaboration with the United India Insurance Company — a public sector enterprise. The annual premium rate is Rs. 200; the government shares 75 per cent of the premium and the rest is borne by the beneficiary or the implementing agency. The health component of coverage includes reimbursement of hospitalisation expenses up to Rs. 15,000 and maternity coverage up to Rs. 750. This scheme offers an innovative way of scaling up SHI for special groups.

Schemes of Public Sector Undertakings

There are 240 Central Public Undertakings established by the Government of India as government companies. As on 2002, the employment in these enterprises was about two million excluding casual workers. These public enterprises provide a range of welfare activities to their employees, in keeping with the spirit of a socially responsible employer. Though housing facilities remain the major element of employee welfare, many of these enterprises are also taking a lead in providing health care facilities.

Health Care under Welfare Funds

Welfare funds have been set up for the benefit of certain classes of workers by the Government of India and also by certain State Governments. The Government of India has set up welfare funds for the welfare of workers in Beedi and Cine industries and certain classes of mines under the following Acts.

- The Beedi Workers' Welfare Fund Act, 1976
- The Cine Workers' Welfare Fund Act, 1981
- The Iron ore, Manganese Ore and Chrome Ore Mines Labour Welfare Fund Act, 1976
- Limestone and Dolomite Mines Labour Fund Act, 1972 and
- Mica Mines Labour Fund Act, 1946

The Acts provide that the Funds may be utilised to defray the cost of measures for the benefit of persons employed in the industries, or mines, as the case may be, directed inter alia towards " the provision and improvement of public health and sanitation, the prevention of disease and the provision and improvement of medical facilities".

The Labour Welfare Organisation of the Government of India in the Ministry of Labour administers these funds departmentally.

The organisation has established and is directly running 13 hospitals with 515 beds and 276 dispensaries spread all over the country under these Acts. They provide basic health care and family welfare measures to the families of eligible workers. A few more 30 bedded hospitals are under construction under the Beedi Workers Welfare Fund.

Any mine which employs 75 or more workers and has a standard hospital, is given grant-in-aid to the extent of 50 per cent of the actual cost for purchase of an ambulance subject to a limit of Rs. 2 lakh. Grants-in-aid are also paid for maintenance of hospitals and dispensaries to mine managements at the rate of Re. 0.10 per MT of iron ore, manganese ore, chrome ore, limestone or dolomite produced or 75 per cent of the expenditure on medicines and establishment charges whichever is less.

Welfare Funds Set up by State Governments

The legislative provisions for the welfare funds set up by the State governments usually provide for payment of lump sum amount by way of financial assistance for meeting the expenditure on medical care, e.g., Kerala Coir Workers Welfare Scheme provides for cash assistance at the rate of Rs. 5 per day for hospitalisation in government hospitals and reimbursement of medical expenses to the extent of Rs. 200.

Kerala Cashew Workers Welfare Fund and Kerala Handloom Workers Welfare Fund provide for reimbursement of medical expenses to the extent of Rs. 200.

The Kerala Labour Welfare Fund provides for payment of Rs. 5,000 for treatment of cancer, etc.

Andhra Pradesh and Karnataka Labour Welfare Funds provide for medical aid for specialised treatment.

The Mathadi Workers Welfare Boards in Maharashtra, however, have set up their own hospital for treatment of head load workers.

Community Based Health Insurance Schemes/Insurance Offered by NGOs

An important part of private health finance in India is the service provided by voluntary and charitable organisations. As noted by Berman (1996) "while such groups do not account for a large share in health care, they are often the only source of health services, or the only trusted ones, for the population they serve". While it is very difficult to estimate even approximately the exact coverage of these varied services, Berman speculates that they cover more than five per cent of the population (Ellis et al 2000). Many NGOs in India are involved in micro-financing initiatives. Some of them have started micro-insurance programmes. There are also some other NGOs that are not into micro-finance but into other developmental activities and they have also started insurance schemes for the poor. Most of these NGOs offer comprehensive assistance packages with the underlying assumption that health is only one aspect of development and should, therefore, be tackled along with other social problems in holistic fashion (Ellis et al 2000). According to one notification, government recognises NGOs and panchayats as intermediaries who can sell insurance.[1]

There are numerous insurance schemes offered by NGOs known as community based insurance schemes. Details of some schemes are given below.

Self-Employed Women's Association (SEWA)

The SEWA is a labour union of 6,00,000 women workers engaged in the informal economy, based in Ahmedabad, Guajarat. SEWA is engaged in a variety of development oriented activities targeted at women. In 1984, SEWA established a community based primary health care programme Aarogya SEWA (or SEWA Health) and Vimo SEWA (or SEWA Insurance) was established in 1992 to complement this primary health care work. SEWA provides a comprehensive insurance package of life, health (hospitalisation) and asset insurance. The scheme is targeted at members of the SEWA union across the districts in Gujarat state, their spouses and their children. Of late, the scheme has also been extended to other states of India. In order to join the scheme, adults must be between 18 and 60 years of age. Under Vimo SEWA's most popular policy, those who pay the annual premium of Rs. 85 (Rs. 37 of which is earmarked for medical insurance) are covered to a maximum of Rs. 2,000 per year in case of hospitalisation. Women also have the option of becoming lifetime members of the social security scheme by making a fixed deposit of Rs 1,000; interest on this is used to pay the annual premium and the deposit is returned to the woman when she turns 60. Exempted from coverage under the medical insurance fund are certain pre-existing diseases (for example, chronic tuberculosis, certain cancers, diabetes, hypertension, piles) and disease caused by addiction. Members are eligible for reimbursement of care taken at any type of hospital (public, private, or trust). At the time of discharge, members must pay for the hospitalisation out-of-pocket, and apply for reimbursement from Vimo SEWA.

Tribhuvandas Foundation

Tribhuvandas Foundation (TF), named after one of the pioneers of the white revolution and founder chairman of AMUL dairy, the late Tribhuvandas Patel, has been actively involved in various development oriented activities, and particularly concerned with the health of women and children in the villages of Kheda and Anand districts of central Gujarat since 1980. The foundation covers 638 villages out of 900 villages of Kheda, Anand district. TF has trained one voluntary health worker (VHW) for work in every village. VHWs are paid an honorarium by the community and they have been trained at TF headquarters to treat primary illnesses and to identify at-risk cases so that they can be referred to TE. In addition to primary health care, TF is also involved in income-generating projects.

The health insurance scheme named as Sardar Patel Aarogya Mandal came into existence on 26 January 2001. TF was already providing primary health care through its infrastructure, but it felt the need of a health insurance scheme that could cover the expensive hospitalisation. So the scheme was created to provide inpatient care. Under this new scheme (TF had already been experimenting with prepayment for more than 20 years), three paisa per litre of milk deposited, plus Rs. 26 (Rs. 25 for TF membership and Re. 1 for the scheme) per year are collected as premium from each household. Originally the purpose behind deducting three paisa per litre of milk deposited was to build up a corpus and the interest on it would pay for the premium. This three paisa per litre, was being collected years before the scheme was started. For those who have paid the premium, 100 per cent of hospitalisation expenses (excluding medicine, transport and other indirect cost) are covered for the entire family. Only those who are members of both, milk cooperative (doodhmandli) as well as TF can enrol in this scheme. They must deposit a minimum 300 litres of milk per year. If they cannot, they are not entitled to the benefits, Another important clause is that members must not sell any amount of milk to AMUL competitors. If they are found selling milk to the competitors, they are disqualified from participating in the scheme.

The Aga Khan Health Services, India

Aga Khan Health Services (AKHS), India a major functionary of the Aga Khan development network, is one of the most comprehensive, non-profit health care systems in the developing world. AKHS is active in Kenya, Tanzania, India and Pakistan. Today more than two million people benefit from AKHS. The organisation derives support from the Aga Khan's secretariat in France and international headquarters in Geneva on policy issues and concerns. AKHS-I (Aga Khan Health Services, India) provides health care to the poor in pockets through the country but mainly the organisation is active in Gujarat, Maharashtra and Andhra Pradesh. In Gujarat AKHS-I is working in Sidhpur taluka of Patan district in north Gujarat and Junagadh district in Saurashtra. AKHS-I believes in providing quality health care to the poor and strives for making all its services financially viable. They charge user fees for all services and have also introduced prepayment or health insurance schemes.

In the first scheme known as cooperative health care financing AKHS-I has tied up with a dairy cooperative and the dairy cooperative deducts three to five paisa per litre of milk and in return provides Rs. 30,000 to AKHS-I. Under the second scheme, known as community health fund (CHF), Rs. 200 is collected as premium from each family that is not a member of dairy cooperatives. Those who are members of any of the two schemes, get waiver in registration fee (which in any case is subsidised, at a cost of only Rs. 2) and medical examination fees (Rs. 5). They get 10 per cent discount in delivery charges. Delivery charges are Rs. 125 plus Rs. 20 per day for in-patient care and for deliveries at home, Rs. 150 is charged. Members receive 20 per cent discounts in all laboratory tests. Moreover all members who are above the age of 35 get free medical checkup and non-communicable disease (NCD) screening once in a year. Females also get breast cancer screening free, AKHS-I does not provide any hospitalisation cover except in case of delivery. The community itself, through a local health sector management committee, decides the premium amount. There is no specific timing period of paying the premium in case of self. Generally people pay the premium during the harvest time.

Navasarjan

The focus of Navasarjan, which was established in 1988, is the dalit community. The main objective 0f the organisation is to unearth atrocities against dalits and fight against these atrocities by providing legal assistance so that dalits can lead a life of self-respect and dignity. One enthusiastic and committed worker of Navasarjan, who belongs to the north Gujarat region, initiated an idea of health insurance. Navasarjan decided to buy the 'mediclaim' policy from New India Assurance (Sanand branch) and pay the premium. The coverage period was from 17 March 1999 to 16 March 2000. The coverage amount was Rs. 15,000 and the premium was Rs. 175 per member. New India Assurance gave a five per cent group discount so per capita premium came to Rs 159. The total premium paid for the scheme was Rs. 91,216. This amount was partly funded by Hivos (a funding agency) and partly from Navasasrjan Social Security membership fund (a larger comprehensive scheme which was also on pilot basis for two years and included accidental death, maternity benefits, etc. The membership fee was Rs. 400 per annum and was paid by individuals). Thus, the scheme was partially financed by the community through the social security fund. Five panel doctors (two orthopedic surgeons, one gynaecologist, one physician and one general surgeon) were approached in Patan town and it was decided that the members, in case of need, would visit them in Patan. The doctors agreed to receive payment after three months, i.e, they would provide treatment on credit. Each member was given a membership card. One staff member of Navasarjan was transferred to

Patan to sit in the premises of the hospital to help the members of the scheme. He looked after all documents like bills and drug prescriptions, and file the mediclaim application form. The village Navasarjan workers often accompanied members to the hospital in Patan. The policy was just for one year and was on pilot basis only.

Yeshaswini

Initiated in early 2003, in the State of Karnataka and targeting the poor farmers regrouped in cooperative societies, the Yeshaswini Cooperative Farmer's Health Scheme was originally designed as a self funding scheme to cover only the most expensive segment of the health expenditure spectrum: the surgical interventions. In its first year of operation, the scheme already succeeded to become one of the largest micro insurance Schemes. The scheme also represents today one of the best examples of efficient public-private partnership in health between a State government, rural cooperatives private and public health providers and a Third Party Administrator.

The development of this partnership over the three years accounted for the following main achievements:

- Setting up of a cost free premium collection mechanism that allows the full face value of the premium to serve for the payment of benefits.
- Organisation of a broad network of hospitals/ nursing homes applying standard reduced tariffs on all interventions covered by the Scheme.
- Provision of subsidies by the State government directly allocated to the payment of benefits.
- Transfer of all health insurance administrative functions to a specialised agency (TPA) at a low cost.

From the perspective of providing quality health care service to poor segments of the population, the scheme proved to be highly successful. Over a three year period, the Scheme could cover some 42000 surgical procedures, many of those lifesaving, with the additional benefit of having allowed some 125,000 people to avail free OPD services provided by a network of 169 health facilities.

From a financial perspective, however, the Scheme shows no sign of having reached some level of stability and still faces major constraints which challenge its long term sustainability. With a premium set at very low level of Rs. 60 per person per year, the Scheme ended its first year with a $725000 surplus. The Scheme, however, experimented with a rapid increase of claims incidence and costs in Year II, a clear indication of a strong adverse selection affect which led it to increase the premium upto Rs. 120 in Year III, while relying on additional subsidies provided by the State Government. As a result of the sudden premium increases the scheme registered a 700,000 membership loss in Year III (from 2.1 million to 1.4 million), while the payout upwards trend did not slow down and even further accelerated.

Answer strategies applied, which focused on extending the outreach and on encouraging family enrolment have had so far a very limited impact, making no dent on the ever increasing benefit expenditure pattern.

Over a three year period, the scheme has renounced its self-funding character and is now found increasingly dependent on State subsidies. The Scheme has still to grasp with this new situation and take appropriate management decisions in order to clearly determine the conditions and extent through which the government should take the responsibility to underwrite the scheme.

While it is not expected, thanks to additional subsidies already received, for the scheme to end up Year III with a cash problem. It is clear that immediate and efficient measures are required to tackle the adverse selection issue before it gets utterly out-of-control, resulting in making the Scheme both cost-effective and unsustainable

The Government of Karnataka has since expanded the scope of the Yeshaswini Health Insurance scheme, which was limited to major surgeries. Chairman of the Yeshaswini Cooperative Farmers' Health Care Trust, recently announced that the medical aid under the scheme would now cover accidental deaths and medical problems faced by farmers in their daily life. It would now cover snake bite, dog bite, drowning, electric shock, goring by bulls, injuries caused while operating agricultural equipment, etc. Benefit under the scheme would be available to women for ensuring normal delivery and for neonatal care.

The definition of the family has been expanded to include dependent father, mother, mother-in-law, father-in-law and all dependent children.

The scheme will cover all members of cooperative societies in rural areas, Stree Shakti groups and self-help groups who are linked to cooperative societies and cooperative banks.

Community Health Insurance Scheme of Karuna Trust, Karnataka

Another successful example of partnership among government, insurance company and an NGO to offer low cost health cover to mainly the poor, comes from Karnataka. The State has collaborated with Karuna Trust, an NGO, and National Insurance Company in two taluks of Karnataka; a health cover for a premium of Rs. 30 for BPL, and between Rs. 30 and 60 for non-BPL population is being offered in these areas. The Government of Karnataka has pledged premium payment for the poor and vulnerable sections of the society. As in the case of the rag pickers' scheme, this scheme too has been successful to a large part due to the presence of Karuna Trust, which has acted as the go-between at all stages of implementation.

Voluntary Health Insurance Schemes or Private-for-Profit Schemes

In private insurance, buyers are willing to pay premium to an insurance company that pools people with similar risks and insures them for health expenses. The key distinction is that the premiums are set at a level, which provides a profit to third party and provider institutions. Premiums are based on an assessment of the risk status of the consumer (or of the group of employees) and the level of benefits provided, rather than as a proportion of the consumer's income. In the public sector, the General Insurance Corporation (GIC) and its four subsidiary companies (National Insurance Corporation, New India Assurance Company, Oriental Insurance Company and United Insurance Company) and the Life Insurance Corporation (LIC) of India provide voluntary insurance schemes.

Of the various schemes offered, Mediclaim is the main product of the GIC. The Medical Insurance Scheme or Mediclaim was introduced in November 1986 and it covers individuals and groups with persons aged 5-80 years. Children (3 months-5 years) are covered along with their parents. This scheme provides for reimbursement of medical expenses (now offers cashless scheme) by an individual towards hospitalisation and domiciliary hospitalisation as per the sum insured. There are exclusions and pre-existing disease clauses. Premiums are calculated based on age and the sum insured, which in turn varies from Rs. 15,000 to Rs. 5,00,000. In 1995-96 about half a million Mediclaim policies were issued with about 1.8 million beneficiaries (Krause Patrick 2000). The coverage for the year 2000-01 was around 7.2 million.

The year 1999 marked the beginning of a new era for health insurance in the Indian context. With the passing of the Insurance Regulatory Development Authority Bill (IRDA) the insurance sector was opened to private and foreign participation, thereby paving the way for the entry of private health insurance companies. The Bill also facilitated the establishment of an authority to protect the interests of the insurance holders by regulating, promoting and ensuring orderly growth of the insurance industry. The bill allows foreign promoters to hold paid up capital of up to 26 per cent in an Indian company and requires them to have a capital of Rs. 100 crore along with a business plan to begin its operations. Currently, a few companies such as Bajaj Allianz, ICICI, Royal Sundaram, HDFC and Cholamandalam among others are offering health insurance schemes.

Employer-based Schemes

Employers in both the public and private sector offer employer-based insurance schemes through their own employer-managed facilities by way of lump sum payments, reimbursement of employee's health expenditure for out-patient care and hospitalisation, fixed medical allowance, monthly or annual irrespective of actual expenses, or covering them under the group health insurance policy. The railways, defence and security forces, plantations sector and mining sector provide medical services and/ or benefits to its own employees. The population coverage under these schemes is minimal, about 30-50 million people.

Micro Health Insurance Schemes

In recent years health micro insurance has emerged in India as an essential tool for removing the financial barriers allowing to an easier access to quality health care services. Wider awareness of the existing social protection gaps as well as the growing demand for adapted benefits emanating from the excluded groups have led to the active involvement of multiple actors of the civil society and to a rapid proliferation of various health micro-insurance schemes across the country

A first national inventory prepared in 2003-04 by ILO/STEP provided detailed information related to each micro-insurance scheme while highlighting the main characteristics of the experiments developed at the country level. Based on a 2005 update of this inventory, the document provides an overview of the various health micro- insurance schemes currently found operational in India as well as a very first assessment of their present and potential contribution to the overall extension strategies still to be fully designed at the national level

There has been a fast growth of micro-insurance schemes since the last inventory was taken. The new inventory could document 60 schemes which was more than twice the number operational in 2001.

NDA Government Schemes

The NDA Government has introduced the following schemes for providing health care to the people:

1) Pradhan Mantri Suraksha BimaYojana

What it offers : Accidental death and disability cover of Rs. 2 lakh.
What it costs: Premium is Rs. 12 per year.
Who is eligible: Anybody who has a savings account in the banks that offer this scheme.
Who should opt for it: Although it is for everybody, this scheme especially suits drivers, security guards, newspaper vendors, vegetable vendors and others who are exposed to the risk of accidental death or disability.

2) Pradhan Mantri Jeevan Jyoti BimaYojana

What it offers: A pure protection term insurance cover which pays Rs. 2 lakh to dependents in the event of the policy holder's death.
What it costs: Premium is Rs. 330 a year.
Who is eligible: Anybody in the age band of 18-70 years who has a savings account in a bank that offers this scheme.
Who should opt for it: This is a must for any member of your staff who is the sole breadwinner in his or her family.

Health Insurance

What it offers: Cover for expenses incurred during hospitalisation due to illness or surgery.
What it costs: Rs 700-800 a year for a cover of Rs. 50,000 for individuals aged between 18 and 40 years.
Who is eligible: All Who should opt for it: Hospitalisation can wipe out the entire savings of those already at a financial disadvantage. Though not offered by the government, affordable policies are available from State-owned non-life insurers like New India Assurance and Oriental Insurance.

Ayushman Bharat

Ayushman Bharat is National Health Protection Scheme, which will cover over 10 crore poor and vulnerable families (approximately 50 crore beneficiaries) providing coverage upto 5 lakh rupees per family per year for secondary and tertiary care hospitalization. Ayushman Bharat - National Health Protection Mission will subsume the on-going centrally sponsored schemes - Rashtriya Swasthya Bima Yojana (RSBY) and the Senior Citizen Health Insurance Scheme (SCHIS).

Salient Features

- Ayushman Bharat - National Health Protection Mission will have a defined benefit cover of Rs. 5 lakh per family per year.
- Benefits of the scheme are portable across the country and a beneficiary covered under the scheme will be allowed to take cashless benefits from any public/private empanelled hospitals across the country.
- Ayushman Bharat - National Health Protection Mission will be an entitlement based scheme with entitlement decided on the basis of deprivation criteria in the SECC database.
- The beneficiaries can avail benefits in both public and empanelled private facilities.
- To control costs, the payments for treatment will be done on package rate (to be defined by the Government in advance) basis.
- One of the core principles of Ayushman Bharat - National Health Protection Mission is co-operative federalism and flexibility to states.
- For giving policy directions and fostering coordination between Centre and States, it is proposed to set up Ayushman Bharat National Health Protection Mission Council (AB-NHPMC) at apex level Chaired by Union Health and Family Welfare Minister.
- States would need to have State Health Agency (SHA) to implement the scheme.
- To ensure that the funds reach SHA in time, the transfer of funds from Central Government through Ayushman Bharat - National Health

Protection Mission to State Health Agencies may be done through an escrow account directly.

- In partnership with NITI Aayog, a robust, modular, scalable and interoperable IT platform will be made operational which will entail a paperless, cashless transaction.

Implementation Strategy

- At the national level to manage, an Ayushman Bharat National Health Protection Mission Agency (AB-NHPMA) would be put in place. States/ UTs would be advised to implement the scheme by a dedicated entity called State Health Agency (SHA). They can either use an existing Trust/ Society/ Not for Profit Company/ State Nodal Agency (SNA) or set up a new entity to implement the scheme.
- States/ UTs can decide to implement the scheme through an insurance company or directly through the Trust/ Society or use an integrated model.

Major Impact

Ayushman Bharat - National Health Protection Mission will have major impact on reduction of Out of Pocket (OOP) expenditure on ground of:

- Increased benefit cover to nearly 40 per cent of the population, (the poorest & the vulnerable)
- Covering almost all secondary and many tertiary hospitalizations. (except a negative list)
- Coverage of Rs. 5 lakh for each family, (no restriction of family size).

This will lead to increased access to quality health and medication. In addition, the unmet needs of the population which remained hidden due to lack of financial resources will be catered to. This will lead to timely treatments, improvements in health outcomes, patient satisfaction, improvement in productivity and efficiency, job creation thus leading to improvement in quality of life.

Expenditure Involved

The expenditure incurred in premium payment will be shared between Central and State Governments in specified ratio as per Ministry of Finance guidelines in vogue. The total expenditure will depend on actual market determined premium paid in States/ UTs where Ayushman Bharat - National Health Protection Mission will be implemented through insurance companies. In States/ UTs where the scheme will be implemented in Trust/ Society mode, the central share of funds will be provided based on actual expenditure or premium ceiling (whichever is lower) in the pre-determined ratio.

Number of Beneficiaries

Ayushman Bharat - National Health Protection Mission will target about 10.74 crore poor, deprived rural families and identified occupational category of urban workers' families as per the latest Socio-Economic Caste Census (SECC) data covering both rural and urban. The scheme is designed to be dynamic and aspirational and it would take into account any future changes in the exclusion/ inclusion/ deprivation/ occupational criteria in the SECC data.

States/Districts Covered

Ayushman Bharat - National Health Protection Mission will be rolled out across all States/UTs in all districts with an objective to cover all the targeted beneficiaries. The scheme is to come into force on 25 September 2018

Endnote

1 'Health Care Financing', Akash Acharya and M. Kent Ranson, *Economic and Political Weekly*, 17 September 2005

5
National Social Assistance Programme

This programme has served the long felt need for uniform national minimum standards for providing social assistance to the weaker sections of society. The programme, however, provides only for three types of benefits, namely, the old age benefit, maternity benefit and survivor benefit. It is desirable that the programme should be redesigned to serve as an effective safety net "to catch the victims of the competitive struggle — such as the temporarily unemployed — and to protect the lowest income groups, the young, the old, and the disabled" *(Human Development Report, 1993)*. The programme should ensure that all the people who are not able to work and earn their living have the necessary means of livelihood and that their basic needs such as food, clothing and shelter are met adequately. The existing food security and housing schemes should be built into the programme. Provision should be made for supply of clothes to those who cannot buy them free of cost or at subsidised prices as in the case of food.

In this connection the following observations contained in the *World Development Report, 1990* devoted to poverty eradication are relevant:

> "The evidence in this report suggests that rapid and politically sustainable progress on poverty has been achieved by pursuing a strategy that has two equally important elements. The first element is to promote the productive use of the poor's most abundant asset — labour. It calls for policies that harness market incentives, social and political institutions, infrastructure, and technology to that end. The second is to provide basic social services to the poor. Primary health care, family planning, nutrition and primary education are especially important.
>
> "The two elements are mutually reinforcing, one without the other is not sufficient....
>
> "Progress has been greatest in the countries that have implemented both parts of the strategy...
>
> "Even if this basic two part strategy is adopted, many of the world's poor — the sick, the old, those who live in resource poor regions and others — will continue to experience severe deprivation. Many others will suffer temporary setbacks owing to seasonal variations in income, loss of the family breadwinner, famine, or adverse macro-economic shocks. A comprehensive approach to poverty reduction, therefore, calls for a programme of well targeted transfers and safety nets as an essential complement to the basic strategy."

The National Social Assistance Programme needs to be reviewed from this perspective. Even the existing programme can be made more beneficial by carrying out the following changes:

1. The programme should be extended to other equally deserving categories of people such as physically and mentally handicapped persons and widows. The old age pensions in many States cover these categories but there is no uniformity in the eligibility criteria or the quantum of benefits. The schemes need to be rationalised.
2. The quantum of the old age pension should be enhanced so as to be adequate at least for basic subsistence. Considering that the minimum wage fixed under the Minimum Wages Act meant to cater to three consumption units is around Rs. 45, the cost of subsistence of one consumption unit comes to Rs. 15 per day or Rs. 450 per month. Granting that a pension may not exceed fifty per cent of a wage, the minimum pension should not be less than Rs. 200 at current prices.
3. The quantum of the benefits should be adjusted to inflation by linking it to the cost of living index so that their real value remains intact. The rate of old age pension under the National Old age Pension Scheme was fixed in 1995. Since then the cost of living has gone up. The rate has not yet been revised although the rates of maternity benefit and family benefit have been renewed and revised.
4. It is seen that the eligibility criteria are not uniform. While destitution is the criterion for old age pension, poverty is the criterion for other benefits. Poverty should be made the criterion for all the benefits under the programme.
5 There is duplication between the National Family Benefit Scheme and the Group Insurance Scheme for Landless Agricultural Workers and others. It could be avoided.

When the benefits are subject to a means test, imposition of numerical and financial ceilings would appear to be discriminatory as they exclude from the benefits those who are in excess of the ceilings. The ceiling should be removed. At any rate, the ceilings appear to be of notional significance as the release of funds and their utilisation have both been very much short of the ceiling. The reasons for the shortfall need to be investigated and steps taken to improve the administration of the schemes.

Historical Development

1995: The NSAP was launched with the aim of providing social assistance to destitutes, defined as any person who has little or no regular means of subsistence from his/ her own source of income or through financial support from family members or other sources. Originally the NSAP included three components: National Old Age Pension Scheme (NOAPS); National Family Benefit Scheme (NFBS); and, National Maternity Benefit Scheme (NMBS).

2000: Annapurna Yojana was introduced to provide eligible beneficiaries, who were not covered under NOAPS, 10 kg of free rice.

2001: NMBS is transferred to the Department of Family Welfare.

2006: Monthly pension amount for NOAPS raised from Rs. 75 to Rs. 200

2007: The NSAP was extended to cover all individuals living below the poverty line. The NOAPS was renamed Indira Gandhi National Old Age Pension Scheme (IGNOAPS).

2009: The NSAP was expanded to include the Indira Gandhi National Widow Pension Scheme (IGNWPS) — for widows aged 40-64 years — and the Indira Gandhi National Disability Pension Scheme (IGNDPS) — for persons with multiple or severe disabilities aged 18-64 years living below the poverty line.

2011: Age limit for IGNOAPS was lowered from 65 to 60 years under IGNOAPS and monthly pension amount for those 80 years and above is raised from Rs. 200 to Rs. 500. Age limits for IGNWPS and IGNDPS were changed to 40-59 and 18-59, respectively.

2012: Monthly pensions under IGNWPS and IGNDPS were increased from Rs. 200 to Rs. 300. Age limits were changed to 40-79 years and 18-79 years, respectively.

2013: Report of the Task Force on Comprehensive Social Assistance Programme submitted to the Government of India. Recommends raising monthly pension and expanding coverage.

Components of National Assistance Programme

The National Assistance Programme consists of five sub-schemes:

Indira Gandhi National Old Age Pension Scheme (IGNOAPS)

Eligibility: Individuals aged 60 years and above living below the poverty line
Amount: Rs. 200 per month for beneficiaries aged 60-79 and Rs. 500 per month for those 80 years and above.

Indira Gandhi National Widow Pension Scheme (IGNWPS)

Eligibility: Widows aged 40 years and above living below the poverty line.
Amount: Rs. 300 per month (Rs. 500 for those 80 years and above).

Indira Gandhi National Disability Pension Scheme (IGNDPS)

Eligibility: Individuals aged 18 years and above with more than 80 per cent disability and living below the poverty line.
Amount: Rs. 300 per month (Rs. 500 for those 80 years and above).

National Family Benefit Scheme (NFBS)

In the event of death of a bread-winner in a household, the bereaved family will receive lump sum assistance of Rs. 20,000. The bread-winner should have been between 18-60 years of age. The assistance would be provided in every case of death of a bread-winner in a household.

Annapurna Scheme

This scheme aims to provide food security to meet the requirement of those senior citizens who, though eligible, have remained uncovered under the IGNOAPS. Under the Annapurna Scheme, 10 kg of free rice is provided every month to each beneficiary.

Administration: The scheme is administered by the Ministry of Rural Development, Government of India. It is fully funded by the Central Government, unlike some other welfare programmes where the Union government shares costs with the State Governments.

Allocation of funds for NSAP by Government of India between 2009-10 and 2014-15 (Rs. in crore)

Financial Year	*NSAP Allocation*
2009-10	5,200
2010-11	5,162
2011-12	6,596
2012-13	8,447
2013-14	9,541
2014-15	10,635

State-Level Initiatives in Social Pensions

The implementation of social pensions varies considerably across states. Through state-level initiatives, many State Governments have expanded coverage beyond BPL households by relaxing eligibility criteria and increased monthly pension amounts using state finances. One such example is Lakshmi Bai Social Security Pension Scheme, launched by Government of Bihar, to cover all widows not covered under IGNWP. This scheme is among one of the many Social Security initiatives taken up by Government of Bihar being implemented by Department of Social Welfare through State Society for Ultra Poor and Social Welfare, also known as SAKSHAM.

Relaxed Eligibility Criteria

Many State Governments have either stopped using the BPL methodology for identifying eligible beneficiaries or launched state-level pension schemes to increase coverage of social pensions beyond those living below the poverty line.

States such as Delhi and Haryana have moved to near-universal coverage by adopting exclusion criteria (for example in Haryana, all residents above 59 years of age with an annual income from all sources less than Rs. 2 lakh are eligible for old-age pension).

Other states have launched state pension schemes that cover individuals from non-BPL households who are not eligible for social pensions under NSAP. In Odisha, for instance, all elderly above 59 years of age and widows whose annual income from all sources is below Rs. 24,000 (US$360) are eligible for the Madhu Babu Pension Scheme.

As the Indira Gandhi National Widow Pension Scheme (IGNWPS) only covers widows aged 40–59, some state governments have launched State widow pension schemes. In Chhattisgarh, the Sukhad Sahara Yojana provides a monthly pension to all widows aged 18-50. The Lakshmi Bai Pension Yojana in Bihar covers all widows above 18 years of age whose annual family income is below Rs. 60,000.

Similarly, the Indira Gandhi National Disability Pension Scheme (IGNDPS) only covers individuals with more than 80 per cent disability. To address this gap in coverage, States like Bihar and Rajasthan have launched State Disability Pension schemes that cover individuals with more than 40 per cent disability.

Increase in Pension Amounts

The Government of India has urged State governments to make matching contributions with the aim of doubling the monthly pension amounts. The table below shows monthly pension amounts in various States:

State	*Old Age Pension*	*Widow Pension*	*Disability Pension*
Andhra Pradesh	1000	1000	1000
Bihar	400	400	400
Delhi	1000	1500	1500
Haryana	1200	1200	1200
Himachal Pradesh	550	550	750
Jammu and Kashmir	400	400	400
Kerala	600	800	800
Maharashtra	600	600	600
Odisha	300	300	300
Rajasthan	500	500	250
Sikkim	600	500	600
Tamil Nadu	400	400	400
Uttar Pradesh	300	400	300

Research and Evaluation

Recent studies of NSAP show that the social pension schemes are performing 'reasonably well' and 'levels of leakage are low and tractable'.

A 2014 study by the National Bureau of Economic Research (NBER) concludes that "the Indian government should increase the pension amount to lower the risk of poverty among the elderly, and work to expand inclusion of the most vulnerable groups."

Based on a study of social pensions in three States (Delhi, Haryana and Uttar Pradesh) in 2014, the World Bank makes a case for scaling up social pensions in India. The study raises four important points regarding expanding coverage of social pensions: "First, an expansion in coverage by adding more numbers (as Haryana has done) is likely to reduce the risk of exclusion of the poor. Second, expansion is unlikely to render the social pension completely regressive in its distribution or change the positive impact it has on vulnerability. Third, an increase in the size of the pension amount (for example, in Delhi) may not necessarily increase the incentive to cheat. Leakages, while present, are likely to be concentrated in particular areas and can be curbed through policy action. Fourth, while bribes have crept in the release of pensions, they can be curtailed through timely and direct disbursement of pension funds into beneficiaries' bank accounts." The study identifies the application process as the 'biggest obstacle' to expanding coverage of social pensions.

According to a 10-State survey of social pensions in 2013, "there is strong evidence to support the fact that the money is reaching the intended beneficiaries without any major leakages ... evaluation of the scheme also brings to the fore issues related to the diminutive amount, inefficient disbursal mechanism, cost of collection and the lack of a fixed pattern of payment."

Report of the Task Force, Ministry of Rural Development (2013)

In October 2012, the Government of India set up a task force to come up with a proposal for a Comprehensive Social Assistance Programme. Some of the recommendations from the report submitted in March, 2013 are listed below:

1. Increase IGNOAPS from Rs. 200 to Rs. 300 per month.
2. Reduce minimum age requirement for IGNWPS from 40 to 18 years.
3. Revise eligibility criteria for IGNWPS to include divorced/ separated/ abandoned women who, according to the report, face the same discrimination as widows.
4. Reduce disability level from 80 per cent to 40 per cent.
5. Assistance to be provided in the event of the death of any adult member (and not just male members) to the bereaved family under NFSB.
6. Pension amount should be indexed to inflation using the criteria adopted for dearness allowance.
7. Coverage should be expanded with the aim of covering all households eligible for benefits under the NFSA.
8. Pro-active identification of beneficiaries with no demand for documentary proof from applicants.
9. Pension payments must follow a fixed monthly schedule — this should be a 'non-negotiable requirement'.
10. Cash payments should be discouraged; States may move to bank or post office based systems.

11. Pension payment method should be adopted keeping in mind that no pensioner should have to travel beyond three km to collect pension; ultimate goal should be to ensure door-step delivery of pensions.

The Government of India is yet to implement most of these recommendations.

Pension Parishad

The Pension Parishad — an initiative to ensure universal pension to all workers in India — has been demanding that the Government of India establish a "non-contributory and universal old age pension system with a minimum amount of monthly pension not less than 50 per cent of the minimum wage or Rs. 2,000 (US$30), whichever is higher."

Other important demands of the Pension Parishad include the following:

- Any individual 55 years or older should be eligible for old age pension; for women, eligibility to be 50 years or older.
- APL/ BPL criteria should not be used for exclusion.

Issues and Debates

Use of BPL Methodology for Identification of Beneficiaries

There has been an ongoing debate in India over the use of BPL status for identifying beneficiaries for social programmes. This is especially true for social pensions where many poor elderly, widows and persons with disability are excluded from the NSAP as their names are not on the BPL list. Many States have expanded coverage of pension schemes by including non-BPL individuals based on their annual income or using a simple exclusion criteria to exclude individuals with government jobs or those owning more than a certain amount of land.

Low Monthly Pension Amount

There has been severe criticism of the Government of India for not increasing the monthly pension provided to the elderly, widows and persons with disability in India. Interestingly, the harshest criticism came from the then Minister of Rural Development, Jairam Ramesh, who described the low monthly pension amounts as 'an insult to the dignity' of the elderly. While the Government of India maintains that State Governments should make a matching contribution to social pensions, the amount would still not account for the rise in living costs over the past decade. The Pension Parishad has demanded that the government raise the monthly pension to half of the minimum wage or Rs. 2,000 whichever is higher. Similarly, the Task Force setup to review the NSAP recommended that pensions be indexed to inflation and increased using a method similar to that of dearness allowance.

Review of the National Social Assistance Programme

The Government of India has recently set up a working group to review the working of the Social Assistance programmes and to suggest measures for revising the same so as to ensure minimal social protection for the socially excluded categories.

The proposals placed before the working Group are set out below.

The Government should adopt a policy for social protection which should aim at achieving two basic objectives during a given period, namely;

- Abolition of hunger
- Eradication of poverty

And adopt the following slogans for the Plan:

Bhukh Mitao Bhikh Hatao

Eradication of extreme poverty and hunger is one of the millennium goals to be achieved. It requires halving between 1990 and 2015 the proportion of people who suffer from hunger. Half the period is over but hunger still exists in India on a large scale.

According to a statement made by the Country Director of the World Food Programme despite the fact that the economy has been growing fast, one in every five Indians suffers from overt or covert hunger. A survey carried out in Karnataka found that a large number of people in the State were homeless, they did not have even one square meal a day for long periods and they survived virtually on crumbs.

According to the WHO, "One in every three world's malnourished children lives in India and about 50 per cent of all childhood deaths in India are attributable to malnutrition. The proportion of low birth weight babies remains high at one third of all births."

The Supreme Court has declared that the Right to Livelihood is a fundamental right; it inheres the Right to Life. The National Human Rights Commission has pointed out that "the citizen's right to be free from hunger enshrined in Article 21 is to be ensured by the fulfillment of the obligations of the State set out in Articles 39(a) and 47".

Poverty eradication has been an important goal of development policy since the inception of planning in India. Various anti poverty, employment generation and basic services programmes have been in operation for decades. These are targeted mainly at persons who are able to work but remain unemployed for lack of employment opportunities. But there are certain classes of people who are unable to work and earn their livelihood. In their case, eradication of destitution and hunger calls for separate and distinct programmes involving direct income transfers by way of social assistance.

Social assistance programmes in the form of old age pensions widow pension , physically handicapped pensions unemployment assistance, etc. have also been in existence at State levels for a long time. Under these programmes cash assistance is given to persons at various rates subject to widely varying conditions. In order to bring about a measure of uniformity in these programmes and to ensure that they conform to certain minimum national standards, a National Social Assistance Programme was introduced in the year 1995.

The NSAP was intended to be a significant step towards fulfillment of the Directive Principles in Articles 41 and 42 of the Constitutions which envisages public assistance in the event of old age disability sickness and other cases of undeserved want. The programme included for the time being three benefits, namely, old age pension family benefit and maternity benefit. It was obviously envisaged that more such benefits would be added in due course to extend protection against other cases of undeserved want.

The scale of benefits provided under the programme initially were as follows:

- National Old age Pension Scheme Rs. 75 per month per beneficiary.
- National Family Benefit Scheme Rs. 5,000 in case of death due to natural causes and Rs. 10,000 in case of accidental death of the primary breadwinner of the bereaved household.
- National Maternity Benefit Scheme: Rs. 300 per pregnancy upto the first two live births.

In the year 1998, the rate of maternity benefit was raised to Rs. 500 per pregnancy and the rate of family benefit due to natural causes was raised to Rs. 10,000, the quantum of benefit in the event of death due to accident remaining the same.

In the year 2000, a new scheme called Annapurna Scheme was added. The scheme provides for supply of 10 kg of foodgrains free of cost to those senior citizens who were eligible for old age pension but had remained uncovered under the National Old Age Pension Scheme.

Many State governments have increased the quantum of old age pension by varying amounts ranging from Rs. 25 to Rs. 225 (total amount of pension ranging from Rs. 100 to Rs. 300)

In the current year (2006) the rate of old age pension was raised to Rs. 200 per month per beneficiary with the request to the State governments to top it up by another Rs. 200 so that each beneficiary may get a total amount of pension of Rs. 400 per month.

The National Maternity Benefit Scheme has been transferred to the Ministry of Health for administration and is renamed as Janani Suraksha Yojana with emphasis on institutional delivery with the help of qualified assistants.

The remaining schemes of the programme which were initially treated as centrally sponsored schemes have been transferred to the States as State Sector Schemes.

Evaluation studies of the National Social Assistance Programme were conducted by the Operational Research Group in 1998 and by the Centre for Management Development, Thiruvanathapuram in 2000. The Programme was also studied by the Jaishanker Memorial Centre. In addition, Dr N.C. Saxena, Commissioner of the Supreme Court and Sri Moneer Alam of the Institute of Economic Growth have made certain observations and recommendations.

The National Commission on Rural Labour as well as the Second National Commission on Labour have also made certain comments and recommendations concerning the Programme.

Having regard to these observations and recommendations the following changes are suggested in the programme.

The National Old-age Pension Scheme

The Scheme is at present applicable to destitutes aged 65 or more. The eligibility criteria for the pension are defined differently by different State governments. The Scheme is also subject to certain numerical and financial ceilings.

The National Policy for Older Persons recognises that a person becomes a senior citizen at the age of 60 and would be eligible for the facilities and concessions available to senior citizens. It is, therefore, suggested that the scheme should be made applicable to all persons of the age of 60 or more. The Government has since accepted this proposal and made the scheme applicable to all persons above the age of 60.

The three schemes introduced under the NSAP, two are applicable to all persons below the poverty line. In the case of the NOAPS only a different criterion of destitution has been prescribed. The various studies conducted in respect of the NOAPS indicate that the criteria of destitution is difficult of application. It has been observed that many States have adopted the poverty line itself to define destitution. It is, therefore, suggested that the NOAPS should also be made applicable to all persons below the poverty line as defined by the Ministry of Rural Development.

The studies have also indicated that the imposition of numerical and financial ceilings have militated against proper implementation of the Scheme and suggestions have been made for reworking of the ceilings. It is felt that the imposition of ceilings in a social assistance programme is unjust and they should be removed.

The NOAPS is subject to certain other conditions such as domicile which were prescribed by the State governments for their schemes. They do not seem to be relevant to a National Scheme. All such restrictive conditions should be removed.

The rate of pension has recently been enhanced to Rs. 200 per month. The State governments have been urged to top it up with another Rs. 200 so that every pensioner would get a minimum pension of Rs. 400. Some State governments have acted on this suggestion and sanctioned an additional pension varying from State to State. Some State governments have not done so. Considering the past experience of the scheme the working group is skeptical whether all the State governments would respond favourably to the exhortation of the Central government. A more correct course of action would be to fix the rate of pension on a uniform basis and require the State Government to make necessary contributions accordingly.

In this connection it may be mentioned that the Pension Portal, an alliance of NGOs representing the pensioners have made a demand that the rate of pension should be enhanced to Rs. 2000. Another recommendation is that the rate of pension should be related to the rate of minimum wage and it should not be less than 50 per cent of the minimum wage.

After the introduction of Aadhar all old age pensions are being paid directly to the bank accounts of the pensioners. There are, however, doubts about efficiency of the scheme.

Annapurna Scheme

The Annapurna Scheme aims at providing food security to meet the requirement of those senior citizens who, though eligible, have remained uncovered under the National Old Age Pension Scheme. The target group receives 10 kg of food grains per month free of cost. Government of India has fixed a numerical ceiling for scheme. It is, therefore, possible that a person may be denied the pension as well as the assistance under the Annapurna scheme if he/ she happens to fall outside both the ceilings.

Introduction of the scheme admits that not all persons eligible for old age pension are covered under the scheme and that those who are not covered would be eligible for assistance under the Annapurna Scheme. The fact that the Government has prescribed certain physical and financial ceilings for application of the scheme confirms that certain number of persons eligible for the pension are denied the same for the reason that they are in excess of the ceilings prescribed. It is needless to say that such an arrangement is socially unjust.

If all the eligible persons can be covered under the NOAPS, there will be no person to be covered under the Annapurna Scheme. It is, however, suggested that this scheme may be merged with the Antyodaya Scheme so that the absolutely poor people who are covered under the Antyodaya Scheme may get a specified quantity of foodgrains free of cost instead of at a concessional price.

National Maternity Benefit Scheme

As the administration of the Scheme has been transferred to the Ministry of Health there is some ambiguity whether it continues to be part of the National Social Assistance Programme. The Working Group is of the view that irrespective of who administers the schemes launched under the NSAP they should remain in that programme unless there is any special reason for removing them from it.

The Working Group does not see any reason why the NMBS should cease to be part of the NSAP.

The WHO, the UNDP as well as the National Family Health Survey have pointed out that the infant mortality rate as well as the maternal mortality rate are unacceptably high in India. The high rate of mortality among mothers and infants can be attributed largely to inadequacy of food and nutrition due to poverty and self-denial by the women of their share of the food in order to feed others in the family. It is, therefore, necessary that women should have adequate income when they are pregnant and also after delivery in order that they are fed with nutritious food at the time when they are nourishing another life. If the women are employed the maternity benefit cannot be less than 75 per cent of their wages as per ILO Convention No. 102. On this basis, if a woman is working on a floor level minimum wage of Rs. 66 per day the maternity benefit payable to her would be about Rs. 3,980. The National Commission on Labour, however, recommended payment of maternity benefit at Rs. 2,000 per delivery. Even if a woman is not working for wages she should be regarded as an unpaid worker in view of the multiple roles she plays in the family and given all the benefits a worker would get. There is, therefore, a strong case for enhancing the rate of maternity benefit to Rs. 2,000

The existing arrangements made by the Department of Women and Child Development for providing supplementary nutrition to women should be improved.

National Family Benefit Scheme

Whenever an accident takes place resulting in death of one or more persons, government has lately been announcing a compensation of Rupees one lakh to each of the bereaved families. Recently, the Railway Minister announced a relief of Rs. 5 lakh each to the kin of the persons who die of a railway accident. In this background, the amount of family benefit paid under this scheme would appear to be too small. It may be adequate to meet the funeral and other incidental expenses incurred by a family when the breadwinner dies. It cannot serve the purpose of income security to the family. The Working Group is, therefore, of the view that while the quantum of the Family benefit may remain as it is, it needs to be supplemented by a family pension scheme which is now being paid in the form of Widow Pension Schemes in many States. The Working Group, therefore, suggests that the government may introduce a National Family Pension Scheme or Widow Pension Scheme whereby every widow may be entitled to a pension equal to one and half times the old age pension payable under the NOAPS, irrespective of her age.

In this connection the following facts may be noted.

- The World Bank, the ADB and the UNDP recognise that widows as a class qualify for social assistance.

- Most, if not all States, have had a widow pension scheme but the rates of pension as well as the eligibility conditions vary widely.
- The National Policy for Empowerment of Women requires special assistance to be provided to women in difficult circumstances including single women in difficult circumstances, women heading households disabled widows, etc.

National Widow Pension Scheme

This scheme was introduced in 2009 effective from February, 2009 subject to the following conditions:

- The age of the beneficiary must be between 40-64 years. This was later revised to 40- for life.
- The beneficiary must belong to family which is below the poverty line as defined by the Government of India.
- The amount of pension shall be Rs. 200 per person per month to be matched by the State Government/ UT. This has been raised to Rs. 300. The amount shall be credited to the account of the beneficiary in the Post office or in Public sector bank.
- The Gram Panchayat or the municipality will play an active role in the identification of the beneficiary
- The number of beneficiaries on the basis of a field survey of all persons satisfying the criteria
- The pension will be discontinued on remarriage or on the person's income going above the poverty line.

National Scheme for Pension to Handicapped Persons

Disability is one of the cases of undeserved want mentioned in Article 41 of the Constitution which requires for public assistance.

According to the National Policy for Disabled Persons, "Disabled persons, their families and care givers incur substantial additional expenditure for facilitating activities of daily living, medical care, transportation, assistive devices, etc. Therefore, there is a need to provide them social security by various means." In particular, the policy specifies rationalisation of the amount of pension and unemployment allowance payable to persons with disabilities.

Most of the State Governments have schemes for payment of pension to physically handicapped persons. They need to be rationalised. The Working Group suggests as follows:

(i) The Persons with Disabilities Act, 1995 requires payment of unemployment allowance to such persons with disabilities who are registered with Special Employment Exchanges for more than two years but could not be placed in any gainful occupation. A few States have introduced schemes for the purpose which provide for payment of unemployment allowance ranging from Rs. 50

to Rs. 500. The eligibility criteria also vary. The Working Group suggests that a National Scheme of Unemployment Allowance to Persons with Disabilities who have some earning capacity but no employment be introduced providing for payment of an unemployment allowance at a uniform rate subject to conditions common to all States.

(ii) In the case of persons suffering from autism, cerebral palsy, mental retardation and multiple disabilities the care givers or the guardians appointed to look after them may be compensated for the cost incurred by them in terms of money, time or effort in discharging their responsibilities at a rate equal to old age pension under NOAPS.

(iii) In respect of all other cases where the persons with disabilities have no earning capacity or whose earning capacity is less than 40 per cent as assessed by a competent medical authority including physically handicapped as well as mentally handicapped persons, another national scheme may be introduced providing for a monthly pension equal to the old age pension under the NOAPS.

Homes

A National Programme may be introduced to establish and to run homes for the maintenance at State cost of the following classes of persons:

(i) The elderly persons who have no family and cannot live alone.
(ii) Orphan and Street children who have no parents or guardians.
(iii) Deserted women who have no one to fall back upon.
(iv) Lepers.
(v) Mentally ill persons who have no guardians.

The homes should provide food, clothing and shelter to the inmates. In the case of children there should be provision for their education and vocational training.

In all cases, there should be provision for appropriate standards of health care through the Public Health care system.

Other Cases of Undeserved Want

The following classes of persons also need social assistance for short periods.

- Persons affected by natural or other calamities
- Displaced persons
- Families of prisoners
- Families of persons suffering from serious diseases such as leprosy
- Families of persons who commit suicide owing to poverty or other reasons
- Workers retrenched from employment without any unemployment benefit
- Labour released from bondage
- Manual scavengers.

There may already be schemes to help these people at the Central or State levels but they need to be standardised.

In some of these cases, assistance is given for rehabilitation of the persons but they need to be given assistance for their subsistence during the gestation period of the respective rehabilitation projects.

Identification and Registration of Beneficiaries: Identification of the beneficiaries can best be done at the local level by the gram sabhas or panchayats. They should also be registered with the panchayats. If possible, the beneficiaries may be issued identity cards so that even if they go out of the locality they may not be deprived of their dues.

Mechanism for Sanction and Maintenance of Accounts

The power to sanction the benefits may also be delegated to the panchayats and the responsibility for disbursing the amount may be entrusted to the local post office which may be required to maintain the accounts of the disbursements they make. If necessary an imprest may be kept with each post office for making the payments and it may be replenished from time to time.

There should be an annual verification of the various kinds of pensioners by a designated official.

The payments made at or by a Post office should be subject to government audit and also social audit through a voluntary organsiation.

Financing of Schemes

All the schemes framed under the National Social Assistance Programme be treated as Centrally Sponsored Schemes and monitored by the Central Government to ensure that all the people entitled to the benefits are getting them. The expenditure on the schemes may be shared by the Central and State Governments in the ratio of 75:25.

Timely Release of Funds

The monetary allocations made by the Government of India for the programme must not fall short of the amount required or estimated for payment to all the registered pensioners and other beneficiaries. The moneys allocated should be transferred to the State Governments in equal quarterly installments. The State governments should put the moneys received from the Central Government for the NSAP into a non lapsable fund in the public account and use it for replenishing the imprests with the post offices.

Flexibility in the Use of Funds

The discretion given to the state governments for reappropriation of funds meant for one scheme and use for another should be withdrawn.

Administration of the Programme

Considering the volume of the funds involved and the number of beneficiaries, it seems necessary to establish or identify a separate Department or Directorate at the Central as well as State level for administration of the programme

An officer designated as a Commissioner of Social Assistance may be appointed by the Central Government for administration of the scheme.

Similarly, at the State level, an officer designated as Director of Social Assistance may be appointed in each State government for administration of the programme.

Necessary staff may also be provided at the lower formations for the programme as required.

Advisory Boards/ Committees at Central, State and district levels may be constituted for advising the administrative authorities on the administration of the scheme.

Research and Studies

The Working Group suggests that studies be commissioned into the conditions of life of the various classes of people for whom social assistance has been proposed to determine whether they need the assistance, and if so, of what orders. The schemes may, if necessary, be modified suitably depending on the findings of such studies.

Provision may be made for social audit and evaluatory studies of the Schemes after they are introduced to determine whether they are being implemented well and whether their purpose has been achieved.

Appointment of an Ombudsman

The possibility of appointing an Ombudsman to hear complaints and grievances regarding the administration of all the schemes under the NSAP may also be considered.

Creation of Awareness

Evaluation studies have shown lack of awareness of the programme among the beneficiaries. Arrangements should be made for giving greater publicity to the programme at frequent intervals in languages understandable by the people through audio visual means. A body or an officer at the district level should be made responsible for the purpose.

6
Land Reforms

According to the Human Development Report 1997, the defining challenge of poverty alleviation is to strengthen people's ability to cope with the adversities — to build resistance and resilience, to seize opportunities for escape . . . . People's assets reduce vulnerability and build resilience against poverty. The more assets they have, the less their vulnerability and the greater their ability to cope with poverty, to resist and to escape it. But any erosion of their assets increases their vulnerability and insecurity. Building people's assets, empowering them to fight poverty, should be the centerpiece of poverty eradication. The State has a responsibility to address structural inequalities in the distribution of assets, especially land, credit housing and social services.

In economic terms, an asset usually refers to capital, whether physical or financial, from which people may derive a future stream of income. But the assets used to resist poverty encompass a broader range of tangible and non-tangible resources classified broadly as economic, social, environmental and personal.

Economic assets include land, livestock, housing, labour and financial capital that provide bases for generating income and production.

Land is critical for rural people — and for three-quarters of the world's income poor who depend on agriculture for their livelihood. About a quarter of the rural labour in developing countries are landless or do not have adequate security of tenure or title. And even those who have land often have holdings too small or unproductive to provide a secure livelihood. Institutions and policy reforms are needed to give better access and secure rights to all the critical assets that are unevenly distributed.

The National Commission on Rural Labour has stated that there is an immediate need to strengthen the land base of the rural poor for raising their income as well as for improving their status and strengthening their bargaining power. The measures include tenancy reforms, distribution of land, development of common property resources, access of land to women, updating land records and vigorous implementation of agrarian reform laws. All these together will have a favourable impact on rural wages tilting the socio-economic structure in favour of rural poor and raising their living standards. This will also result in change of the power structure in Panchayat Raj institutions.

Land reforms are, therefore, regarded as an important social protection measure.

The Commission has reviewed the performance of land reform measures in various States and observed that the situation could be classified under four types:

(a) Semi-feudal areas like Bihar where the barriers to reform inherent in the prevailing structure of society are too strong to be overcome by the scale and intensity of the efforts for land reforms made so far. Bihar, UP, Madhya Pradesh and Rajasthan have been placed in this class.
(b) Areas with less formidable barriers to land reforms and stronger thrust for reforms as compared to semi feudal areas but having mixed and on the whole modest results of land reforms. Karnataka, Tamil Nadu, AP, Maharashtra and Gujarat have been placed in this class.
(c) Areas with strong political mobilisation and effective land reforms but where the growth performance has been too weak to complement the reforms to bring about enduring structural change. West Bengal and Kerala are in this class.
(d) Green Revolution areas where capitalist farming is firmly entrenched and where reform is needed mainly to improve wages, work environment and economic condition of labourers. Haryana and Punjab are in this class.

It is, therefore, clear that land reforms have not been carried out uniformly in all the States. The Commission has further concluded that whatsoever may have been the implementation of land reforms, they have not helped the rural poor to obtain secure and equitable access to land nor has an enduring improvement in their economic status been brought about. The Commission has, therefore, made several recommendations for better implementation of the reforms. There is, however, no evidence that they have been implemented so far. Indeed there is no mention of the recommendations or the action taken thereon in the Annual Reports of the Ministries concerned.

Land title formalisation has been part of India's State policy from the very beginning. Independent India's most revolutionary land policy was perhaps the abolition of the Zamindari system (feudal land holding practices). Land reform policy in India had two specific objectives: "The first is to remove such impediments to increase in agricultural production as arise from the agrarian structure inherited from the past.... The second object, which is closely related to the first, is to eliminate all elements of exploitation and social injustice within the agrarian system, to provide security for the tiller of soil and assure equality of status and opportunity to all sections of the rural population." (Government of India, 1961 as quoted by Appu, 1996)

Categories of Reforms

There are four main categories of reforms:

- Abolition of intermediaries (rent collectors under the pre-Independence land revenue system);
- Tenancy regulation (to improve the contractual terms including security of tenure);

- A ceiling on landholdings (to redistributing surplus land to the landless);
- Attempts to consolidate disparate landholdings.

History

Since independence in 1947, there has been voluntary and State initiated/mediated land reforms in several States with dual objectivity of efficient use of land and ensuring social justice. The most notable and successful example of land reforms are in the States of West Bengal and Kerala. Other than these State sponsored attempts of reforming land ownership and control, there was another attempt to bring changes in the regime which achieved limited success; famously known as Bhoodan movement (Government of India, Ministry of Rural Development 2003, Annex XXXIX). Some other research has shown that during the movement, in Vidarbha region, 14 per cent of the land records were incomplete thus, prohibiting transfer to the poor. A considerable amount of land which is 24 per cent of the land promised had never actually become part of the movement. The Gramdan, which arguably took place in 160,000 pockets, did not legalise the process under the State laws (Committee on Land Reform 2009, 77, Ministry of Rural Development).

After promising land reforms and elected to power in West Bengal in 1977, the Communist Party of India (Marxist) (CPI(M)) kept their word and initiated gradual land reforms, such as Operation Barga. The result was a more equitable distribution of land among the landless farmers, and enumeration of landless farmers. This has ensured an almost lifelong loyalty from the farmers and the communists were in power till 2011 assembly election.

In land reforms in Kerala, the only other large State where the CPI(M) came to power, State administrations have actually carried out the most extensive land, tenancy and agrarian labour wage reforms in the non-socialist late-industrialising world. Another successful land reform programme was launched in Jammu and Kashmir after 1947.

However, this success was not replicated in other areas like the States of Andhra and Madhya Pradesh, where the more radical Communist Party of India (Maoist) or Naxalites resorted to violence as it failed to secure power. In the State of Bihar, tensions between land owners militia, villagers and Maoists have resulted in numerous massacres.

All in all, land reforms have been successful only in a few pockets of the country, as people have often found loopholes in the laws that set limits on the maximum area of land that is allowed to be held by any one person.

7

Mahatma Gandhi National Rural Employment Guarantee Act (MNREGA)

National Rural Employment Guarantee Act 2005 (or, NREGA No. 42) was later renamed as the "Mahatma Gandhi National Rural Employment Guarantee Act" (or, MGNREGA), is an Indian labour law and social security measure that aims to guarantee the 'right to work'. It aims to ensure livelihood security in rural areas by providing at least 100 days of wage employment in a financial year to every household whose adult members volunteer to do unskilled manual work.

Starting with 200 districts on 6 February 2006, the NREGA covered all the districts of India from 1 April 2008. The statute is hailed by the government as "the largest and most ambitious social security and public works programme in the world". In its World Development Report 2014, the World Bank termed it a "stellar example of rural development".

The MGNREGA was initiated with the objective of "enhancing livelihood security in rural areas by providing at least 100 days of guaranteed wage employment in a financial year, to every household whose adult members volunteer to do unskilled manual work". Another aim of MGNREGA is to create durable assets (such as roads, canals, ponds, wells). Employment is to be provided within five km of an applicant's residence, and minimum wages are to be paid. If work is not provided within 15 days of applying, applicants are entitled to an unemployment allowance. Thus, employment under MGNREGA is a legal entitlement.

MGNREGA is to be implemented mainly by gram panchayats (GPs). The involvement of contractors is banned. Labour-intensive tasks like creating infrastructure for water harvesting, drought relief and flood control are preferred.

Apart from providing economic security and creating rural assets, MNREGA can help in protecting the environment, empowering rural women, reducing rural-urban migration and fostering social equity, among others."

The law provides many safeguards to promote its effective management and implementation. The Act explicitly mentions the principles and agencies for implementation, list of allowed works, financing pattern, monitoring and evaluation, and most importantly the detailed measures to ensure transparency and accountability.

The trends during 1980 to 2000 in employment and unemployment have been summarised as follows:

1. Trends in work participation rates at the All India level show:
   (a) Stability in crude Worker Participation Ratio
   (b) Decline in WPR standardised for age distribution
   (c) Rise in WPR for males and females if we consider daily status
2. Growth rate of employment during the period 1972-73 and 1987-88 showed deceleration. It increased during 1988-94 but the rate of growth was still lower than that of the '70s. The elasticity of employment also showed similar trends. The growth of employment over the past two and a half decades has, on an average, been lower than the rate of growth in the labour force;
3. There has been a slow change in the structure of the work force. The share of Agriculture in total workforce started declining only in the early 1990s. The share of Agriculture declined by 9 per cent during the period 1972-73 and 1993-94. During the same period, there has been a significant increase in the share of rural non-agricultural employment.
4. The proportion of the self-employed has shown a steady decline over the years. The corresponding increase has mostly been in the informal sector of casual labourers.
5. Though the shares of organised and unorganised sectors in aggregate employment have remained constant at 10 per cent and 90 per cent respectively, the proportions of the unorganised sector have significantly increased in manufacturing, construction and transportation sectors.
6. The unemployment rates for the period 1973-88 show that open unemployment increased while daily status rates declined. During the period 1987-94, there was no sign of increase in open unemployment as well as CDS unemployment rate at the All India level except in the case of rural males under daily status. The share of educated in total unemployment has been increasing.

Structural adjustment programme which has encouraged multinational companies using sophisticated technology to enter the country freely could displace people engaged in traditional sectors. Workers occupied in the traditional processing sector suffer from competition from the large-scale industry. They face unemployment and destitution, as they cannot be absorbed in the new economy. There is growing casualisation of labour.

The current trends like slowing rate of growth in rural non-farm employment, the rising share of casualisation, especially the sharp rise in the proportion of casual labour among the educated work force, the stagnant (jobless growth) or declining share of organised sector in total employment levels in urban areas, particularly among females, slow growth in rural real wages call for corrective steps. The existing employment programmes are not adequate to meet these problems.

High labour intensive pattern of economic growth is important for creation of productive employment. The approach treating employment as a mere byproduct of growth or seeking solutions to the unemployment problem in special employment programmes is inadequate. It is necessary that a relatively rapid growth of employment be built into the growth strategy itself. Whether the new economic policy permits this is questionable.

There can, however, be no doubt that special employment programmes have a crucial role to play in providing short-term employment and preventing starvation. These programmes coupled with the increase in food production and the PDS have been able to successfully prevent famines in India. Programmes like the Maharashtra EGS have acted as an insurance mechanism.

There is an intellectual debate whether the employment programme should concentrate on wage employment or self-employment. This debate appears to be somewhat sterile. The programmes should be designed to suit the aptitude of the workers. Not everyone will be able to run self-employment programmes. Provision of facilities to bonded labour as their release from bondage has not been an unmixed success. Any of them could have been rehabilitated better by provision of wage employment.

An attendant problem concerning wage employment relates to the quantum of wages. In many areas the market wages are lower than minimum wages. The minimum wages fixed in many States in turn are lower than minimum subsistence wages. The wages fixed are very low and they do not take into consideration the minimum requirements of a worker's family. While promoting wage employment, the States have, therefore, to adopt and enforce a rational minimum wage policy.

The *Human Development Report*, 1994 has set out the strategy for creation of employment as follows:

> "Creating sufficient opportunities for productive employment and sustainable livelihood is one of the most important — and most difficult — tasks in any society. Based on experience, the central elements of an effective national employment strategy are likely to include:
>
> *Education and Skills:* To compete in a fast changing global economy, every country has to invest heavily on education, training and skill formation of its people;
>
> *Access to assets:* A more equitable distribution of physical assets (land) and better access to means of production (credit and information) are often essential to ensure sustainable livelihood;
>
> *Labour intensive technology:* Developing countries have to be able to make the most efficient use of their comparative advantage of abundant labour. Tax and price policies should try to encourage labour intensive employment;
>
> *Public Works programme:* Where private markets fail to produce sufficient jobs, it would be necessary for the State to offer employment through public works programmes to enable people to survive;
>
> *Disadvantaged groups:* Where markets tend to discriminate against particular groups such as women or certain ethnic groups, the State may need to consider targeted intervention or programmes of affirmative action;

Job sharing: With the phenomenon of jobless growth it has become necessary to rethink the concept of work and to consider more innovative and flexible arrangements including job-sharing."

India has undoubtedly built up a vast network of training institutions. In the absence of a system of manpower planning, it is doubtful whether the institutions fulfil the training needs adequately. Recommendations have been made in various forums for setting up a Skill Development Fund. It is necessary to assess the training needs scientifically and to make adequate arrangements satisfying those needs, if necessary, by setting up a 'Skill Development Fund.

The need for land reforms for a more equitable distribution of land has been accepted and a reform package has been introduced. But its implementation has been stalled by vested interests. A more determined effort is necessary to carry out the reforms as in West Bengal and Kerala.

The need to encourage labour intensive employment is recognised by the planners and the policy makers but in actual practice, however, India appears to be moving in the direction of high technology development, especially after the introduction of economic reforms.

Public Works programmes have long been recognised as effective policy instruments of poverty alleviation in rural areas. The Maharashtra Employment Guarantee Scheme is a prime example of such programmes. But these programmes have tended to provide only short-term employment and lack the long-term perspective of permanent labour absorption. In so far as these programmes are designed to create infrastructure, they are expected to contribute to long term growth of the economy, which will lead to permanent absorption of labour.

India has done very well in reducing, if not eliminating, the discrimination against disadvantaged groups in so far as numerous programmes have been introduced for providing education, training and employment to Scheduled Castes, Scheduled Tribes, Backward Classes, Minorities, Women and the Disabled people.

It does not appear, however, that much thought has been given to the question of making flexible working arrangements so as to provide additional employment. It is also doubtful if it is feasible to introduce such programmes.

The responsibility for promotion of employment in the Central Government is diffused over several Ministries and Departments. The arrangement is not conducive to the formulation of a comprehensive or coherent policy or programmes for promotion of employment. It is desirable that it should be made the exclusive responsibility of one Ministry.

Telangana

Rythu Lakshmi Scheme

Rythu Lakshmi scheme also Farmers' Investment Support Scheme (FISS) is a welfare program to support farmers input subsidy for a crop by the Government of Telangana. The government will provide Rs. 4000 per acre per season to take care of the expenditure on inputs. This is the first ever such scheme in India.

The Rythu Lakshmi scheme offers a financial help of Rs. 8,000 per year to each farmer (two crops). There is no cap on the number of acres as over 97 per cent of farmers have less than 10 acres per person. It will launch just before kharif season in April 2018 and for Rabi in November.

Benefits

- Financial assistance of Rs. 8,000 per acre to be provided to all the farmers in the State
- The amount will be provided in 2 installments of Rs. 4,000 each
- Rs. 4,000 to be provided at the start of Kharif season
- Remaining amount Rs. 4,000 will be provided at the start of Yasangi season
- With the financial assistance farmers dont need to take any loans for sowing
- The money can be used to buy seeds, fertilizers, pesticides, labour etc
- Since major cost of agriculture is covered by the Rythu Lakshmi Scheme, loan waivers etc are not required and farmers can use their own money for other developmental purposes
- The scheme is expected to reduce farmer suicides
- RLS/ FISS is expected to increase the farmers earnings
- Insurance cover of Rs. 5 lakh each is provided to all the farmers in the State

Implementation

- A budget of Rs. 12,000 crores is allocated for the scheme
- The cheques will be distributed in 3 phases
- The cheques distribution will begin on April 19th 2018
- The government has established Rythu Samanvaya Samiti to identify the beneficiaries and distribute cheques
- Mr. Gutha Sukhender Reddy is appointed as chairman of the committee
- The scheme will benefit all 1.43 crore farmers in the State
- The scheme covers 1.63 crore acres of land in the State

Eligibility

- All the farmers who are residents of the State of Telangana are eligible for the scheme
- There is no minimum or maximum cap on the land holding. All farmers rich or poor or belonging to any caste or socio-economic status are eligible for the scheme

Rythu Bandhu Scheme

Within six weeks, the government of Telangana has distributed Rs. 5000 crore to over 47.5 lakh land-holding farmers of the State. The programme launched on May 10 is basically a "crop investment support" scheme. A year ahead of the Lok Sabha and Assembly elections in Telangana, the scheme is being seen by analysts as a "masterstroke" that will help the ruling K Chandrasekhar Rao-led TRS party comfortably beat the Opposition.

At a time when the Central government led by Prime Minister Narendra Modi is promising to double farmers' income by 2022, Telangana government's popular scheme needs to be seen closely for its simple and efficient features. Moreover, when demand for farm loan waivers get regularly made across several States, and with examples like Uttar Pradesh where such steps have failed to please all farmers, the impact of the Rythu Bandhu scheme is remarkable in view of the minimal criticism that it has faced since its launch.

The Financial Express reported earlier citing an official source from the Telangana government as saying that Rs. 5000 crore of Rs. 6000 crore has been encashed by over 47.5 lakh farmers of the State within 6 weeks of the launch of the scheme.

What is Rythu Bandhu scheme?

Rythu Bandhu scheme aims at farmer's empowerment. It is also India's "first ever farmer investment support" scheme. Some of the key features of the scheme include:

- Grant of Rs. 8000 per acre to all Telangana farmers with land titles every year, i.e. Rs. 4000 per crop season.
- The money is disbursed by two equal pay-order cheques issued ahead of the two crop seasons.
- Telangana government allocated Rs. 12000 crore in the current budget for the scheme.
- The scheme aims to benefit around 58 lakh farmers of Telangana.
- Under the scheme, there is no upper limit of land holding for farmers to avail benefit of the scheme.
- The scheme is expected to benefit around 1.42 crore acre land of the State.
- As part the scheme, the State government also offers 'Pattadar Dharani' passbooks to every farmer. The passbooks assist in identifying ownership of the land, and replace all other farm ownership documents.
- All payments are done via bank accounts.

Rythu Bandhu Scheme vs Loan Waivers, crop compensation

There are at least two popular ways in which the government tries to compensate farmers. First, through loan waivers to loss-making farmers. Second, through ensuring Minimum Support Price support for major crops. In the Union Budget this year, the Centre promised MSP to farmers at 1.5 times the cost of production of the crop. However, farmers in many parts of the country are yet to realise this promise.

Several Indian States have announced farm loan waivers worth around Rs 1.5 lakh crore since March last year. However, the rollout of loan waivers were partial in many States. This is so because the loan waiver schemes have tried to address only a certain class of farmers, not all.

Reports say the government is still mulling over compensating farmers the difference of the (lower) market prices and MSPs irrespective of whether the administration buys the products or not.

As compared to loan waivers and partial compensation being mulled by the Modi government, Rythu Bandhu scheme is simpler to administer and also less inflationary to the farmer's choice of crops.

8
Water Supply

National Rural Drinking Water Programme (NRDWP)

Provision of safe drinking water is a basic necessity for every human being. Rural drinking water supply is a State subject and has been included in the Eleventh Schedule of the Constitution of India, among the subjects that may be entrusted to Panchayats by the States. To accelerate the pace of coverage of problem villages with respect to provision of drinking water, the Government of India introduced the Accelerated Rural Water Supply Programme (ARWSP) in 1972-73, to support States and UTs with financial and technical assistance in implementing drinking water supply schemes in such villages. In order to address the major issues like sustainability, water availability and supply, poor water quality, etc., the Rural Drinking Water Supply Guidelines have been revised w.e.f. 1.4.2009. The revised programme known as National Rural Drinking Water Programme (NRDWP) focuses on the following areas:

- Moving forward from achieving habitation level coverage towards household level drinking water coverage.
- Moving away from over dependence on single drinking water source to multiple sources, through conjunctive use of surface water, groundwater and rainwater harvesting.
- Ensuring sustainability in drinking water schemes and preventing slip back.
- Encouraging water conservation methods including revival of traditional water bodies.
- Convergence of all water conservation programmes at the village level.
- Ensuring household level drinking water security through water budgeting and preparation of village water security plans.
- Consciously moving away from high cost treatment technologies for tackling arsenic and fluoride contamination to the development of alternative sources in respect of arsenic contamination and alternate sources/ dilution of aquifers through rainwater harvesting for tackling fluoride contamination.
- Developing the capability of preliminary drinking water testing at the Gram Panchayat level.
- Establishing Water Testing Laboratory facilities with respect to drinking water, at the district and subdivision level.
- Linking of Water Quality Monitoring and Surveillance with the Jalmani guidelines for implementation of stand-alone drinking water purification systems in rural schools.

- Encouraging handing over of management of rural drinking water schemes (RWS) to the Panchayati Raj Institutions (incentive of 10 per cent of the NRDWP allocation for the States that transfer the management, is introduced). [NRDWP Guidelines to meet the emerging challenges in the rural drinking water]

According to the Approach to the Ninth Plan document, an investment of around Rs. 10,000 crore at current prices made over the successive Five Year Plans has resulted in significant achievements in this sector. While about 82 per cent of the population has access to safe drinking water facility in rural areas, the accessibility in urban areas is around 85 per cent. However, the access in most of the cities and towns is still inadequate, particularly in slums inhabited by the poorer sections of society.

National Rural Drinking Water Programme, 22 April 2013

The National Rural Drinking Water Programme (NRDWP) is a flagship programme of the Government and a component of the Bharat Nirman with the objective of ensuring provision of safe and adequate drinking water supply through hand pumps, piped water supply, etc. to all rural areas, households and persons. This programme was launched after merging the three erstwhile programmes on: Accelerated Rural Water Supply Programme — ARWSP Swajaldhara National Rural Water Quality Monitoring and Surveillance. Under this centrally sponsored scheme, financial assistance is provided to States/ UTs for coverage of all rural habitations, including quality affected habitations with safe drinking water provision; Sustainability measures for drinking water sources and systems; Operation and Maintenance of existing rural water supply schemes. Support activities like IEC, training, MIS and Computerisation etc. and Water Quality Monitoring and Surveillance.

Funds Components, Involvement of PRIs, Objectives/Norms for providing drinking water funds.

In the Union Budget 2013-14, an amount of Rs. 11,000 crore has been made for NRDWP and the rural water supply sector including Rs. 1,100 crore earmarked for North-Eastern Region and Sikkim. Further, 22 per cent of the total allocation i.e. Rs. 2,420 crore and 10 per cent amounting to Rs. 1,100 crore is earmarked for meeting expenditure on Scheduled Caste Sub-Plan and Tribal Sub-Plan respectively.

Components: The NRDWP has following six components: NRDWP (Coverage), NRDWP (Sustainability), NRDWP (Water quality) NRDWP (DDP areas), NRDWP (Natural calamity), NRDWP (Support). In accordance with the policy of Government of India, the Department of Drinking Water Supply has earmarked 10 per cent of the total Central outlay for the programme for the NE States.

Involvement of PRIs: As per the 73rd Amendment to the Constitution, the responsibility for drinking water may be devolved to the Panchayati Raj Institutions (PRIs). In many States, rural drinking water schemes have been transferred to PRIs for operation and maintenance. To encourage this aspect and involve PRIs in O & M, the Government of India has revised its guidelines for the rural water supply scheme to provide for a 10 per cent weightage in allocation of funds to States. This weightage is given for the rural population managing their water supply schemes.

Objectives/Norms for Providing Drinking Water: The objectives of this programme is to provide:

- 40 litres per capita per day (lpcd) of safe drinking water for human beings.
- 30 lpcd additional for cattle in the Desert Development Programme Areas.
- One hand-pump or stand post for every 250 persons.
- The water source should exist within the habitation/ within 1.6 km in the plains and within 100 mtrs. elevation in the hilly areas.
- Performance of the projects.
- According to the Economic Survey for 2015-16 only 46.6 per cent of households in India have access to drinking water within their premises. A far lower, 43.5 per cent of households have access to tap water.

In order to improve availability of drinking water in rural areas, National Rural Drinking water programme initiated a new project supported by the World Bank, the Rural Water Supply and Sanitation Project, low income States with a total cost of Rs. 6,000 crore. The project aims to provide safe 24x7 piped drinking water supply to 7.8 million rural population in four low income States – Assam, Bihar, UP and Jharkhand that have the lowest piped water supply and sanitation facilities.

9
Sanitation

Nirmal Bharat Abhiyan renamed as Total Sanitation Campaign, (or TSC) was a programme following the principles of community-led total sanitation (CLTS) initiated by the Government of India in 1999. It was a demand-driven and people-centred sanitation programme. It evolved from the limited achievements of the first structured programme for rural sanitation in India, the Central Rural Sanitation Programme, which had minimal community participation and was not following the principles of CLTS. The main goal of Total Sanitation Campaign was to eradicate the practice of open defecation by 2017. Community-led total sanitation was not focused on building infrastructure, but on changing cultural norms to prevent open defecation. In Maharashtra, where the programme started, more than 2000 Gram Panchayats achieved "open defecation free" status. Villages that achieved this status received monetary rewards and high publicity under a programme called Nirmal Gram Puraskar. The campaigning ambassador for Nirmal Bharat Abhiyan is Vidya Balan.

Swachh Bharat Abhiyan

On 2 October 2014 the Nirmal Bharat Abhiyan campaign was relaunched as Swachh Bharat Abhiyan (Clean India Mission).

Swachh Bharat Abhiyan (Clean India Mission and abbreviated as SBA or SBM for "Swachh Bharat Mission") is a national campaign by the Government of India, covering 4,041 statutory cities and towns, to clean the streets, roads and infrastructure of the country.

The campaign was officially launched on 2 October 2014 at Rajghat, New Delhi, where Prime Minister Narendra Modi himself cleaned the road. Modi said that the best memorial to Mahatma Gandhi would be to achieve a "Clean India" by 2019, his 150th birth anniversary. It is India's biggest ever cleanliness drive and three million government employees and school and college students of India have participated in this event. The mission was started by Prime Minister Modi, who nominated nine famous personalities for the campaign, and they took up the challenge and nominated nine more people and so on. It has been carried forward since then with people from all walks of life joining it.

Prime Minister Narendra Modi spoke of the need for toilets in his 2014 Independence Day speech.

> "Has it ever pained us that our mothers and sisters have to defecate in open? Poor womenfolk of the village wait for the night; until darkness descends, they can't go out to defecate. What bodily torture they must be feeling, how many

> diseases that act might engender. Can't we just make arrangements for toilets for the dignity of our mothers and sisters?" — *Narendra Modi*

Modi also spoke of the need for toilets in schools during the campaign for 2014 Jammu and Kashmir State elections stating,

> "When the girl student reaches the age where she realises this *lack of female toilets in the school* she leaves her education midway. As they leave their education midway they remain uneducated. Our daughters must also get equal chance to quality education. After 60 years of independence there should have been separate toilets for girl students in every school. But for the past 60 years they could not provide separate toilets to girls and as a result the female students had to leave their education midway.".— *Narendra Modi*

Objectives

This campaign aims to accomplish the vision of a 'Clean India' by 2 October 2019, the 150th birthday of Mahatma Gandhi. Specific objectives are:

1. Eliminate open defecation by constructing toilets for households, communities
2. Eradicate manual scavenging
3. Introduce modern and scientific municipal solid waste management practices
4. Enable private sector participation in the sanitation sector
5. Change people's attitudes to sanitation and create awareness.

The programme plans to construct 12 crore toilets in rural India by October 2019, at a projected cost of Rs. 1.96 lakh crore (US$29 billion).

Finance

Swachh Bharat Mission envisages an investment of Rs. 62,009 crore (US$9.3 billion), of which Rs. 14,623 crore (US$2.2 billion) will be provided by the Centre. The rest is expected to be raised by States, urban local bodies, and from private players. For FY 2015-16, the Government has allocated Rs. 3,625 crore (US$540 million) for Swachh Bharat Mission, an increase of 27 per cent over the previous financial year.

For funding the mission, a *Swachh Bharat Cess* has been imposed on Service Tax at the rate of 0.5 per cent since 15 November 2015. The programme has also received funding and technical support from the World Bank, corporations as part of corporate social responsibility initiatives, and by State governments under the Sarva Shiksha Abhiyan and Rashtriya Madhyamik Shiksha Abhiyan schemes.

The Ministry of Urban Development (MoUD) has released cleanliness rankings for all 476 Class 1 cities with a population of over one lakh. The cities were graded based on their performance on two major indicators in the Mission:

efforts to end open defecation, and solid waste management practices, which were assigned 20 and 22 marks, respectively. The country was divided into five zones (South, North, West, East and Central) and market research agencies were appointed to collate data from urban local bodies on individual, public and community toilets and the door-to-door collection, transportation and disposal of waste generated in each city. This was followed by field visits and interviews in five sample railway stations, bus stations, slums, markets, commercial areas and planned and unplanned localities, before marks were assigned for various categories.

According to the *Economic Survey 2015-16* while access and coverage of latrine facilities is as high as 95 per cent in Kerala, 91 per cent in Mizoram, and 89 per cent in Manipur, less than 25 per cent of households have access to latrine facilities in Bihar, Jharkhand and Odisha.

As per Census 2011 Bihar, Chhattisgarh, Jharkhand and Odisha are States with more than 75 per cent households having no latrine facilities at all. In this context, the Swachh Bharat Mission is accelerating efforts to achieve universal sanitation coverage and eliminate open defecation in India by October 2019.

The progress in sanitation has witnessed a spurt since the launch of the Swachha Bharat Mission. More than 122 lakh toilets have already been constructed in rural areas under the Mission. Sanitation coverage which stood at 40.60 per cent as per NSSO data has risen to around 48.8 per cent as on 31.12 2015

10
Social Protection of the Elderly

Aging of the population is a global phenomenon. In 1950, there were about 200 million persons aged 60 and over in the world, constituting 8.1 per cent of the total global population. It is projected that by the year 2050, there will be a nine fold increase in the population of the aged to 1.8 billion representing about 20 per cent of the total population.

India is no exception to this trend. According to the 1991 census, the proportion of the elderly persons has risen from 5.3 per cent in 1961 to 6.58 per cent in 1991 and is expected to be 9.08 per cent in 2001 and 9.87 per cent in 2021. The number of elderly persons in India is expected to be about 136 million and that of the old — old (70+) accounts for 52 million. More than four fifths of the elderly persons live in rural areas and the female elderly outnumber the male elderly. The current elderly are most illiterate working beyond 60 years of age and most of them are widowed.

World Population Ageing 2013 UN

In addition to the core demographic aspects of population ageing, the present edition of World Population Ageing introduces new sections and information on trends in the economic support ratio, the demographic dividend, independent living among older persons, international differences in the main causes of deaths among older persons, health expenditures, intergenerational transfers, the sources of financial support in old age, and the prevalence of poverty among older people in different regions of the world.

Major Findings: This report includes the following major findings.

1. Population ageing is taking place in nearly all the countries of the world. Ageing results from decreasing mortality, and, most importantly, declining fertility. This process leads to a relative reduction in the proportion of children and to an increase in the share of people in the main working ages and of older persons in the population. The global share of older people (aged 60 years or over) increased from 9.2 per cent in 1990 to 11.7 per cent in 2013 and will continue to grow as a proportion of the world population, reaching 21.1 per cent by 2050.
2. Globally, the number of older persons (aged 60 years or over) is expected to more than double, from 841 million people in 2013 to more than two billion in 2050. Older persons are projected to exceed the number of children for the first time in 2047. Presently, about two thirds of the world's older

persons live in developing countries. Because the older population in less developed regions is growing faster than in the more developed regions, the projections show that older persons will be increasingly concentrated in the less developed regions of the world. By 2050, nearly 8 in 10 of the world's older population will live in the less developed regions.

3. Population ageing has major social and economic consequences. The old-age support ratios (number of working-age adults per older person in the population) are already low in the more developed regions and in some developing countries, and are expected to continue to fall in the coming decades with ensuing fiscal pressures on support systems for older persons. In a number of developing countries, poverty is high among older persons, sometimes higher than that of the population as a whole, especially in countries with limited coverage of social security systems. While people are living longer almost everywhere, the prevalence of non-communicable diseases and disability increase as population's age.
4. On the positive side, population ageing and the increased prevalence of non-communicable diseases originate in the mostly positive trends of drastically reduced child and adult mortality, and declining fertility. Also, older persons can increasingly live independently (alone or with their spouse only), and in most countries, they support themselves financially with their own labour earnings, income from their assets, and through public transfers. In most countries with pertinent data, older persons make net financial contributions to younger family members until rather advanced ages.
5. Most developed countries already have aged populations. By contrast, a large number of developing countries are projected to experience high and increasing economic support ratios for years or decades to come, and can, therefore, benefit significantly from the "demographic dividend", provided that appropriate labour market and other policies allow for a productive absorption of the growing working-age population and for increased investments in the human capital of children and youth. United Nations Department of Economic and Social Affairs I Population Division

Other Specific Findings

The older population is itself ageing. Globally, the share of older persons aged 80 years or over within the older population was 14 per cent in 2013 and is projected to reach 19 per cent in 2050. If this projection is realised, there will be 392 million persons aged 80 years or over by 2050, more than three times the present.

The older population is predominantly female. Because women tend to live longer than men, older women outnumber older men almost everywhere. In 2013, globally, there were 85 men per 100 women in the age group 60 years or over and 61 men per 100 women in the age group 80 years or over. These sex ratios are expected to increase moderately during the next several decades, reflecting a slightly faster projected improvement in old-age mortality among males than among females.

Globally, 40 per cent of older persons aged 60 years or over live independently, that is to say, alone or with their spouse only. Independent living is far more common in the developed countries, where about three quarters of older persons live independently, compared with only a quarter in developing countries and one eighth in the least developed countries. As countries develop and their populations continue to age, living alone or with a spouse only will likely to become much more common among older people in the future.

Many older persons still need to work, especially in developing countries. In 2010, the labour force participation of persons aged 65 years or over was around 31 per cent in the less developed regions and eight per cent in the more developed regions. Labour force participation among older men is decreasing in the less developed regions, but it is increasing in the more developed regions. In both development groups, despite their numerical disadvantage, men made up a large majority of the total labour force among older persons.

The labour earnings of older persons are an important source of economic support in old age, especially in developing countries. Public transfers are a major source of old age support in developed countries and in some developing countries with substantial social security coverage, while income from their own assets finances another substantial part of the consumption of older persons, especially in countries with less expansive public transfer systems. In most countries with available data, older persons are net givers of familial transfers.

In much of Africa, the prevalence of poverty among older persons is either lower or only slightly higher than the total population average, while in Latin America the prevalence of poverty among the older population varies widely, from levels much lower than average in countries of the Southern Cone, to significantly higher than average in some Central American countries. Although older persons in most countries of the Organisation of Economic Co-operation and Development (OECD) are well covered by social protection systems, the poverty rate of older persons tends to be higher than population average.

Situation of Elderly in India—2011

Highlights

- The elderly population (aged 60 years or above) account for 7.4 per cent of total population in 2001. For males it was marginally lower at 7.1 per cent, while for females it was 7.8 per cent. Among States the proportion vary from around 4 per cent in small States like Dadra and Nagar Haveli, Nagaland Arunachal Pradesh, Meghalaya to more than 10.5 per cent in Kerala.

- Both the share and size of elderly population is increasing over time. From 5.6 per cent in 1961 it is projected to rise to 12.4 per cent of population by the year 2026.
- The sex ratio among elderly people was as high as 1028 in 1951 but subsequently dropped to about 938 in 1971 and finally reached 972 in 2001.
- The life expectancy at birth during 2002-06 was 64.2 for females as against 62.6 years for males. At the age 60, average remaining length of life was found to be about 18 years (16.7 for males, 18.9 for females) and that at age 70 was less than 12 years (10.9 for males and 12.4 for females).
- There is sharp rise in age-specific death rate with age from 20 (per thousand) for persons in age group 60-64 years to 80 among those aged 75-79 years and 200 for persons aged more than 85 years.
- The old-age dependency ratio climbed from 10.9 per cent in 1961 to 13.1 per cent in 2001 for India as a whole. For females and males the value of the ratio was 13.8 per cent and 12.5 per cent in 2001.
- About 65 per cent of the aged had to depend on others for their day-to-day maintenance. Less than 20 per cent of elderly women but majority of elderly men were economically independent.
- Among economically dependent elderly men 6-7 per cent were financially supported by their spouses, almost 85 per cent by their own children, 2 per cent by grand children and 6 per cent by others. Of elderly women, less than 20 per cent depended on their spouses, more than 70 per cent on their children, 3 per cent on grand children and 6 per cent or more on others including the non relations

According to the 42nd round of the NSS, 34 per cent of the rural elderly were financially independent against 28.94 per cent in urban areas. The economically dependent elderly are mostly living with and supported by their children and in some cases by the grandchildren. Though living within the family is most common among Indian elderly, 12 per cent of the male elderly were staying alone and this percentage was a little above 1 per cent for females.

Currently majority of older people live with their children. Due to industrialisation of the society coupled with urbanisation, the family system is breaking up and the children are not able to keep their parents with them for a variety of reasons. The current trend, therefore, is to supplement traditional informal family support with formal social protection.

There are three ways in which social protection is provided to the elderly — namely, social assistance, social security and provident funds.

Social assistance programmes in the form of old age pensions operate in all the States. With the introduction of the National Old Age Pension Scheme, a minimum standard has been established for these schemes. Unfortunately, this standard is a little too low. In the absence of a provision for adjusting the rate of pension to the rise in the cost of living, the real value of the pension has tended to be eroded. It is, therefore, necessary to revise the rates of pension payable under the Social Assistance Programme periodically.

Destitution is the basic criterion for payment of old age pension under the Social Assistance Programme. It is also subject to a numerical and financial ceiling. As there is no other scheme to provide retirement benefit to them who are above the level of destitution and are not covered by the Employees' Pension Scheme, the eligibility criterion for the old age pension payable under the Social Assistance Programme needs to be liberalised so as to bring within its scope all persons who are below the poverty line. In fact, poverty is the criterion for the other social assistance schemes. There is no reason why the same criterion should not be adopted for the National Old Age Pension Scheme also.

In this connection, the following findings of a study of the old age pensions conducted by the Jai Shankar Memorial Centre are relevant and, therefore, they are reproduced in extenso:

Old Age Pension (OAP) Beneficiaries by State, District and Village

The State-wise distribution of the number of beneficiaries in 1997-98 shows wide disparities—from a high of 67.9 per cent of total aged population in Haryana to a low 1.3 per cent in Uttar Pradesh. Bihar leads the list with a total of 1.5 million beneficiaries, covering 26.1 per cent of the total aged population. It is not sure whether this level of assistance was kept up in later years. Even at Rs. 50/- p.m., the old age pension scheme would have cost the Bihar State Government something in the region of Rs. 900 million that year. As for Haryana — at one stage, in 1987 — all persons above the age of 65 were made eligible for a monthly pension of Rs. 100/-. This decision was modified in 1991 under which all persons above the age of 60 but satisfying an income criterion were made eligible; as a result, the numbers came down from 700,000 to 500,000. The number swelled again to 650,000 in 1993-94 but the Government was able to disburse old age pension only for seven months in the Year. The budget provision of Rs. 128 crores for 1994-95 in the Haryana budget will not, it is stated, be adequate to clear the arrears of the previous years.

At the State level, the total number of beneficiaries, district-wise and even block-wise, (as in Odisha) is fixed and communicated to the districts. Availability of funds with the State governments is the main consideration in fixing the number of beneficiaries at the State level and from that, at the district level and below. Even here, there is a lack of system. For example, in Andhra Pradesh, it is seen from the figures for 1993-94 furnished by the State Government, that, whereas numbers of OAP beneficiaries vary considerably from district to district, almost a uniform 2,700 widows' pensions have been sanctioned for each district except for Hyderabad (6,100) and Ranga Reddy (3,200) districts. The numbers fixed for landless agricultural workers' pension seem to follow a totally different pattern and has no, relation to the numbers of OAP beneficiaries; this is surprising because there cannot be that marked difference in a district in the incidence of beneficiaries under the OAP scheme and under the pension schemes for landless agricultural workers. Even the amounts released for the latter pension cases do not seem to correspond to the target fixed in terms of numbers.

Finally, our field study has shown that the incidence of OAP pension payments can be quite different from one village to the other. It is difficult to say how far these differences are due to lack of stringent administrative supervision or by differential pressures on inclusion of beneficiaries at the local level. Unless a detailed study is made State-wise of these issues, it is not easy to identify the kind of administrative problems that are faced in the field in the matter of identification of beneficiaries and implementation of the schemes in general.

Eligibility Criteria

The income criteria that has been accepted for purposes of targeting, are not the same in all the States. Gujarat has prescribed a maximum personal income of Rs. 2,400 per annum or a family income of Rs. 4,500 and a Niradhar (without support) status for OAP. Odisha has prescribed a maximum income of Rs. 3,200 per annum as well as the Niradhar Status. And Uttar Pradesh has indicated a maximum income of Rs. 2,700 per annum coupled with the stipulation that the person should not own more than 2.5 acres of land; the latter, namely 2.5 acres of land, can in certain locations, for example irrigated land in Western Uttar Pradesh, may result in an annual income which will be a high multiple of the maximum income limit prescribed. Other States also have prescribed criteria of income.

In actual practice, these carefully calibrated criteria are not very relevant for the simple reason the coverage is usually so low, compared to the number of deserving cases, as to make these criteria subordinate to the whims and fancies of the lower rungs of administrations including the village level staff; and in quite a few cases, the local political heavy-weights have a hand in deciding who the beneficiaries should be. So our field teams had occasion to come across beneficiaries who, in their opinion, were not eligible to be included within the criteria prescribed; also, even among the eligible, the more deserving, in terms of destitution, have been passed over in favour of the less deserving.

In prescribing criteria for eligibility to old age pension, some States have indicated that the claimant should not have a major son (for support); e.g. Gujarat and Uttar Pradesh. The condition is a little difficult to understand, as this does not take note of the fact whether the son or sons are in a position to support the father and/ or whether they themselves are below the poverty line. It may as well be that sons above 21 years of age are staying away from their elderly parents and that their financial situation is such they cannot help their parents financially. In Gujarat it was found that — with a view to helping needy old people through OAP — the local authorities sometimes resort to deleting the names of the elderly from the common family ration card so that they can become eligible for the OAP. Be that as it may, this raises an important question of social policy, namely, whether it is not desirable, if not necessary, for old age care to be provided as far as possible within the family. In our view, social assistance should not only target individuals (indigent old people), but also the families that take care of them. It is, therefore, proposed to remove the eligibility criterion. According to which poor elderly people with close relatives are excluded from the OAP scheme (*see* also Midgley, 1993).

As far as widows' pension is concerned, it was found that there are substantial differences in age eligibility criteria. Some States include all eligible widows above the age of 18, others include widows above the age of 15 and so on. Gujarat has a unique scheme whose eligibility criteria have the potential of becoming the national norm. In Gujarat, widows' pension is available only for one year during which the widow is given training on acquiring a skill which she can, on completion of training, use to earn a livelihood for which purpose an equipment grant of Rs. 1, 000 is given; during the period of pension, the amount is enhanced by Rs. 80 per month per minor child, subject to a maximum of two minor children. It is also understood that during the period of training, the widow is also eligible to get a stipend of Rs. 80 per month, though this is restricted to widows not belonging to the "upper castes". (In passing, it may be mentioned that of the two cases of below 60 widows' pension recipients in the sample in Gujarat, none had chosen to opt for the training as they were tribals who preferred to continue to be agricultural labourers in their villages).

If Gujarat's widows' pension scheme were to be applied at the national level, it would have to be decided whether eligibility for continuous pension should be fixed at 50 or 55 years. In addition, the lower age eligibility criterion would have to be placed at 18 years, being the legal marriage age. For widows between 18 and 50 or 55 years old, it would be recommendable to allow a pensionable period of two years. The idea of paying a small amount towards maintenance expenditure of minor children up to a maximum of two is sound and may be retained.

As far as the disabled are concerned, all those above the age of 60 will automatically get covered as part of the OAP scheme. Several States have extended pension benefits to other younger disabled, as part of the OAP or as in Orissa under a separate scheme. Some have not prescribed any minimum age limit. Degree of disability has also been a relevant criterion for eligibility in certain States.

In general, a national scheme should be restricted to total disability and disability resulting in at least 70 per cent loss of earning capacity. In order to avoid uncertainty or dispute about the extent of loss of earning capacity, it is suggested to follow the Working Group on Economic and Social security of the National Commission on Rural Labour (1991) which recommended to adapt those injuries which, under Schedule I to the Workmen's Compensation Act, 1923 and the Second Schedule to the Employees' State Insurance Act, 1948 result in 70 per cent or more loss of earning capacity. Of the several disabilities, visual disability and locomotion disabilities are generally considered greater handicaps than hearing or speech disability, particularly in respect of earning capacity.

Access to the OAP Scheme

Being aware of, and eligible to, the schemes by itself is not enough to get the benefit. Even getting copies of the application forms can be a hurdle. Our survey showed that sufficient copies of forms are not being made available to the local officialdom by the government, compelling the local officials to get them photocopied and sold, of course, not at the minimum cost, to the applicants. Filling of the forms can be a second hurdle, sometimes calling for "expert" help from the public authorities and, may be, at a price. It was found during our field study that cases are not uncommon where the Sarpanch or any other village level functionary 'manages' to help persons whom he favours, by filling in their forms and 'processes' them through the official channels, more often out of turn.

The system followed is such that the actual sanction is to be accorded at a fairly high level for this purpose — either at the sub divisional level or even at the district level as in Andhra Pradesh where the sanctioning authority is the District Collector. No wonder the ordinary individual, however deserving, may have to wait, sometimes endlessly, for the sanction of his or her pension.

The real and lasting solution to this question of prompt and proper selection seems to lie in entrusting this work and responsibility to the village or at the block level. It may not be possible to evolve a system that is fool-proof but given the experience so far and considering the relevance of Panchayats at the local level as organs of 'local Government', selection of persons as beneficiaries under a given set of criteria is best left to be made by the Gram Sabha at an open meeting and to have the lists periodically revised, say twice a year or once a year. Perhaps, a variation of this system could be the preparation of 'provisional' lists by the Panchayat in consultation with the village officials and to leave it to the Gram Sabha to make such changes to the list as it considers necessary. In addition, the identified beneficiaries should be registered at the village level and provided with identity cards (which can also be in the form of an additional colour card attached to the ration card). And if selection of beneficiaries and the revision of the list is to be at the Panchayat level, logic demands that payment must also be at that level.

Till 1996, provident funds were the main source of protection of the workers in the organised sector in their old age. They were found to be inadequate for the purpose. Many of them have, therefore, been partially converted into pension schemes. The most important of these schemes is the Employees' Pension Scheme.

The Employees' Pension Scheme is somewhat complex. It is difficult to appreciate its merits or demerits. The scheme has been welcomed by the organisations of workers generally with some exceptions.

Given the rate of contribution, the nature and quantum of benefits can be varied depending upon the system of financial organisation that is adopted. Usually every such scheme indicates the system of financial organisation recommended. There are various methods of financing a scheme depending on whether any fund is created and if so the extent of funding. In the case of pension schemes, the system of funding recommended by the International Association of Actuaries and Statisticians is the Scaled Premium Method which seeks to ensure an equilibrium between the assets and liabilities over comparatively a short period as against the General Premium Method which seeks to ensure equilibrium over an indefinite period. The Employees' Pension Scheme is silent about the system of financial organisation recommended. Actuaries who have framed pension schemes in India are generally overcautious and have tended towards full funding. This was the case with the Employees' Family Pension Scheme and it appears to be the case with the Employees' Pension Scheme as well. There is, therefore, a general dissatisfaction with the quantum of benefits in both cases. The scheme calls for a review from this point of view.

In this connection an ILO Technical Assistance Appraisal Mission (November, 1996) is reported to have commented on certain aspects of the scheme and to have made certain recommendations which include the following:

- Withdrawal option shall be abolished or modified.
- Pensions should be adjusted to inflation.
- Provision regarding return of capital should be withdrawn.
- The option to commute part of the pension should be withdrawn.
- The minimum pension age should be raised to 50 and the reduction factor should be modified.
- The financial sustainability of the current standard age of 58 should be assessed actuarially.
- Pension should be calculated on the basis of the earnings for a longer period instead of last year's earnings.
- Provision should be made that no insured person will receive more than one benefit for the same category.
- Provision to pay pension to a non-relative nominee should be reviewed.

As regards the financial system of the scheme, the Mission has observed that the objectives of guaranteeing the actuarial soundness of the schemes, an acceptably stable contribution rate and adequate protection of pensioners against inflation can be achieved with partial funding.

There is great merit in these recommendations of the ILO and they need to be considered objectively.

Many countries around the world are facing difficulty in running their pension schemes and are contemplating reform of the schemes. There is no system that can escape from problems of moral hazard, adverse selection agency costs and free riding. All pension systems require good governance and good management to function well. All pension schemes have to cope with the uncertainty that characterises human existence, and the single but inescapable fact that we do not know the future. All systems are exposed to the vagaries of macro-economic imbalances, the peculiarities and unpredictability of fundamental demographic trends, and the implications of changes in the relative scarcity of labour and capital. The current trend all over the world is, therefore, not to pin all hope on one scheme but to have a mixed system of two or more schemes. They are known as the complementary schemes. The ILO has described the trend as follows:

> "Numerous countries have retirement income policies that refer to three tiers or pillars of protection. The first is the National Pension Scheme, the second is the Complementary or Occupational Pension Scheme, and the third is an Individual Retirement Account. Favourable provisions often apply to savings deposited in these accounts from which withdrawal cannot be made before retirement age."

A proposal called Swiss Chilampore based on a combination of the best features of the pension schemes of three different countries, namely, Switzerland, Chile and Singapore was put forward at the General Assembly of the International Social Security Association held a few years back. This is a multi-pillar system comprising of two compulsory pillars and one or two voluntary ones.

The World Bank has also made a similar proposal. The difference between the proposal of the World Bank and the other multi-tiered systems lies in the approach to the second tier, the form of that tier and about its management. There is no dispute about the desirability of introducing a three tier system.

In fact, the existing schemes in India could be built into a three tier system; the National Old age Pension Scheme and the State Old Age Pension Schemes could form the first tier, focusing on redistribution, alleviating old Age poverty and a multitude of risks such as inflation, recession and low investment returns; the Employees' Pension Scheme and the variants thereof could constitute the second tier based on contributions but managed by a public authority; the schemes of the LIC, UTI and others may constitute the voluntary pillar based on occupational or other basis.

In the year 2014, the government decided to pay a minimum pension of Rs. 1000 under the Employees Pension Scheme. Simultaneously, the government also decided to enhance the minimum wage ceiling for application of the Scheme to Rs. 15, 000 per month. The decision to pay a minimum pension of Rs. 1000 was effective from 1 September 2014 but subject to renewal after 1 April 2015

Later, in April 2015 Government decided to continue its Rs. 1,000 per minimum monthly pension scheme in perpetuity.

"Providing a minimum pension of Rs. 1,000 per month is an effort to provide meaningful subsistence to pensioners who have served in the organised sector. The present proposal is likely to benefit approximately 20 lakh pensioners under EPS, 1995," release issued on Wednesday *(The Hindu*, 29 April, 2015).

The Cabinet also approved corresponding grant of continuous annual budgetary support for implementing the minimum pension, which will be to the tune of Rs. 850 crore per year on a tapering basis.

A large number of member pensioners under the EPS, 1995 receive low pensions, which is not commensurate with the growing cost of living.

The primary reason behind a meagre pension is that it is calculated on the basis of pensionable service and average of last sixty months' wages.

If either of them is low, the pension amount will also be low. This is largely seen in the cases of employees of seasonal industries.

In this connection it must be noted that self-employed persons who constitute more than 50 per cent of the workforce did not have any social security pension scheme for providing them an old age benefit. They had to depend entirely on voluntary insurance schemes of the LIC and the UTI. In the year 2010, the government introduced a new scheme called Swavalamban Yojana to help the self-employed to provide for their retirement.

Swavalamban Yojana

It was a government-backed pension scheme targeted at the unorganised sector in India. It was applicable to all citizens in the unorganised sector who joined the National Pension Scheme (NPS) administered by the Pension Fund Regulatory and Development Authority (PFRDA) Act, 2013.

Under the scheme, the Government of India contributed Rs. 1,000 (US$15) per year to each NPS account opened in the year 2010-11 and for the next three years, that is, 2011-12, 2012-13 and 2013-14. The benefit was available only to people who joined the NPS with a minimum contribution of Rs. 1,000 (US$15) and maximum contribution of Rs. 12,000 (US$180) per annum.

The scheme was announced by the Finance Minister in Budget 2010-11. It was funded by grants from the Government of India.

This scheme has been replaced with Atal Pension Yojana, in which all subscribing workers below the age of 40 are eligible for pension of up to Rs. 5,000 (US$74) per month on attainment of 60 years of age.

Atal Pension Yojana

Introducing the new scheme the Government made the following statement:

1. The Government of India is extremely concerned about the old age income security of the working poor and is focused on encouraging and enabling them to join the National Pension System (NPS). To address the longevity

risks among the workers in unorganised sector and to encourage the workers in unorganised sector to voluntarily save for their retirement, who constitute 88 per cent of the total labour force of 47.29 crore as per the 66th Round of NSSO Survey of 2011-12, but do not have any formal pension provision, the Government had started the Swavalamban Scheme in 2010-11. However, coverage under Swavalamban Scheme is inadequate mainly due to lack of clarity of pension benefits at the age after 60.

2. The Finance Minister has, therefore, announced a new initiative called Atal Pension Yojana (APY) in his Budget Speech for 2015-16. The APY will be focussed on all citizens in the unorganised sector, who join the National Pension System (NPS) administered by the Pension Fund Regulatory and Development Authority (PFRDA) and who are not members of any statutory social security scheme. Under the APY, the subscribers would receive the fixed pension of Rs. 1,000 per month, Rs. 2,000 per month, Rs. 3,000 per month, Rs. 4,000 per month, Rs. 5,000 per month, at the age of 60 years, depending on their contributions, which itself would vary on the age of joining the APY. The minimum age of joining APY is 18 years and maximum age is 40 years. Therefore, minimum period of contribution by the subscriber under APY would be 20 years or more. The benefit of fixed pension would be guaranteed by the Government. The Central Government would also co-contribute 50 per cent of the subscriber's contribution or Rs. 1,000 per annum, whichever is lower, to each eligible subscriber account, for a period of five years, i.e., from 2015-16 to 2019-20, who join the NPS before 31 December 2015 and who are not income tax payers. The APY would be launched from 1 June 2015. The existing subscribers of Swavalamban Scheme would be automatically migrated to APY, unless they opt out.

Brief Particulars of the new Scheme – Atal Pension Yojana (APY)

Benefit: Fixed pension for the subscribers ranging between Rs. 1,000 to Rs. 5,000, if he joins and contributes between the age of 18 years and 40 years. The contribution levels would vary and would be low if subscriber joins early and increase if he joins late.

Eligibility: Atal Pension Yojana (APY) is open to all bank account holders who are not members of any statutory social security scheme.

Age of joining and contribution period: The minimum age of joining APY is 18 years and maximum age is 40 years. Therefore, minimum period of contribution by the subscriber under APY would be 20 years or more.

Focus of APY: Mainly targeted at unorganised sector workers.

Enrolment and Subscriber Payment: All bank account holders under the eligible category may join APY with auto-debit facility to accounts, leading to reduction in contribution collection charges.

*Enrolment agencies***:** All Points of Presence (Service Providers) and Aggregators under Swavalamban Scheme would enrol subscribers through architecture of National Pension System.

*Operational Framework***:** It is Government of India Scheme, which is administered by the Pension Fund Regulatory and Development Authority. The Institutional Architecture of NPS would be utilised to enrol subscribers under APY.

*Funding of APY***:** Government would provide (i) fixed pension guarantee for the subscribers; (ii) would co-contribute 50 per cent of the subscriber contribution or Rs. 1,000 per annum, whichever is lower, to eligible subscribers; and (iii) would also reimburse the promotional and development activities including incentive to the contribution collection agencies to encourage people to join the APY.

This a voluntary pension Scheme. Except for the fact that the government subscribes 50 per cent of the premium limited to Rs. 1,000 per annum for a period of five years, it cannot be regarded as a social security Scheme. It is necessary to design a contributory social insurance scheme for providing the self-employed persons a retirement income. One way is to amend the Employees' Provident Funds Act to enable the self-employed persons to join the Employees' Pension Scheme. Another is to introduce a separate social insurance scheme for the purpose.

Old Age Homes

This brings us to the next question relating to the shelter needs of the elderly. While ordinarily the elderly persons live with their children and grandchildren, circumstances are developing in such a way that many of them have had to live independently or under institutional care. Sometimes the health condition of the persons may be such that the concerned families may not be able to provide the necessary care. In some cases there may be no family at all. At the worst, the families might have abandoned them. The elderly persons would need institutional care in such circumstances. A WHO seminar of Health experts is reported to have concluded as follows:

> "The emergent need for some basic provision of institutional care is now evident in most countries of the region (Western Pacific countries). The seminar identified the need for Governments to take account of this trend to enact legislation and regulations to ensure good quality, appropriate, equitable, and cost-efficient provision of institutional services whether by the Government, non-Governmental organisations or the private sector."

The National Policy for older persons recognises this need. The national policy is to consider institutional care as the last resort when personal circumstances are such that old age homes become absolutely necessary. The policy provides for giving assistance to voluntary organisations for construction and maintenance of old age homes.

According to information available there are over 300 old age homes in this country. Some of these are maintained by the State governments and most are run by non-government organisations with assistance from government. There are also some institutions run by private charitable institutions without any assistance from government. The total number of inmates in these institutions is about 15,000. Assuming that at least 1 per cent of the aged require institutional care, facilities would have to be created for providing institutional care to about five lakh persons. (It has been reported that nearly 5 per cent of the elderly live in these institutions).

It is doubtful if voluntary organisations will come forward to set up so many old age homes. There is, therefore, no alternative for the Central and State Governments except to take the initiative to set up their own homes in sufficient numbers.

One cannot be content with the setting up of the homes. The quality of service provided in these homes needs to be monitored. The existing arrangements in this regard are less than adequate.

The elderly people are apt to develop health problems as they grow older.

The National Policy for Older Persons recognises that with advancing age, old persons have to cope with health and associated problems some of which may be chronic, of a multiple nature, requiring constant attention and carry the risk of disability and consequent loss of autonomy. There is no special scheme for the health care of the elderly except the ESI and the CGHS which are applicable to a small number of persons who have been in service with the Central Government or an insurable employment. In all other cases the old persons have to depend upon public medical services or private doctors and hospitals. The health insurance schemes of the GIC do not cover persons who are above the age of 70 who require greater attention. It is necessary to develop appropriate social health insurance schemes for the elderly which may be linked to pension insurance.

The National Programme for Health Care of the Elderly (NPHCE) has been introduced recently. It is an articulation of the international and national commitments of the government as envisaged under the UN Convention on the Rights of Persons with Disabilities (UNCRPD), National Policy on Older Persons (NPOP) adopted by the Government of India in 1999 and Section 20 of "The Maintenance and Welfare of Parents and Senior Citizens Act, 2007" dealing with provisions for medical care of Senior Citizen.

The programme has envisaged to provide promotional, preventive, curative and rehabilitative services in an integrated manner for the Elderly in various Government health facilities. The range of services will include health promotion, preventive services, diagnosis and management of geriatric medical problems (out and in-patient), day care services, rehabilitative services and home based care as needed. Districts will be linked to Regional Geriatric Centres for providing tertiary level care.

- Main objective of the programme is to provide preventive, curative and rehabilitative services to the elderly persons at various levels of health care delivery system of the country.
- Other objectives are to strengthen referral system, to develop specialised man power and to promote research in the field of diseases related to old age.

Achievements of the programme is yet to be assessed.

With the growth of the population of the aged, the associated problem of caring for the aged is becoming increasingly important. Lately it has been systematised in the form of social care insurance as a part of social security. It has been reported that in 1991, in Germany, approximately one-third of the social security expenditure was devoted to care provision. The concept of care dependency is distinct from treatment for illness and covers help with daily tasks that do not fall under any medical treatment plan, e.g., personal hygiene, feeding, mobility or housework.

The normal and preferred arrangement for taking care of the aged is to encourage them to live with their families. Where there are either no families or the families cannot look after them, they would have to be provided with institutional care.

It has been reported that in China a law has been enacted that children must support their elderly parents failing which they would be liable to punishment. In India, too, in a trail blazing move the Himachal Government has recently enacted a law which makes it binding on the children to take care of the parents. The Government of Maharashtra also is planning to enact a similar law. The Central Government should consider a Central Law on the subject.

Social security is a basic human right. It is based on the principle that society has an obligation to provide livelihood to every one of its members by providing work to those who can work and by other means to those who cannot work. Right to work and right to social security are complementary social rights. The object of social security is thus to provide livelihood to those who cannot work and earn their living.

According to the Supreme Court, Right to Livelihood inheres the Right to Life a fundamental right enshrined in Article 21 of the Constitution of India. It follows, therefore, that social security is also a fundamental right.

The need for social security may be chronic or temporary. It is chronic in the case of the persons who are unemployed and who are unemployable because of their age or other disabilities. It may be temporary in the case of others. In the latter case, the need for social security arises when a contingency arises such as sickness, accident, maternity, loss of employment due to retrenchment or closure of a unit, old age or death of a breadwinner. These occurrences may be normal incidences of life or may be the result of natural or manmade disasters or catastrophes.

It is desirable that every individual or group of individuals should make their own arrangements for meeting these contingencies. It should be the primary objective of public policy to enable the individuals to make such arrangements. Every society would, however, have many sections of people who cannot make their own arrangements for protecting themselves against such contingencies, because of poverty caused by lack of or low income. The State has to make provision for their protection.

There are various ways of providing social security of which the preferred ones are social assistance and social insurance. Actually different combinations of social assistance and social insurance schemes are in vogue in different countries.

Broadly speaking, social insurance types of schemes will be appropriate in respect of those for whom contributions may be made by the beneficiaries themselves or others. In respect of those for whom no contributions can be recovered, social security protection will have to be provided under social assistance schemes.

The appropriate strategy for providing social security in India particularly for the elderly, therefore, requires classification of the people according to their economic status.

From the point of view of social security, the first priority has to be given to people of the last category, namely the old, the infirm and the young persons who are destitute and constitute the liability of the State and the first charge on the resources of the State. Admittedly social security for this class of people has necessarily to be provided by means of social assistance.

Above this class are those for whom social security may be provided by means partly of social insurance and partly of social assistance. Next in the order would be those for whom social security may be provided entirely on a contributory basis. Above them would be those who do not need social security being able to make their own provision for meeting the contingencies that arise including old age.

Thus, the system of social security in India would consist of a multi-tiered structure. Indeed, there is already such a structure though in a rudimentary form. In the first tier, there is the National Social Assistance Programme and other social assistance programmes. At the second tier, there are the social insurance schemes, namely, the ESI Scheme, the Schemes framed under the EPF Act, the employers' liability schemes and such others. At the next level are the numerous voluntary health insurance and old age pension schemes which are being run by LIC, GIC, the UTI and other financial institutions. Lately a new set of schemes have appeared on the scene and they are the welfare funds, subsidised insurance schemes, self-help groups, micro-credit, micro- finance and micro-insurance schemes, etc. meant to provide social security to the workers in the unorganised sector. Each of these tiers needs to be expanded to cover the whole population, especially the vulnerable sections.

The National Social Assistance Programme consists of three separate schemes, namely, the National Old Age Pension Scheme, the National Maternity Benefit Scheme and the National Family Benefit Scheme. We are here concerned with the National Old Age Pension Scheme.

National Old Age Pension Scheme

The National Old Age Pension Scheme provides for a pension of Rs. 75 per month to the old people living in conditions of destitution. This rate was fixed in 1995 and has not been revised since then despite the fact that the real value of the pension has been reduced by steadily rising prices. Some State Governments have, however, on their own raised the level of old pension. Considering that the floor level of minimum wage suggested to the State governments for adoption by the Central Government is Rs. 45 per day catering to three consumption units the amount required for bare subsistence would be Rs. 15 per day per person. By this reckoning the minimum amount required for subsistence would be Rs. 450 per month per person. Granting that the amount of pension is usually limited to 50 per cent of the last wage drawn the amount of minimum pension cannot be less than Rs. 225 per month. The rate of pension payable under the National Old Age Pension is, therefore, totally inadequate for the subsistence of the pensioners and needs to be raised.

Under another scheme, the elderly are also entitled to supply of 10 kg of food grains free of cost to supplement the pension. The eligibility conditions for the two schemes are not the same. They need, therefore, to be integrated.

There are complaints about the implementation of both the schemes. They need to be addressed.

Subsidised Insurance Schemes

One of the models for providing a measure of social security for workers in the unorganized sector is insurance. The Government of India as well several State governments have launched a variety of schemes for the benefit of the weaker sections of the people through the Life Insurance Corporation of India and the General Insurance Corporation of India.

The Government of India had launched the following schemes through the LIC:

1. Landless Agricultural Labour Group Insurance Scheme'*
2. Group Insurance Scheme for the beneficiaries of the IRDP.*
3. Group Insurance Scheme for the weaker sections.*
4. Rural Group Insurance Scheme.*
5. Jeevan Suraksha.

The following schemes had been introduced by the Government of India through the General Insurance Corporation and its subsidiaries:

1. Personal Accident Social Security Schemes for poor families.*
2. Hut Insurance Schemes.*
3. Solatium Funds Scheme.
4. Jan Arogya.
5. Public Liability Insurance Act, 1991.
6. Railway Passengers' Insurance Scheme.
7. Comprehensive Crop Insurance Scheme.

   * *Discontinued Schemes*

Some of the State Governments have also introduced a few Insurance Schemes. These schemes provided limited benefits and were, therefore, not very popular.

Of these the schemes marked* have since been discontinued and merged in a new scheme called Jan Shree. The new scheme was introduced in August, 2000. Under this scheme; insurance benefit has been raised to Rs. 20,000 for natural death, Rs. 25,000 for partial disability and Rs. 50,000 for accidental death or permanent disability. The premium is Rs. 200 which is subsidised to the extent of 50 per cent; the insured person has to pay a premium of Rs. 100 per annum and the balance is paid out of the Social Security fund maintained by the LIC.

The Government of India has also introduced another insurance scheme for the benefit of agricultural workers called Khetihar Mazdoor Bima Yojana. The introduction of this scheme was announced on 18 May 2001 at the end of the inaugural session of the 37th Indian Labour Conference and it is reported to have been actually launched with effect from 1 July 2001. To begin with, the scheme was to be implemented in clusters of 5 to 6 villages each in 100 carefully chosen districts. It is understood to have been introduced in fifty chosen districts to begin with. The following benefits will be provided under the Scheme:

- Lump sum payment of Rs. 20,000 on natural death.
- Lump sum payment of Rs. 50,000 in case of death due to accident.
- Lump sum payment of Rs. 50,000 in case of permanent disability or Rs. 25,000 in case of partial disability due to accident.
- If the agricultural worker survives the age of 60, he will be entitled to a pension ranging from Rs. 100 to Rs. 1,900 per month depending on age entry in case of death after the age of 60.
- On death after commencement of pension the family will be paid a lump sum amount ranging from Rs. 13, 000 to Rs. 2,50,000 depending on the age of entry to the scheme.
- The insured person has to pay a premium of Re. 1 per day or Rs. 365 per annum and the Central Government will pay double this amount, that is Rs. 730 per annum

The differential rates of subsidy payable under the two schemes may be open to the criticism of discrimination, unless the distinction sought to be made between the different target groups can stand the test of reasonable classification. It is, therefore, desirable to rationalise the subsidised insurance scheme providing for a uniform rate of subsidy and for differential rates of contribution by the insured persons The scheme will be administered by project societies.

It is also desirable to extend the application of the scheme to all classes of workers in the unorganised sector over a course of time, if not immediately.

It has been the experience of Insurance companies in India that, however low the rates of premium may be, the take up of subsidised voluntary insurance policies has not been encouraging. There is no reason to believe that the response to the new insurance schemes introduced by the LIC will be better. It would, therefore, be necessary to make them mandatory by linking with the welfare funds or welfare boards so that the insured persons' share of the premium is paid by the welfare fund as in the case of the groups insurance scheme for beedi workers.

Pension Insurance Schemes

In so far as workers in the organised sector are concerned retirement benefits are presently being provided through provident fund schemes. There are numerous provident fund schemes in India of which the Employees Provident Fund Scheme established under the Employees Provident funds and Misc. Provisions Act, 1952 is the largest in terms of the number of persons covered and the volume of the Fund. The Scheme provides for payment of contribution to the Provident Fund by the workers and their employers at a minimum of 10 per cent each. Some of the specified industries are required to pay contribution at a higher rate of 12 per cent. Till recently, the accumulation in the Provident Fund released on retirement was expected to provide income security in old age. As, however, the average balance available in the individual Provident Fund accounts of the members at the time of retirement was found to be small because of the provision permitting premature withdrawals from the fund for various purposes to be adequate to provide any such security. There was, therefore, a demand for introduction of a pension scheme. Eventually, the EPF Scheme was restructured and an Employees Pension Scheme was established. The contribution of the employers to the extent of 8.33 per cent of wages are transferred to a pension fund established under the Employees Pension Scheme. This scheme has been in force for over six years and a large number of members of the PF are now drawing pension under the scheme. The scheme is, however, not popular. Some of the trade unions have gone to court on the ground that the benefits admissible under the EPS Scheme are less favourable than those of the Provident Fund. The matter is now before the Supreme Court whose judgement is awaited.

The EPS has also been criticised as not viable and that it is under funded. The current decline in interest rates is making the scheme less and less viable. There are many suggestions for reform of the Employees Pension Scheme.

It seems necessary to have the scheme reviewed by an independent valuer and to put it on a sound footing.

Dave Committee Report

The Ministry of Social Justice set up a committee under the Chairmanship of Shri S.A. Dave to suggest measures for providing income security in old age of workers in the unorganised sector. The Committee has recommended the introduction of a new pension system based on individual contributions. The Union Finance Minister in his last budget speech endorsed these recommendations and asked the Insurance Regulatory and Development Authority to draw up a Pension Scheme on that basis. The IRDA is reported to have submitted a draft scheme for consideration of the Government.

The details of the proposals have not been disclosed. Decision of the government on the proposals of the IRDA is awaited.

The main thrust of the Dave committee report is that the State as well as the employers should be relieved of the responsibility for income security of the elderly and that the new pension system should be based on contributions by the insured persons themselves. What the Committee has recommended is a voluntary private pension insurance scheme in place of a State supported social security scheme. There can be no objection to the introduction of a private insurance scheme which people have the option to join or not. But it will not be a social security scheme and it cannot be a substitute for a social security scheme.

The history of social security tells us that before the introduction of social security there were private insurance schemes which provided a measure of protection against the contingencies which tended to deprive people of their income. It was, however, found that the workers struggling for survival, day by day, had neither the means nor the motivation to save for the future and it became necessary for the State to intervene to protect them. The condition of labour in India has not changed much to warrant the suggestion that they may be required to make their own arrangements for the old age security and that the State may be absolved of its responsibility to provide social security. Basic social security has to be provided by the State. Voluntary pension schemes can only be supplementary to the basic schemes.

Another major point made by the Dave committee is that the mangement of pension funds should be entrusted to professional fund managers. A similar recommendations is understood to have been made by a team of experts who conducted a study of the Employees Provident Funds Scheme and the Employees Pension Scheme in India. This team has mooted the idea that the management of EPF funds should be outsourced "to private accredited fund managers under liberalised investment guidelines and appropriate regulatory oversight".

The principal argument in favour of private management of pension schemes is that private managers can obtain better investment returns. This argument is questionable in the context of the various scams and scandals that have to come to light in the working of the money markets. It has been the experience of many investors that their investments in the mutual funds have mostly lost value and there has been little or no return from those investments. There is , therefore, a great deal of scepticism about the idea of investment of public funds by private managers.

Where a person joins a private scheme fully conscious of the risks involved he enjoys the benefit of high return when the management is able to achieve it. At the same time he should also be prepared to suffer losses if the investments fail. But where a person make a contribution under a mandatory scheme he does so in the firm belief that his money will be safe in the hands of the government and he will not like that the investment of his hard earned money should be exposed to unnecessary risk, it does not permit any unnecessary risk. There is no dispute about the efficiency of private management but private management by definition operates for its own benefit but it cannot be expected to serve the public interest.

Maintenance

Maintenance is a civil right available to give economic support to the needy persons from those who are liable to protect and maintain their spouse, children, parents, etc. In law, parents are bound to maintain minor children, major children their parents, husband his wife, and vice versa. The quantum of maintenance varies depending on the economic status of the parties.

The various personal laws such as Hindu Marriage Act, 1955, the Hindu Adoption and Maintenance Act, 1955, the Indian Divorce Act, 1859, the Parsi Marriage Act, 1954, the Shariat Laws, etc., provide for maintenance, also known as alimony or allowance. Civil Courts take long time to dispose of cases. Even if a competent Civil Court passes a judgement and decree, execution takes months and even years due to cumbersome legal procedures. Even before the maintenance is realised the decree holder may die of starvation.

Realising the above, the right to maintenance has been incorporated in Chapter IX of the Criminal Procedure Code (Cr.P.C)

It is a chapter for "order for maintenance of Wives, Children and Parents" Under Section 125 of the Cr. P. C., "if any person having sufficient means neglects to maintain (a) his wife, unable to maintain herself, or (b) his legitimate or illegitimate minor child, whether married or not, unable to maintain itself, or (c) his legitimate or illegitimate child (not being a married) who has attained majority, where such child is, by reason of any physical or mental abnormality or injury unable to maintain itself, or (d) his father or mother, unable to maintain himself or herself a magistrate of the first class, may upon proof of such neglect or refusal, order such person to make a monthly allowance for the maintenance of his wife or such child, father or mother, at such monthly rate not exceeding five hundred rupees in the whole, as such magistrate thinks fit, and to pay the same to such person as the magistrate may from time to time direct."

Thus, Rs. 500 per month is allowed as maintenance. Section 125 provides the procedure to be followed and the jurisdiction of the courts. The cases could be filed in the magistrate's court within which the petitioner resides or where the parties lastly resided together, etc. Summons case procedure has to be adopted for disposal of cases. This paves the way for expeditious remedies. Section 127 is for alteration in the allowance under changed circumstances, but the monthly rate of five hundred rupees in the whole should not be exceeded.

A ceiling of Rs. 500 per month towards maintenance will not prevent vagrancy which is the object of the provision. Various women's and civil rights organisations and other activists raised their voice against this ceiling. In West Bengal the amount was raised to Rs. 1,500.

In Tamil Nadu, after a long debate with various sections of society and women's organisations and the Tamil Nadu Women's Commission, it was decided to amend Cr.P.C. and remove the ceiling and to invest the power on the magistrate to grant maintenance in his discretion taking into account the capacity of the person to pay and the need of the person seeking maintenance. The Legislative Assembly unanimously passed a bill to amend the Cr.P.C. accordingly and it was sent to the Central government for getting President's assent. In the meantime, the Government changed and the bill has been withdrawn on the ground that the Central Government itself is contemplating a similar amendment.

The Union Law Minister has announced that the Government of India is planning to enhance the interim maintenance limit for an estranged wife from the existing Rs. 500 to Rs. 5000 on the recommendation of the Law Commission. He is reported to have said that a proposal to enhance the outer limit of the interim maintenance from the existing Rs. 500 to Rs. 5,000 by means of an amendment to Section 125 of the Cr.P.C. is being given final touches by the Law Ministry and the Home Ministry and a draft of this would soon be prepared for the Cabinet.

The right approach appears to be removing the ceiling on the amount to be paid for maintenance of dependants as was proposed by Tamil Nadu and to leave it to the courts to decide the amount depending on the facts of the case.

Health Care

The elderly people are apt to develop health problems as they grow older.

The National Policy for older persons recognises that with advancing age old persons have to cope with health and associated problems some of which may be chronic, of a multiple nature, requiring constant attention and carry the risk of disability and consequent loss of autonomy. There is no special scheme for the health care of the elderly except the ESI and the CGHS which are applicable to a small number of persons who have been in service with the Central Government or an insurable employment. In all other cases the old persons have to depend upon public medical services or private doctors and hospitals. The health insurance schemes of the GIC do not cover persons who are above the age of 70 and who require greater attention.

Appropriate schemes would, therefore, need to be designed for the health care of the elderly similar to the Medicare and Medicaid programmes of the USA.

Providing Gainful Occupation to the Elderly

In order that the elderly people keep healthy it is necessary that they should remain gainfully active. Their service should, therefore, be utilised in various activities of the community such as manning child care centres, cultural clubs, vocational training centres, etc. for which they may be paid appropriate remuneration.

There is a Medicare National Health Insurance System in the US to provide medical care.

Medicare Programme

It is a federal government programme which was introduced in 1965. Under the Scheme assistance is given to older and disabled people to pay for their medical costs. The scheme is in two parts. Part A is called hospitalisation insurance. It covers most of the costs of a stay in hospital as well as some follow up costs. Part B called Medical Insurance, pays for the cost of doctors and outpatient care. The service is provided by certain private companies called carriers or intermediaries under contract with the government. Most of the people of the age 65 and above are covered under the Scheme free of cost based on their work records. Those who are not eligible for such coverage will be covered on payment of a prescribed premium.

The medicare programme does not, however, meet the entire cost of medical care of the elderly. It does not pay for certain types of costs and services. It is said that broadly speaking it covers only 50 per cent of the medical costs. The balance has to be paid for by the insured persons themselves by way of yearly deductibles or copayments. There is, therefore, another scheme called Medicaid under which those who cannot make such payments are given assistance. This is a State level programme the deatils of which vary from State to State. In many States, Medicaid covers costs which are not paid for by Medicare, including the premium for Medicare, the annual deductibles, etc.

A similar programme needs to be introduced in India.

Long Term Care

With the growth of the population of the aged, the associated problem of caring for the aged, is becoming increasingly important. Lately, long term care of the elderly in some of the developed countries has been systematised in the form of social care insurance as a part of social security. It has been reported that in 1991, in Germany, approximately one-third of the social security expenditures was devoted to care provision. The concept of care dependency is distinct from treatment for illness and covers help with daily tasks that do not fall under any medical treatment plan, e.g., personal hygiene, feeding, mobility or housework.

In the US there are many home health care agencies providing care for patients who do not need high level hospital care but still require part time nursing or physical therapy.

There may be terminally ill patients who cannot be cured of their maladies but need comfort so that they may die in peace. Hospitals provide such care.

There are many voluntary organisations providing medical care as well as long term care and Hospital care to the elderly in India but they are not adequate. Considering the size of the elderly population in India, their care cannot be left entirely to voluntary organisations. The State has to come in a big way and support private efforts so that they may expand their services.

11
Social Protection Schemes of Women

Women, though they make up half the world's population, constitute the largest group which is excluded from the benefits of development. In many industrial countries, female development is around 80 per cent of that of males. Women's participation in employment is less and their earnings lesser than those of men. The situation in developing countries is worse. In many of these countries women are excluded from participation in political as well as economic activities due to tradition, discriminatory laws or lack of education. The development index of women is, therefore, less than 60 per cent of that of men in these countries.

In India, the work participation rate of women is less than half that of men as shown below:

Work Participation Rate (as per 2011 census)	
Male	51.7 per cent
Female	25.6 per cent

Annual rate of growth of employment has been rising but it is not enough to bridge the huge gap.

This is because much of the work women do, especially at home is not regarded as economic activity and, therefore, omitted from statistics.

Women play multiple roles in society. They are principally home makers, child bearers and rearers. They are also earners of income. Their function as home makers and child bearers/ rearers come in the way of their participation in any productive work. There is, therefore, a growing demand that the responsibility of women in housekeeping and child rearing should be shared by men so that they may be able to devote more time for economic activities.

Women constitute a substantial part of the agricultural labour force. But they have no access to the resources which are necessary to make them independent. They play a subordinate role. The vast majority of rural women in the unorganised sector is landless; they work in the fields, they look after the animals, they are actively involved in food production, food processing and forestry. In spite of their role in agricultural production, the land reform measures have not benefited them because land has rarely been in the name of women.

The Working Group on Labour Policy for the Ninth Five Year Plan in the report has stated:

> "Notwithstanding laudable pronouncements in the Constitution backed by several laws of the land such as Protection of Civil Rights Act, Equal Remuneration Act, etc., women of all ages, classes and individuals in general and those belonging to SC community in particular have for generations been subjected to varying degrees of discrimination and exploitation at home as well as at the place of work. The stratified structure of society, the sexual division of labour and control over women's sexuality have all combined to assign women the traditional role of mother and wife and have also made women as receivers of these roles for generations. The culture of acquiescence has led to a state of helplessness for women and is responsible for many of the aberrations which afflict society such as child marriage, unlimited family size, absence of leisure, freedom and relaxation leading to a drudgerous existence and denial of the basic dignity, equality and respect to which every woman is entitled. The twin problems of invisibility (of poor women in rural areas) and insensitivity (of bureaucracy at all levels) have been tellingly brought out by the National Commission on Self Employed Women and women in the informal sector".

The Eighth Five Year Plan laid emphasis on efforts to ensure that the fruits of development do not bypass women, on building greater gender sensitivity into the development process and on carving out special complementary programmes which can improve the status and condition of women. The flow of benefits to women in the three core sectors of education, health and employment were to be monitored as they together could contribute a great deal towards mainstreaming women into the national developmental process. Employment and income generation activities including self employment along with necessary training for skill upgradation would constitute the most important intervention for raising the status of women.

In pursuance of these objectives, the Government of India as well as the State Governments have introduced several measures for improving the condition of women in India. The importance of these measures cannot be underestimated but their impact would appear to have been minimal. The Human Development in South Asia, 1998, contains the relevant indicators of development in India. The following table shows the gender disparity profile which is also indicative of the level of development of men as well as women:

Gender Disparity

Population	
Male	627 Million
Female	586 million
Sex ratio	918 for every 1000 males
Life Expectancy (As per WHO 2013)	
Male	64.7
Female	68.2
Average	66.4
Maternal Mortality per 100,000	174 (2015)
Literacy	
Men	82.14 per cent
Women	65.46 per cent
Women in Parliament	12 per cent
Females over 25 with secondary education	27 per cent
Women in labour force	29 per cent
Global Gender Gap Index	
Value	0.644
Rank	108 out 145

The average female life expectancy is low compared to other countries.
Maternal Mortality is the 56th highest.
42 per cent of live births are supervised in medical institutions.

India's Rank in WEF's Gender Index

At 108, out of 145 countries, India's ranking in the global gender index, compiled every year by the World Economic Forum (WEF), has climbed six places, primarily on account of political representation, but continues to be abysmal on the economic and health fronts.

India's improved overall ranking (up from 114 of the 142 countries examined last year) reflects the fact that there are more women in positions of political leadership, particularly Ministers and Members of Parliament. With the number of women ministers jumping from 9 per cent to 22 per cent of the cabinet, India ranks among the most improved countries in the region in terms of political representation.

Prime Minister Narendra Modi's cabinet has six women ministers, including in the key portfolio of defence and external affairs. The 16th Lok Sabha also saw a rise in the number of women parliamentarians from 11.4 per cent to 12.15 per cent. That's the good news.

Equally, there are many causes for concern.

India fell five places in terms of women in the workforce to hit nearly the bottom of the rankings at 139 of 145 countries, its worst rank in this category since 2006.

Indian women have also regressed in terms of health and survival, placed at a low 143 out of 145. India is one of the three countries that have declined the furthest on the health and survival sub-index, the other two being China and Albania.

The WEF's assessment of India's ranking in terms of sex ratio at birth (143), a sub-indicator in the health and survival category, is unchanged from last year and is ahead only of China and Armenia.

On educational attainment — a fourth parameter in the overall gender index after political representation, economy and health — India has improved marginally, going up one place from 126 in 2014 to 125 this year.

The report said the female to male ratio in India's labour force participation is 0.35 now against 0.36 last year. Income disparity is also high, with women earning an estimated average of $2,257 per year, compared to $9,175 for men. While South Africa has narrowed its labour force participation gap by 18 per cent and Japan by 11 per cent, in India, the gap has widened by 7 per cent.

Overall, India's fall in rank is not only relative to other countries, it also marks a decline in absolute terms — the gap is wider today than 10 years ago.

Ironically, even as India's gender ranking in education reflects an improvement — 119 in primary education enrolment, 118 for secondary and 104 for tertiary education — women continue to be missing from the workforce.

At 53 percentage points, India has one of the worst gender gaps in the world when it comes to labour force participation, 2015 World Bank data shows. Not only other countries in the BRICS (Brazil, Russia, China and South Africa) grouping, but other emerging economies in Asia such as Indonesia fare much better than India when it comes to employing women, according to the World Bank data.

India's female labour force participation rate fell nearly seven percentage points to 22.5 per cent between 2004-05 and 2011-12, according to India's NSSO data (http://bit.ly/1jenLeB), *Mint* reported in November 2013.

It would be seen from the foregoing table that the level of achievement with respect to females has been lower than that of males on all counts.

Reasons for the disparity were investigated by the National Commission for Self-employed women (1988) and their findings are as valid today as they were when they submitted the report. The following recommendations of the Commission are relevant:

> The Commission strongly recommends that if we are serious about substantially improving the economic status of poor women working in the informal sector of the economy, we have to devise concrete strategies which can help to enhance the ownership of and control over productive assets of these women. Perhaps it will be the single most important intervention towards both their empowerment and economic well-being. Some of the assets that women can be given are a plot of land, housing, tree pattas, joint ownership of all assets transferred by the State to the family, livestock assests, bank accounts, membership of organisations and identity cards.

Similar views were expressed at a workshop on widows held in 1994 at Bangalore where the following demands were put forward:

> Housing: including automatic transfer of the conjugal house to the widow's name upon the death of her husband, or allotment of house site and housing by the Government.
>
> Law: including automatic transfer of land and other property to the widow's name upon the death of her husband.
>
> Jobs: including automatic transfer of the husband's job to the widow (or her son) and training plus subsidies for self-employment.
>
> Children's Education: including scholarships, stipends to cover the cost of books, uniforms and transport and boarding facilities.

It would appear from the foregoing recommendations and demands that the improvement in the social and economic conditions of women calls for fundamental changes in law regarding the right to property of women. In this connection Martha Chen has observed as follows:

> "In rural India, even today, most social groups follow customary norms rather than modern statutory laws. In regard to property, there is a widespread tradition joint patrimonial ownership under which widows are entitled to use rights (if they have no adult sons) or maintenance rights (if they have adult sons) over their husbands' share of ancestral land. However, the use rights of widows are often violated in practice. When a widow tries to manage the land as her own, without adult sons, her in-laws often insist on sharecropping or managing her land themselves or simply attempt to deprive her of her rightful share of the land. In their attempt to gain control of her land, in-laws or other rival claimants may go so far as to forcing a widow to leave the village or even — in extreme cases — arranging her murder. Once her sons (if any) grow up, a widow may have to forfeit her use rights to her husband's land in exchange for a right to maintenance by one or more of her sons. Even maintenance rights are often uncertain."

The problems do not appear to have been addressed by all the governments. The Government of Maharashtra has amended the Hindu Succession Act, whereby women have been given co-partner rights. The Government also intends to amend the Hindu Marriage Act to provide that a woman on solemnisation of marriage will become a joint owner of the properties and assets earned by the husband. Similar laws will need to be enacted in other states if they have not done so already.

The Ninth Five Year Plan document says that empowerment of women would be a primary objective of the Plan but it falls short of spelling out the measures that would be taken to confer the legal rights on women to function as equal partners in decision making and to enhance their capacity to earn, besides the access to and control/ ownership of all family/ community assets.

The National Commission on Rural Labour has made several recommendations for improving the work participation rate of women and their income but it does not appear that the recommendations have been acted upon.

In a paper titled *Labour Force Participation of Women in India: Some Facts, Some Queries,* published by the London School of Economics' Asia Research Centre, Surjit Bhalla and Ravinder Kaur point out that discrimination against women, starting from practices such as sex-selective abortion, is a possible reason for poor participation of women in the workforce.

In addition, the lack of safety and supporting infrastructure plays a role in deterring many educated, urban women from pursuing careers.

"India is a very peculiar case where despite increases in incomes and the economy, female labour-force participation has declined. Barring a few metros and some companies, workspaces are not women-friendly. Lack of safety and infrastructural issues have been reasons why women are staying away," said Shamika Ravi, a fellow at Brookings India, a think tank.

Some have questioned the WEF's methodology, which they say is anomalous because it looks at political empowerment through representation even though Parliament itself has failed for 20 years to pass a bill seeking to reserve 33 per cent parliamentary seats for women.

"I am not sure how much weightage can be given to having a female prime minister or president as there is no direct link with women in power and feminist notions of empowerment," said Mary E. John, senior fellow and associate professor, Centre for Women's Development Studies at Delhi University.

Globally, the gender gap has closed by 4 per cent in the 10 years since WEF began measuring the global gender gap in 2006.

The economic gap has closed only by 3 per cent with wage equality and labour force parity stalling from 2009-10.

The WEF estimates that at this rate, the economic gender gap worldwide will not be bridged until 2033.

As with India, globally, too, the area where the most progress has been made over the past decade is political representation.

For 2015, the top 10 ranked countries in terms of gender include the Scandinavian trio of Iceland, Finland and Norway.

One African country, Rwanda, comes in at No. 7 and an Asian country, the Philippines ranks 9.

The Asia-Pacific top 10 include two South Asian countries — Bangladesh at 64 and Sri Lanka at 84.

Under Article 15(3), the Constitution of India allows for positive discrimination in favour of women and children. The article, under right to equality, states: "Nothing in this article shall prevent the State from making any special provision for women and children." In addition, the directive principles of State Policy 39(a) state that: "The State shall, in particular, direct its policy towards securing that the citizens, men and women equally, have the right to an adequate means of livelihood."

More recent programmes initiated by the Government of India include the Mother and Child Tracking System (MCTS), the Indira Gandhi Matritva Sahyog Yojana Conditional Maternity Benefit plan (CMB), and the Rajiv Gandhi Scheme for Empowerment of Adolescent Girls.

Mother and Child Tracking System (MCTS): The Mother and Child Tracking System, launched in 2009, helps to monitor the health care system to ensure that all mothers and their children have access to a range of services, including pregnancy care, medical care during delivery and immunisation. The system consists of a database of all pregnancies registered at health care facilities since 1 December 2009, and all births since 1 December 2009.

The Indira Gandhi Matritva Sahyog Yojana, Conditional Maternity Benefit Plan (CMB): It is a scheme sponsored by the national government for pregnant and lactating women age 19 and over for their first two live births. The programme, which began in October, 2010, provides money to ensure the good health and nutrition of the recipients. As of March 2013 the programme is being implemented in 53 districts around the country.

Rajiv Gandhi Scheme for Empowerment of Adolescent Girls — Sabla: The Rajiv Gandhi Scheme for Empowerment of Adolescent Girls – Sabla is an initiative launched in 2012 that targets adolescent girls. The scheme offers a package of benefits to at-risk girls between the ages of 10 and 19. It is being offered initially as a pilot programme in 200 districts. The programme offers a variety of services to help young women become self-reliant, including nutritional supplementation and education, health education and services, and life skills and vocational training.

Rashtriya Mahila Kosh

Rashtriya Mahila Kosh (The National Credit Fund for Women) was created by the Government of India in 1993. Its purpose is to provide lower income women with access to loans to begin small businesses.

Priyadarshini

Priyadarshini, initiated in April 2011, is a programme that offers women in seven districts access to self-help groups. This scheme is being pursued by Government.

Tamil Nadu is a forward looking State with a whole range of programmes for the welfare of all sections of the State. The State has a well developed infrastructure of roads and communication, electricity and commercial services. The social infrastructure of the State in the Sherrie of education, health, rural water supply and housing have also made impressive strides in the last four decades, providing a reasonable quality of life for the people. The current phase of development in Tamil Nadu is characterised by its accent on "Gender" concerns in every sector. Tamil Nadu is the first State to declare a policy for women. The emphasis on the gender concern in the last decade has improved several factors constituting the Human Development Index for the State. Specifically these relate to female literacy, infant mortality, expectation of life at birth and income generation activities for women. A plethora of well orchestrated activities have contributed to improve the standard of living for the people and the status of women in particular. In an advertisement on the achievements of Dr. M. Karunanidhi's Government in three years which appeared in the *The Hindu* of 13 May 1999, the State has claimed to be a trendsetter among the States in implementing Welfare Schemes for Women. In that connection the number of persons benefited and the amount distributed among them under the various Marriage Assistance Schemes and the Pregnant Women Assistance Scheme have been highlighted. It is, however, doubtful if such schemes which provide assistance for current consumption expenditure would help to improve the standard of living of the people in the long term.

Maharashtra is another State where a comprehensive policy for welfare of women has been formulated and is being implemented. The objective of this policy is to ensure an improvement in the physical, mental and emotional quality of life of the women of the State as also to make them economically independent and self-reliant. The most important step the government has taken to promote the development of women is to provide them free education up to the highest level.

State Government Schemes

Kerala

The Kudumbashree story: How Kerala women's grassroots scheme grew into a multi-crore project (Megha Varier, Saturday, October 15, 2016 - 15:21)

The Kudumbashree project started off as a neighbourhood group in 1992 in the Alappuzha municipality. A notification in the regional newspapers was sent out, resulting in the formation of around hundred groups consisting of 20 women each.

The women were imparted training to set up micro-enterprises like cattle-rearing and poultry farming.

After a successful two year-stint in Alappuzha under the guidance of officer Gopinath, a State-government employee, a pilot project was implemented in Malappuram in 1994.

Close to 4,000 groups, comprising 20 women each, were formed in the district. Activities included goat-rearing, and setting-up of poultry and dairy units.

A year after the project was implemented in Malappuram, James Varghese IAS took charge as the district collector and the in-charge of the project for his tenure of a year and a half.

A group of 15 women settled themselves in a small two-room house in Perinthalmanna in Malappuram. Some sat on red plastic chairs pooled from the neighbourhood, while others sat on the floor for their first meeting with the district collector before enrolling themselves for the programme.

"The group brought the best chair in the house for me to sit on and they patiently listened to my address for the next half an hour," recalls Varghese, while speaking to The News Minute.

The programme was in its nascent stage, and it would be another three years before it would be formally registered.

"At that time, it was a matter of joy and curiosity to even catch a glimpse of the district collector," says Varghese, as he fondly remembers the many Kudumbashree meetings that he coordinated.

"It took us a hell lot of effort to convince the womenfolk in Malappuram. There was opposition from family and political parties against women venturing out for work. We were still able to do well in Malappuram, a district that was heavily bound by religious constraints too. News of our success soon spread to other districts," recollects Varghese.

After the project was formally registered in 1998, James Varghese took over as its first executive director.

"This for me was personally a matter of immense joy, especially since I was associated with the pilot project in Malappuram, and I had seen the women make their way in life, and learning to stand up for themselves."

Starting with micro-financing and poultry-farming, the project later diversified into organic farming, tailoring units, catering units, household-waste management and Kudumbasree travels.

KB Valsala Kumari who served as its Executive Director from 2012-15 says that more than the fact that the programme has helped eradicate poverty, Kudumbashree has over the years become a household name.

"Unlike the schemes in other States, Kudumbashree is not a self-help group. It is instead a neighbourhood group that drastically differs from the former. The basis of this programme is the idea that, for a woman, other women living in the same neighbourhood is more likely to provide support than any random group of women," she avers.

Tamil Nadu

SGSY, a major anti-poverty programme is being implemented since 1999, with the prime objective of bringing the assisted poor families above the poverty line by ensuring reasonable and sustained level of income over a period of time. This scheme adopts SHG approach and aims to graduate them from micro credit stage to micro-enterprises stage by providing skill development training, bank credit, infrastructure facilities and much needed marketing support to the products produced by them. Government of India and the State Government are sharing the costs in the ratio of 75:25.

In order to ensure that there is greater convergence of activities taken up for the benefit of SHGs in the State, monitoring of the implementation of SGSY scheme has been transferred to TNCDW from 2008-09.

The SGSY fund is used to provide subsidy for the Revolving fund and Economic assistance to Self Help Groups. Part of the Scheme component is also utilised for formation of groups and conduct of training for their basic orientation and skill upgradation. Upto 20 per cent of the total allocation can also be spent on putting up of Infrastructure required for promotion of activities of SHGs. The SHGs, after the first grading, are provided with a revolving fund of Rs. 50,000 for first linkages (bank loan of Rs. 50,000 and Rs. 10,000 as subsidy) Rs. 1.00 lakhs for second linkages and Rs. 1.5 lakhs for third and subsequent linkages. After the second grading, the successful groups are provided with economic assistance, the maximum eligible subsidy being 50 per cent of the project cost with a ceiling of Rs. 1.25 lakhs.

In 2010-11, a sum of Rs. 133 crores is likely to be allocated for the implementation of the scheme with a credit target of Rs. 220 crores. In order to implement the scheme in a more purposeful manner, the following initiatives will be undertaken in 2010-11:

1) A sum of Rs. 50.00 crores will be utilised for disbursing the subsidy component of Revolving Fund to 50,000 eligible SHGs formed in rural areas.
2) 6,500 SHGs will be provided with economic assistance with maximum eligible subsidy being 50 per cent of the project cost with a ceiling of Rs. 1.25 lakh.
3) Greater emphasis will be laid to encourage SHGs to opt for major key activities around which suitable clusters can be created at District/ Block levels. Necessary infrastructural facilities will be created for these clusters and activity based federations.
4) Qualitative skill development training through reputed institutions will be imparted to the assisted SHGs.

Women Empowerment

Launched in 1997-98, Mahalir Thittam was implemented with the support of NGOs and deployment in a network of self help groups (SHGs).

Like Rajeshwari, the women, who are part of the group, are imparted skill development training, enabling them to set up their own businesses.

It is not the only successful women-centric scheme from the State government; it is one among many, making Tamil Nadu unique in State sponsored gender empowerment.

In 1987, the State government introduced financial assistance to pregnant women who are poor. The idea behind the Dr Muthulakshmi Reddy Maternity Benefit Scheme (DMRMBS) was to compensate for wage loss during pregnancy, help them in getting nutritious food and avoiding low birth weight babies.

Analyzing the scheme, a 2010 study by Public Health Resource Network, M.S. Swaminathan Research Foundation and Tamil Nadu-Forum for Crèche and Childcare Services pointed out that DMRMBS was "nearly universal in application, with hardly any exclusion, no evidence of corruption or leakages, and (with) few difficulties reported in applying for or getting the money or opening bank accounts."

This scheme was implemented by Tamil Nadu more than two decades before the centre introduced The Indira Gandhi Matritva Sahyog Yojana, a maternity benefit programme providing conditional cash transfer for pregnant and lactating women of 19 years or older.

In 1992, during her first stint as chief minister, J. Jayalalithaa launched the cradle scheme under which young mothers could leave their children under the government's care. Families that did not want a girl child were invited to leave them in cradles outside social welfare centres. The aim was to address the State's skewed sex ratio and check large-scale sex-selective abortions.

In 2015, the State government inaugurated more than 350 breastfeeding rooms at bus terminals across the State—the first in India. It then set up breast milk banks in seven government hospitals across the State.

Not surprising then that Tamil Nadu has India's second-best record in minimizing infant mortality and maternal mortality. As per the Sample Registration System Survey (2014), the Infant Mortality Rate of Tamil Nadu decreased from 24 in 2010 to 20 per 1,000 live births in 2014. And the Maternal Mortality Ratio, during 2014-15 in Tamil Nadu was 687 maternal deaths amounting to a MMR of 67 per lakh live births as against an MMR of 90 in 2010-12.

The Method

The State's remarkable record on women's empowerment is no happy accident, instead it is the outcome of meticulous planning together with a sustained makeover of the social justice system.

> "To see why policies for women are persistent in Tamil Nadu, we need to study bureaucracy. It is very systematic, and the bureaucrats here are trained as deliverers, not just planners. This approach by the bureaucracy in turn helps the political parties in power. There is mutuality in recognizing that their responsibility is much higher than party cadres' social movements. It is also important to note that the bureaucracy itself has seen transformation due to the reservation policy, and is hence highly sensitive to the social class they have come from," says S. Anandhi, Associate Professor at the Madras Institute of Development Studies in Chennai.

The first half of the 20th century saw the rise of many mass movements aimed at mobilizing the lower castes in the southern states, especially in Tamil Nadu.

As Neeta Pillai from the Centre for Women's Development Studies, New Delhi says, "Women's issues and women were a central part of the social movements that took place in Tamil Nadu. The policy makers took these social issues into account and made policies accordingly." This led to greater democratisation of public services—making it available to the underprivileged communities, castes as well as women.

The results are visible. With 73.4 per cent of its women literate, Tamil Nadu—third among larger States after Kerala and Maharashtra—has India's largest number of establishments run by women, according to the Economic Census 2012. And has among the lowest crime rates against women and children. It introduced all-women police stations—a concept that picked up in the rest of the country only after the 2012 Delhi gangrape.

In March this year, the country celebrated the passing of The Maternity Benefit (Amendment) Bill, 2016 which raises paid maternity leave for women employees in the organized sector to six months. But the fact is that Tamil Nadu increased maternity leave for women government employees from six to nine months in September last year.

In addition, the government offers schemes like Amma baby care kits (a kit having basic essentials like a towel, mosquito net, an infant mattress, napkin, baby shampoo for mothers delivering in government hospitals), gold for economically backward women (Thalikku Thangam Thittam, gold for marriage scheme, launched in 2011) or those providing grinders, mixer-grinders and table fans to families.

However MIDS professor Anandhi broaches circumspection. "Women cannot talk about re-entitlement but only accept what the State can offer them. Women take on several responsibilities through these schemes, but are not entitled to their rights."

Anandhi is right, yet the success story of Rajeshwari cannot be overlooked. Not just because what it has done for her personally, but the multiplier effect it is generating. For someone who has studied till class eight, Rajeshwari has assisted over 300 women in becoming financially independent. *First Published: Sep 07 2017.*

Karnataka

Department of Women and Child Development, Karnataka is implementing various schemes, programmes, social welfare schemes, health and nutrition, scholarship for women empowerment, girl child pregnant women, mothers, ward members, Anganwadi workers, women health volunteers, the women living in the rural and tribal areas, ex-servicemen, physically handicapped, nursing women, lactating mother, widows/ destitutes, old age women, women self-help group (SHG), women entrepreneurs and adolescent Girls'.

Also special assistance is given to the women and child belonging to Scheduled Caste (SC) and Scheduled Tribes (ST), Other Backward Classes (OBC), Socially and Educationally Backward Classes (SEBC) Minority Category and below poverty line (BPL).

It gives assistance in the form of:

1. Subsidy on the loans
2. Education, Training
3. Financial assistance/ Cash
4. Scholarship
5. Nutrition
6. Self employment
7. And others much more, etc.

The schemes have been initiated in order to:

1. To encourage women empowerment.
2. To promote development and empowerment, gender equality and gender justice of women.
3. To ensure women's social, economic and political empowerment, fulfillment of their rights, promoting their participation and leadership.
4. To protect women from domestic violence.
5. For child development, empowerment and protection.
6. To the Child Sex Ratio, Child Care.

Women and Child Schemes of Karnataka Government are listed below:

- Karnataka Mahila Abhivrudhi Yojane (KMAY)
- Kittur Rani Channamma Award
- Santhwana Scheme
- Scheme of assistance to women for taking up job oriented courses
- Scheme of financial assistance for remarriage of destitute widows and marriage of devadasis
- Skill development programme
- Stree shakthi programme

West Bengal

Kanyashree Prakalpa

State Intervention to Prevent Child Marriage

The conditional cash transfer scheme of the Government of West Bengal, Kanyashree Prakalpa, has been hailed as a much-needed intervention to combat the high rate of child marriage in the State, and has received numerous awards since its inception. The scheme incentivises girls to continue education, while simultaneously delaying early marriages. However, an examination of the working of the scheme highlights the fact that rather than promoting higher education of women, the scheme has ended up entangled in the marriage economy of rural Bengal. (Ishita Savina Chowdhury, Jadavpur University)

On 24 June 2017, the Government of West Bengal was declared the winner of the United Nations Public Service Award at The Hague for its flagship scheme known as Kanyashree Prakalpa, which provides educational support to unmarried girls through conditional cash transfers. India stood first in the Asia–Pacific group for the category "Reaching the Poorest and Most Vulnerable through Inclusive Services and Participation," with the Government of West Bengal being the receiving institution. The scheme was introduced by Mamata Banerjee in 2013, and her government celebrated the award with much fanfare. In the four years since its inception, the scheme has gained national and international recognition, and has received six different awards, including the National Awards for e-Governance 2014-15 by the Narendra Modi government's Department of Administrative Reforms and Public Grievances.

Currently, over 40 lakh girls are beneficiaries of the scheme, which attempts to combat the increasing rate of child marriages in West Bengal. The State ranked high in terms of underage marriages of girls according to the District Level Household and Facility Survey–3 (DLHS–3), conducted during 2007-08, and the National Family Health Survey (NFHS–3), conducted during 2005-06. This prompted the Government of West Bengal to intervene in the education sector. Considering the relationship between child marriages and the dropout rate of girls, the objective of the scheme was to both tackle the rate of girl dropouts from school, as well as delay the marriages of girls. According to the State government website, the aim is to ensure that girls remain in school, so that they gain requisite skills and knowledge, which will allow them to become economically independent. It states:

Even if girls do get married soon after they turn 18, it is expected that their education and enhanced social and emotional development will give them a better foundation for in their adult lives [...] as entire generations of women begin to enter marriages only after attaining some degree of economic independence, the practice of child marriage will be eradicated.

Kanyashree Prakalpa targets girls between the ages of 13 and 19 years, studying in Classes VIII-XI, as the dropout rate is the highest for this age group. The intervention has been a clever move, since it is introduced just as the central government-sponsored support for the Sarva Shiksha Abhiyan (SSA)—which provides for free and compulsory education till Class VIII — ceases. In a survey in rural West Bengal conducted by the School of Women's Studies, Jadavpur University, during the months of June–September, 2016 in four districts of West Bengal, namely South 24 Parganas, Birbhum, Purba Medinipur and Jalpaiguri, it was found that the dropout rate peaked after Class VIII. Girls who have dropped out of school and are no longer pursuing any form of education because of the expense involved, are usually married off.

Tailoring Policy

In all four districts a similar pattern was observed. Among the 222 girls interviewed only 68 of them have been enrolled in Classes IX–X. Given that employment opportunities are scarce, girls drop out after Class VIII and are asked to assist their mothers in the family's unpaid labour. Parents feel that spending money on a daughter's education is a bad investment, as the returns will be enjoyed not by them, but by her marital family. Respondents were cynical of the benefits of higher levels of education. The lack of employment opportunities for women rendered such education infructuous. In the case of male children, however, there is always the possibility of migration for employment, an option not open to women, and one which prompts optimistic parents to continue to support a son's education even at considerable sacrifice to their present comfort. Since even highly educated women are mostly involved in the family's unpaid labour, women's education is viewed as economically unrewarding.

If girls are not in school or working at a job, unmarried, "idle" daughters are considered a social problem, since they attract, and may become prey to unwanted male attention. With increasing access to television, internet and mobile phones, parents have grown increasingly anxious about the control and surveillance of young women in the family. Many report their suspicions about the mobile phone. In the villages, the phone is the modern cupid, allowing young men and women to establish connections and develop relationships, which often end in underage elopements. In our field survey, we found 44 cases where underage marriages had taken place due to elopement. Parents say that they marry off daughters at a young age out of fear of elopements, even though the rate of child marriage has remained quite static in West Bengal during the last few decades. Unlike in some other parts of the country, the parents we met in the districts of West Bengal display a tolerant attitude towards elopements, agreeing in most cases to arrange what they term "social marriages" post facto. This is not to dismiss the high premium attached to arranged marriages, or the limits to what parents will accept in the form of a bride or groom. In our survey we found a higher degree of acceptance of inter-caste marriage than expected, as well as a very strong sanction against Hindu–Muslim marriages.

Kanyashree Prakalpa attempts to retain girls from dropping out after Class VIII with a promise of an annual grant, as well as a larger one-time grant if the girl is still unmarried at 18 years. It aims to push girls towards education, as well as take some of the expense away from the family. The benefits can be availed by families with an annual income of Rs. 1.2 lakh or below, and the scholarship is given in two tiers. At first, an Annual Scholarship (K1) of Rs. 750 is given to unmarried girls between the ages of 13 and 18, enrolled in any government recognised educational institution. Second, a One-time Grant (K2) of Rs. 25,000 is given to unmarried girls on completion of 18 years of age, who are part of an academic institution, vocational institution, or a sports institution. The scheme also makes provisions for girls with special needs, orphaned girls, and girls residing in juvenile homes by waiving the income criterion, as well as allowing them to apply for the scholarship even before they reach Class VIII. Thus, the social inclusiveness of the scheme ensures that all girls benefit.

The annual report of Kanyashree Prakalpa for 2015-16 bears witness to the fact that an increasing number of beneficiaries are being encouraged to continue their schooling and are targeting the one-time grant of Rs. 25,000 (Department of Women Development and Social Welfare 2016). According to a rapid assessment made by government in nine schools in three districts of West Bengal, namely Purulia, Malda, and North 24 Parganas during April-June, 2015, it was found that the enrollment of girls between Classes VIII-XII has increased from 9,021 in 2013-14, to 9,329 in 2014-15 (an increase of 3 per cent). The increase in enrolment rate has significantly improved the presence of girls at the secondary and higher secondary levels (Classes IX and XI) which signifies that more students are graduating from secondary to higher secondary.

The number of girls dropping out of school has reduced from 161 in 2013-14 to 71 in 2014-15 (a decrease of 56 per cent). It was also found that in the schools evaluated, in 2013-14, 132 girls had been married prior to attaining the legal age. This figure reduced to 89 girls in 2014-15, showing a 33 per cent decrease in child marriage rate.

Ground Realities

However, this celebratory narrative is not wholly supported by field experience. In the four districts that were surveyed, of the total 204 households, most were aware of the Kanyashree Prakalpa Scheme, but very few were its beneficiaries. Only 5 of the 42 households availed the Kanyashree benefits in South 24 Parganas. Similarly, only 5 of 30 households in Birbhum; 5 of 67 households in Jalpaiguri; and 4 of 65 households in Purba Medinipur availed the benefits. These figures are of the recipients who have received K1 benefits. Though the decision to increase the K1 sum from Rs. 500 to Rs. 750 was to be effective from the financial year 2015-16, all our respondents had received an annual sum of either Rs. 500 or less.

There also appears to be lack of clarity regarding K2 benefits. In some cases, families were not aware that marriage before the age of 18 years disqualifies a daughter from the grant. Recently-married women were aggrieved that they would not be able to claim the benefit. Equally, in some cases, girls claim the benefit after marriage. They remain in school, and without a marriage registration, there is no proof of marriage. They drop out on receiving the grant. Families have retained daughters in school until they get the benefit, in order to use the money for marriage expenses. This last observation is quite prevalent thinking, and parents often plan their daughter's marriage taking into account the K2 benefit. Thus, rather than promoting higher education, the scheme has ended up entangled in the marriage economy of rural Bengal.

Part of the problem with the scheme is the small amount involved. Respondents spoke of the annual benefit as paltry, and unable to cover even basic educational expenses. Further, a number of girls from the locality fill the form to avail the benefits, but grow impatient due to the lengthy process that precedes the receipt of money. In the case of one respondent, her marriage took place after she had filled the form. The benefit took too long to arrive, and her parents refused to wait any longer. Moreover, since the money is directly transferred into the bank account of the recipient it often gets utilised for purposes other than the daughter's education. As mentioned above, a number of parents save even the annual grants for marriage expenses. Respondents say that the daughter's marriage is more important than waiting for a one-time grant of Rs. 25,000. The view of several mothers is that while such a sum of money does not take care of the daughter for life, marriage on the other hand, does.

In each of the districts it was found that the level of education had increased, but only at primary and secondary levels. A significant increase in the number of girls pursuing education beyond Classes IX-X was not supported by this survey. Though the level of education among girls has increased over generations, the level of higher secondary education is still very low. Interestingly, this overlaps with findings regarding the age of marriage. While occurrences of child marriage in its true sense are increasingly rare in rural West Bengal, the concentration is between the ages of 16-17 years, still legally child marriage, but involving adolescents, rather than children. Girls in this age range are eligible, if they were willing to defer marriage for a year or two, to claim the K2 benefit from the scheme. Yet, many women and their families opt to marry at 16-17 years, rather than wait until they are 18 years and avail the benefit.

In West Bengal, the rate of child marriage has not decreased significantly, when compared to the national average. According to NFHS–3, the rate of child marriage in West Bengal was 53.3 per cent in contrast to the country's 40.7 per cent. Ten years later NFHS–4, conducted in 2015-16 shows that the rate of child marriage in India has decreased to 26.8 per cent while that of West Bengal is 40.7 per cent. In NFHS–3, the percentage of child marriage was 60.3 per cent in Bihar, 63.2 per cent in Jharkhand, and 65.2 per cent in Rajasthan. These proportions declined respectively to 39.1 per cent, 38 per cent and 35.4 per cent in NFHS–4. While other States display significantly declining rates of child marriage, West Bengal seems to lag behind. This could be due to the lack of employment opportunities for the young in the State. The State is experiencing a severe brain drain, with a large number of its youth migrating to greener pastures in search of opportunities. In the rural areas, there is landlessness, poor employment opportunities, and increasing rates of poverty. In almost all the households examined, there was at least one male member who was based outside the State. In such a scenario, investing money or time on education is considered futile, since earnings have little relation to the level of skill or education.

Challenges Ahead

Women are limited to very few badly paid jobs and possess limited opportunities for migration. In the absence of any employment opportunities, parents visualise a future for their daughters through marriage, rather than through education. Whether Kanyashree Prakalpa will be able to make a dent in this rigid cultural and economic logic remains uncertain. Also, the small amount given as benefits may prove an insufficient incentive for parents to alter set patterns. Some parents are wary of "overeducating" their daughters out of a marriage market in which even the men have a very limited scope for education. An equally qualified groom is both difficult to find and is considered to be a greater expense, in terms of higher demands for dowry.

To be successful, Kanyashree Prakalpa may need to explore greater connections with regard to employment for young women. On receiving the award from the UN, Mamata Banerjee announced that the scheme would be extended to benefit postgraduate students as well, so that women enrolled in higher educational institutes can avail a monthly benefit of Rs. 2,000 (arts) and Rs. 2,500 (science). These more substantial amounts may work better as incentives, but even then, linkages with jobs and economic opportunities are necessary. Making women economically independent will not only give them a voice, but also offer an alternative to marriage as the only means of securing a future. Through the inclusion of this objective, Kanyashree Prakalpa may see greater success in targetting child marriage in West Bengal.

Widows

Among women, widows are the most vulnerable sections of the society.

There are about 33 million widows in India representing 8 per cent of the total female population (as per 1991 census). The proportion of widows in the female population rises sharply with age reaching over 60 per cent among women aged 60 and above and close to 80 per cent among women aged 70 and above.

Several studies have pointed out that female widowhood in India tends to be associated with economic deprivation. Households headed by widows have a lower than average consumption level and a higher than average poverty level.

Yet the amelioration of the socio-economic condition of the widows in India has not been given due consideration at the level of the Central Government. Some State Governments have introduced special pension schemes for widows but the rates of pension are low, the actual coverage is also low. The eligibility criteria are restrictive and the bureaucratic hurdles are difficult to overcome. It needs to be investigated whether the pension schemes as they exist today can be said to be an effective instrument of social security to women.

Maternity Benefit

Maternity benefit is one of the important social security benefits provided to women. There are several legislative and other measures under which this benefit is given but their coverage is limited. In some cases the quantum of benefit is also lower.

The Government of India has recently introduced the National Maternity Benefit Scheme. Under the scheme maternity benefit is provided as a lump sum cash assistance to women of households below the poverty line. It is subject to a numerical ceiling of about 46 lakhs and a financial ceiling of Rs. 138 crores. The amounts released to the States for implementation of the scheme were Rs. 68 crores in 1996-97 and Rs. 50 crores in 1997-98. The amounts utilised by the States were lesser being Rs. 52 crores in 1996-97 and Rs. 40 crores in 1997-98.

The statutory schemes under the ESI Act and the Maternity Benefit Act are applicable to limited classes of establishments specified thereon. The National Maternity Benefit Scheme is applicable only to those who are below the poverty line. There could be many women who fall between the two stools, mainly in the unorganised sector. It is, therefore, necessary to take steps to extend the scope of the statutory scheme on the one side and the National Scheme on the other.

Even within the limited coverage the benefits of the schemes are not being fully utilised. This could be due to ignorance, cumbersome procedures and other reasons. It is, therefore, necessary to simplify the procedures and to create greater awareness among the beneficiaries. NGOs can render better service in this regard. It should be tapped.

The Government of India has also introduced another measure which benefits women who have lost their husbands. That is the National Family Benefit Scheme. Under the scheme, a lump sum family benefit is paid to households below the poverty line on the death of the primary breadwinner. This benefit accrues mainly to single parent families headed by widows. Initially the quantum of family benefit was Rs. 5,000. It has since been raised to Rs. 10,000 which is a substantial amount. Here again the benefit is subject to a numerical and a financial ceiling and the actual utilisation has been less than the amount provided for. For example, the financial ceiling for the National family Benefit is Rs. 251 crore. The amount released in 1996-97 was Rs. 107 crore and the amount utilised was Rs. 92 crore. Similarly, in 1997-98, the amount released was Rs. 118 crores and the amount utilised was Rs. 106 crore. The shortfall could only be due to lack of awareness of the bureaucratic hurdles. These problems need to be remedied.

There are several other survivour benefit schemes under the insurance schemes introduced by the Government for the benefit of agricultural workers and other people belonging to weaker sections. In these cases the quantum of benefits are small and the disbursal of the benefits is also small. The schemes need to be liberalised and better publicised.

Some States have taken the initiative to introduce innovative measures for the welfare and development of women. Of these, Tamil Nadu and Maharashtra need to be specially mentioned.

The Government has since introduced a Widow Pension Scheme under the National Social Assistance Programme. Brief particulars of this scheme are given below:

Widow Pension Scheme

Indira Gandhi National Widow Pension Scheme: The scheme is known as 'Indira Gandhi National Widow Pension Scheme' (IGNWPS). It came into existence from February, 2009.

Eligibility Criteria of Beneficiary : For purpose of claiming central assistance, the following criteria shall apply:

a) The age of the widow shall be between 40-64 yrs.
b) The applicant must belong to a household below the poverty line according to the criteria prescribed by the Government of India.

Amount of pension: The central assistance under IGNWPS will be provided at the rate of Rs. 300 per month per beneficiary. The State governments are urged to contribute at least equally towards the pension amount.

Specific condition regarding sanction of pension: Sanction of pension to a beneficiary has to be made only after placing the database of beneficiary in the public domain/ website of the Ministry or State.

Indira Gandhi Matritva Sahyog Yojana (IGMSY) - *a Conditional Maternity Benefit (CMB) Scheme*

(already discussed in previous pages).

Janani Suraksha Yojana (JSY): It was launched in 2005 with an objective to increase institutional deliveries. Under the scheme, the government provides a cash incentive for pregnant mothers to have institutional births as well as pre- and ante-natal care. The JSY primarily aims at promoting institutional delivery while NMBS component (payment of Rs. 500/-) within the Scheme is fairly limited. According to the October, 2006 JSY guidelines, all women in Low Performing States (LPS) receive cash assistance if they have their baby in a government health centre or accredited private institution. In rural areas they receive Rs. 1,400 and in urban areas Rs. 1,000. The money is to be dispersed at the time of delivery in the institution. The cash assistance to the mother is mainly to meet the cost of delivery. Under JSY, below poverty line pregnant women above 19 years of age also receive Rs. 500 cash assistance for their first two births if these deliveries are at home. The cash is to be given at birth or around seven days before for "care during delivery or to meet incidental expenses of delivery".

Beti Bachao, Beti Padhao

Save girl child, educate a girl child is a social campaign of the Government of India that aims to generate awareness and improve the efficiency of welfare services intended for girls. The scheme was launched with an initial funding of Rs. 100 crore (US$16 million). It has been the target of fraudsters in Uttar Pradesh, Haryana, Uttarakhand, Punjab, Bihar and Delhi.

According to census data, the child sex ratio (0–6 years) in India was 933 girls per 1,000 boys in 2001, which dropped to 918 girls for every 1,000 boys in 2011. A 2012 UNICEF report ranked India 41st among 195 countries. In the Population Census of 2011 it was revealed that the population ratio of India 2011 is 943 females per 1,000 of males. The Sex Ratio 2011 shows an upward trend from the census 2001 data.

Speaking on the occasion of International Day of the Girl Child in 2014, the Prime Minister, Narendra Modi had called for the eradication of female foeticide and invited suggestions from the citizens of India via the MyGov.in portal.

The Beti Bachao, Beti Padhao (BBBP) scheme was launched on 22 January 2015 by Modi. It aims to address the issue of the declining child sex ratio image (CSR) and is a national initiative jointly run by the Ministry of Women and Child Development, the Ministry of Health and Family Welfare and the Ministry of Human Resource Development. It initially focused multi-sector action in 100 districts throughout the country where there was a low CSR.

In 26 August 2016, Olympics 2016 bronze medallist Sakshi Malik was made brand ambassador for BBBP.

The hashtag #SelfieWithDaughter was promoted on social media in June, 2015, which started when Sunil Jaglan the sarpanch of the village Bibipur in Haryana took a selfie with his daughter Nandini and posted on Facebook on 9 June 2015. The hashtag garnered worldwide fame.

Sukanya Samriddhi Yojana

Sukanya Samriddhi Yojana is a savings scheme for the girl child launched as a part of the Government's 'Beti Bachao Beti Padhao' campaign, in 2015. A Sukanya Samriddhi Account can be opened any time before the girl child turns 10 years old. Under this scheme, a minimum of Rs. 1,000 and a maximum of Rs. 1,50,000 can be deposited in a year.

There are a number of benefits of saving through Sukanya Samriddhi Yojana. Let us highlight five of them:

High Interest Rate: Sukanya Samriddhi Account offers an interest rate of 8.6 per cent for current financial year, i.e. FY 2016-17. When compared to other Small Savings Schemes, the interest rate offered by this plan is the highest.

Every year, the Government of India declares the Interest Rate for the current Financial Year. Interest on this is compounded yearly, which means that it will be credited yearly. The interest is accrued every month on the lowest balance between 5th and last day of the month.

Income Tax Savings: Income tax is exempted from the contribution to this account under Section 80C of the Income Tax Act. Exemption on this scheme is available on the interest and also at the time of withdrawal. This scheme is under the authority of Department of Revenue (DOR). DOR will go for a legislative amendment. Moreover, this scheme will also be one of the most tax efficient ones.

Lock-in Period: Lock-in period is one of the best features of this scheme. Twenty one years is the maturity age of the account and this starts from the date when the account was opened or the Marriage of the Girl Child (either of the earlier one). Make sure that the age of the daughter is 18 years at the time of marriage.

The account cannot be operated after the marriage of your child. Parents are required to go for a premature withdrawal once their girl child attains 18 years of age and this can be done only if you require funds for Higher Education.

Only 50 per cent of the account balance can be withdrawn in case of premature withdrawal at the end of the previous financial year. One can deposit money in the account till 14 years from the date of opening of the account. Moreover, the maturity period of the account is 21 years from the date of opening the account.

Guaranteed Maturity Benefits: When your Sukanya Samriddhi Account reaches the maturity date, the account balance including the interest accumulated will be directly paid to the policyholder (Girl Child in this case). This is primarily required to render financial independence to the Girl child and , therefore, acts as an efficient tool to empower them in India.

Interest even after Maturity: Sukanya Samriddhi Account gives interest to the policyholder even when the scheme reaches the maturity. A unique feature of Sukanya Samriddhi Account is that the interest is accrued on the account even after it is matured and this keeps on going till it is finally closed by the account holder.

Wrapping Up

One of the best ways to build up a sufficient corpus for the education of your girl child is to keep aside a major portion of your savings or invest in equities. However, you only need to invest a small portion of the savings in Sukanya Samriddhi Account and reap the benefits in the long run. Looking at the high-interest rate, one can certainly build an adequate corpus to provide a brighter future to your girl child.

Government Schemes available for Economic Empowerment of Women in India

In its capacity as the nodal Ministry, the Ministry of Women and Child Development seeks to promote economic empowerment of women through policies and programmes cutting across sectors, mainstreaming gender concerns, creating awareness about their rights and facilitating institutional and legislative support for enabling them to develop to their full potential. The important programmes in different areas are:

Skill Upgradation

Support to Training and Employment Programme for Women (STEP)

A Central Sector Scheme launched in 1986-87, it seeks to upgrade skill of poor and assetless women and provide employment on sustainable basis by mobilising them in viable cooperative groups, strengthening marketing linkages, support services and access to credit. The scheme also provides for enabling support services in the form of health check-ups, legal and health literacy, elementary education, gender sensitisation and mobile crèches. The ultimate endeavour of each project is to develop the group to thrive on a self-sustaining basis in the market place with minimal governmental support and intervention even after the project period is over. Since inception, around 250 projects have been provided financial assistance under the scheme.

The ten traditional sectors identified for project funding under STEP comprise of agriculture, animal husbandry, dairying, fisheries, handlooms, handicrafts, khadi and village industries, sericulture, waste land development and social forestry. The scope and coverage of the scheme is being broadened with introduction of locally appropriate sectors being identified and incorporated into the scheme.

Rajiv Gandhi Scheme for Empowerment of Adolescent Girls (RGSEAG) - 'SABLA'

A centrally-sponsored scheme was approved by the Government on 16.8.2010. The scheme is being implemented in 200 districts across the country on a pilot basis. In the remaining districts, Kishori Shakti Yojana (KSY) continues to be operational as before. However, SABLA has completely replaced Nutrition Programme for Adolescent Girls (NPAG) as all districts of NPAG are now part of the SABLA. The scheme, interalia, aims at vocational training for girls above 16 years of age for their economic empowerment.

Sabla is being implemented through the State Governments/ UTs with 100 per cent financial assistance from the Central Government for all inputs other than nutrition provision for which 50 per cent Central assistance to States is provided. Anganwadi Centre is the focal point for the delivery of the services.

Objectives:

- Life Skill Education and accessing public services,
- Vocational training for girls aged 16 and above under National Skill Development Programme (NSDP)
- The successful implementation of SABLA requires convergence with development activities/ schemes of other Departments such as Health, Education, Youth Affairs, Labour, PRIs, etc.
- Nearly 100 lakh adolescent girls per annum are expected to be benefitted under the scheme. Against the allocation of Rs. 350 crore for the year 2010-11, a sum of Rs. 330 crore(approx.) has been released to States/ UTs. The year 2011-12 will be the first complete year of implementation of the scheme after which the physical and financial achievements made vis-à-vis the target would be assessed. A sum of Rs. 750 crore has been allocated for Sabla for 2011-12.

Central Social Welfare Board (CSWB)

In order to address the socio-economic needs of the women and children of selected eight most backward districts in the North Eastern region in the economic arena, Central Social Welfare Board has formulated the Integrated Scheme for Women Empowerment (ISWE). The scheme is being implemented on pilot basis since 2008 and has the objective of meeting the felt needs of the area by mobilising community action, converging available services and resources of the area, income generation through feasible and sustainable activities for women and to provide services for health awareness, career counselling vocational training, preventing child trafficking and other social evils.

Economic Improvement

National Mission for Empowerment of Women

The extent of empowerment of women from a holistic and macro-point of view is largely determined by three factors viz. economic, social and political identity. These factors are deeply intertwined and linked with many cross cutting linkages. It implies that if efforts in any one dimension remains absent or weak, the outcome and momentum generated by the other components cannot be sustained. It is only when all these three factors are addressed simultaneously and made compatible with each other, can women be truly empowered. Therefore, for the holistic empowerment of women, an inter-sectoral approach has to be adopted. The vision for socio-economic empowerment of women is to empower women economically and socially to end exploitation and discrimination enabling them to develop their full potential to be active participants in nation building, sharing the benefits of economic growth and prosperity. To achieve this vision, the National Mission for Empowerment of Women (NMEW) was launched on 8th March, 2010. The objectives of the Mission are to:

1. Ensure economic empowerment of women,
2. Ensure that violence against women is eliminated progressively,
3. Ensure empowerment of women with emphasis on health and education,
4. Oversee gender mainstreaming of programmes, policies, institutional arrangements and processes of participating mininstries, institutions and organisations, and
5. Undertake awareness generation as well as advocacy activities to fuel the demand for benefits under various schemes and programmes and create, if required, structures at district, tehsil and village level with the involvement of Panchayats for their fulfillment.

Economic Empowerment of Women is to be achieved through convergence of the schemes and programmes having focus on formation and promotion of SHGs so as to enable women to have access to micro-credit and micro-finance. Programmes like National Rural Livelihood Mission (erstwhile SGSY) of MoRD, Smayamsidha of MWCD and similar programmes of other Ministries and organisations would need to be converged to help the identified SHGs in a coordinated fashion. The Mission would see that access to credit by women SHGs under schemes of NABARD, Rashtriya Mahila Kosh, financial institutions like NSCFDC/ NBCFDC/ NSKFDC of MoS&ME and nationalised banks, is coordinated well and delivery of credit is timely.

In order to promote self-employment opportunities and create livelihood options for women, it would ensure that training and skill up-gradation under schemes/ programmes of MoS&ME, MoL&E, MoRD, MWCD, etc.

are available to the women beneficiaries of SHGs. Sustainability of income generation activities by women would be looked at and they would be ensured provision of adequate forward, backward and horizontal linkages. The relevant programmes of NABARD, RMK and participating ministries as well as organisations with components of processing, storage, distribution and market networks would be put in a convergent mode to strengthen the livelihood of women.

The existing monitoring systems in place at the State and district levels would be utilised by the National Mission for tracking the effectiveness of convergence efforts in the area of economic empowerment. While at the district level, the District Collector as per the existing arrangement of the DRDA would be responsible for monitoring convergence efforts at the district level, the Chief Secretary of the State Government with technical inputs from the State Resource Centre to be set up for women (SRCW) will be made responsible at the State level. At the national level, the National Mission Authority (NMA) will be responsible for overall monitoring of actionable agenda requiring convergence and for which it will take the inputs from both the Mission Directorate and the National Resource Centre for Women (NRCW).

Rashtriya Mahila Kosh - (National Credit Fund for Women)

The Rashtriya Mahila Kosh (National Credit Fund for Women) was set up in 1993 with a corpus of Rs. 31 crore, against the backdrop of socio-economic constraints faced by poor women to access micro – credit from the formal financial system in the country, especially those in the rural and in unorganised sectors. The principal corpus has increased to Rs. 100.00 crore by 2009-10.

The main objective behind the setting up of the Rashtriya Mahila Kosh (RMK) under the Department of Women and Child Development (now Ministry) was to provide micro-credit to poor women for various livelihood support and income generating activities at concessional terms in a client-friendly procedure to bring about their socio-economic development. The RMK is now being restructured as a NBFC with a corpus of Rs. 500.00 crore.

Till 31.3.2011, 6,87,512 women beneficiaries have been sanctioned Rs. 307.52 crore and disbursed Rs. 251.82 crore. However, with the proposed induction of funds and conversion to NBFC, the projected yearly number of beneficiaries and loans are at the end of five year period in FY 2015-16 is likely to be 2,19,500 and Rs. 492.02 crore, respectively. Thus, there would be a quantum jump in the business volume of the organisation through this restructuring.

Further, the fact that RMK extends loan up to maximum of 18 per cent interest per annum to SHGs/ beneficiaries as against loans disbursed to beneficiaries through Micro- Finance Institutions (MFIs) under the NABARD's SHG – Bank Linkage Programme at the interest rate ranging between 30 and 40 per cent per annum and even higher and 60 to 70 per cent rate charged by traditional moneylenders, would mean that the impact by way of higher incomes and welfare of the beneficiaries at such an expanded scale of finance and at affordable rate, would be much more pronounced.

An RMK sponsored 'Impact Study' of 2008 shows 84 per cent beneficiaries from rural areas and 16 per cent from urban areas had undertaken activities like Animal husbandry (41 per cent), Petty Shops (19 per cent) and Agriculture (17 per cent). Their monthly income has increased between Rs. 2000 and Rs. 4000. 54 per cent reported increase in household expenditure, 96 per cent reported improvement in food consumption pattern, and 87 per cent reported increase in household assets. Access to medical facility increased for majority of beneficiaries (88 per cent). There was increase in social status of 87 per cent of beneficiaries. 98 per cent women beneficiaries reported increase in their self-confidence and security with increased income through RMK. Majority (95 per cent) of the beneficiaries reported improvement in their standard of living and participation in micro finance led to decrease in domestic violence.

Gender Budgeting and Economic Empowerment of Women

Budgets, which influence the overall level of national income and employment and reflect the priorities of the government regarding public investment, also promote gender equality within the national development framework. The Government of India is committed to promoting gender equality and has adopted Gender Budgeting (GB) as a tool to address the inequalities faced by women. The purpose is to ensure the translation of Government's policy commitments on gender equity into budgetary allocations.

To institutionalise the process of Gender Budgeting, the Government had initiated the formation of Gender Budget Cells (GBCs) within all Central Ministries/ Departments in 2005. These Cells are required to take up evaluation of existing Government programmes and schemes from a gender perspective and identify new areas of intervention for addressing the existing gender gaps. The flow of funds under certain women specific schemes/ programmes are also being monitored through a Gender Budget Statement (Statement 20) as a part of the Union Budget Document since 2005.

MWCD, as the nodal agency, is pursuing with other Ministries/ Departments to build their capacity so as to integrate gender concerns across sectors/ schemes/ programmes/ and ensure proper allocation and/ or reprioritisation of resources. The number of Ministries reflecting their allocations in the Gender Budget Statement have gone up from nine in 2005-06 to 29 in 2011-12, with a magnitude of Gender Budget (BE) increasing from Rs. 14,379.00 crore (2.79 per cent) in 2005-06 to Rs. 78,251.00 crore (6.22 per cent) in 2011-12.

Support Services

Hostel for Working Women

a. *The Scheme of Working Women Hostel* envisages provision of safe and affordable hostel accommodation to working women, single working women, women working at places away from their home-towns and for women being trained for employment.

The scheme has been revised with following salient features:

- Financial assistance for construction of hostel building to be given only on public land.
- Financial assistance available for rent of the hostels which are run in rented premises also.
- Provision for maintenance grant of hostel building (maximum Rs. 5 lakh) and one-time non-recurring grant for furnishings (@ Rs. 7,500 per beneficiary).
- State Government agencies, Urban Municipal Bodies, Cantonment Boards, Civil Society Organisations, Panchayati Raj Institutions, Self Help Groups, Recognised Colleges/ Universities, and Corporate or associations like CII, ASSOCHAM and FICCI have been included under the revised scheme.
- The State Governments have been advised to disseminate and send project proposals as per the revised guidelines the Scheme. Since its inception in 1972-73, 890 hostels have been sanctioned under the scheme all over the country benefiting about 66,000 working women.

b. *Working Women Hostel at Jasola, New Delhi*: In view of increasing incidents of assault on women from the North-eastern States, the Ministry of Women and Child Development had undertaken construction of a working women hostel in the year 2008-09 exclusively for the working women of North East region working in and around Delhi. The six storied hostel building has 167 living rooms with a capacity to accommodate 500 working women. This hostel also has provision of a day care centre for the children of working mothers.

Rajiv Gandhi National Crèche Scheme – With a view to encourage women to join/ continue with gainful employment, Rajiv Gandhi National Crèche Scheme for children of working mothers (RGNCS) was introduced in 2006. The scheme seeks to provide day care facilities to children in the age group 0-6 years from families with a monthly income of less than Rs. 12,000. In addition to being a safe space for the children, the crèche provide services like supplementary nutrition, pre school education, emergency health care, etc.

The scheme provides for grant of Rs. 3,532 per month for a crèche, limited to 90 per cent of the schematic pattern or actual expenditure whichever is less, and the remaining expenditure is borne by the implementing agencies. Honorarium to crèche workers is fully funded under the scheme. Funds are separately provided to the implementing agencies for one time training of crèche workers.

The Central Sector scheme is implemented through Central Social Welfare Board (CSWB) and two national level mother NGOs i.e. Indian Council for Child Welfare (ICCW) and Bharatiya Adimjati Sevak Sangh (BAJSS).

Indira Gandhi Matritva Sahyog Yojana (IGMSY) **– Conditional Maternity Benefit (CMB) scheme** is a Conditional Cash Transfer scheme for pregnant and lactating women to contribute to better enabling environment by providing cash incentives for improved health and nutrition to pregnant and nursing mothers. It is being implemented initially on pilot basis in 52 selected districts using the platform of ICDS. IGMSY is a Centrally Sponsored Scheme introduced in the FY 2010-11, under which the grant-in-aid is released to States/ UTs. The Scheme envisages providing cash directly to P&L women during pregnancy and lactation in response to individual fulfilling specific conditions. It would address short term income support objectives with long term objective of behaviour and attitudinal change. The scheme attempts to partly compensate for wage loss to pregnant and lactating women both prior to and after delivery of the child.

12
Social Protection Schemes for Children

The report on Human Development in South Asia for 1997 describes the plight of children in South Asian countries which include India, as follows:

"To be a child in South Asia is to suffer a life of constant denial. Children are often born without their mothers being attended by trained health personnel. In fact, nearly 70 per cent of the mothers struggle alone, surrounded by untrained though anxious relatives, at the time of their greatest need. It is, therefore, not surprising that, far too often this miracle of birth turns into a nightmare of death, with too many children losing their mothers at the time of their arrival on this earth. The maternal mortality rate is nearly 600 per 100,000 live births in South Asia, and as high as 850 in Bangladesh, 1500 in Nepal, and 1600 in Bhutan (It is 570 in India). These are among the highest maternal mortality rates in the world, when compared to a mortality rate of only 28 in industrialised countries, and a sad commentary both on the status of women in these societies and on the prospects confronting children at birth.

In their survival and development, these children face even more formidable hurdles than those they face at birth. Half of the world's malnourished children (83 million) are to be found in just three countries: Bangladesh, Pakistan and India (The number of malnourished children in India is 62 million representing 53 per cent of the number of children under-five years). Almost two-thirds of all under-five deaths in South Asia are associated with malnutrition. The infant mortality and under-five child mortality rates in this region still remain high, despite a reduction by one-half over the last three decades. The infant mortality rate is still 82 per 1,000 live births, compared to 63 in the developing world (excluding South Asia) and the child mortality rate is 122, compared to an average of approximately 95 in the developing countries (excluding South Asia). (In India under-five mortality rate is 119 per thousand live births; infant mortality rate is 79 per 1000 live births). Far from being a pleasant dream, childhood becomes a constant nightmare for too many innocent children.

About 85 million children in South Asia have never seen the inside of a school. Only half of the total number of school-age children enrol in schools. Of these, 42 per cent drop out before reaching Grade 5. (In India the percentage of primary enrolment went up to 102 in 1992 but the percentage of children drop out of schools before Grade 5 was as high as 34). While many children are forced to leave school due to family circumstances and the compulsion to provide economic support to the household at a tender age, one of the main reasons for the high rates of school drop-out in South Asia is that both parents and children realise the poor quality of education they receive. Ultimately, drop-outs from schools can be reduced, and primary school enrollment rates raised, if efforts at human development focus not just on the number of schools but on the quality of education that these schools provide. Dramatic improvements are required in teacher training and supervision, in learning materials and school facilities, in the design and relevance of the curriculum content, in the formulation of the examination system, and in catering to the special needs of the 10 per cent of the children in most classrooms who have mild or moderate learning difficulties. Only when the quality of education is raised to a level that meets the needs and circumstances of poor children, and when that education is relevant to their present difficulties and future aspirations, will the education system in South Asia provide an adequate basis for greater economic prosperity and higher human development in the region.

Even more worrying than the state of education is the fact that there are an estimated 134 million children in South Asia employed as working children, sometimes in inhuman conditions and for a paltry wage. (In India the number of child labour is reported to have been 100 million in 1994).

Many children have to work over fifteen hours a day and are often physically abused. Rape and beatings are frequent. Once bonded, these children are traded like livestock and sometimes shipped to distant areas. Many of the children suffer from nutritional deficiencies, and most rarely have the opportunity to visit their families. Some children are simply kidnapped by employers and chained to their looms.

Seventy per cent of South Asia's children are employed in agriculture, mainly victims of an entrenched system of bonded labour, where whole families are enslaved in order to pay off debts. Others work in hazardous industries such as mining, brick-making, fireworks, brass handicrafts, carpet weaving and gem-polishing — industries which might not survive without the cheap labour provided by children.

Pressures are now emerging, both from governments and from civil society organisations within these countries, to stop the use of child labour.

The carpet industry is a prime example of demand-driven reform where India, Pakistan, and Bangladesh have observed a sudden decline in orders following a media outcry about the violation of children's rights in the industry. As a result, in January, 1996, carpet exporters and human rights groups in India launched the Rug-mark label, which certifies that carpets have been made without child labour.

Many governments in South Asia have ratified the convention on the Rights of the Child (CRC), adopted by the UN General Assembly on 20 November 1989, which sets minimum standards for children's rights. Some governments are now devising stricter child labour regulations, but results are generally poor due to a lack of effective implementation and enforcement.

Another shocking problem in South Asia is the sexual exploitation of children for profit. Child prostitution is a virtually invisible form of abuse in South Asian societies, but every day more and more children in the region fall victim to it.

Child protection laws are often inadequate to prevent the exploitation of children. In Pakistan, for instance, when legal help is sought, initial rape charges can sometimes result in a case of adultery against the female child *victim* under the country's offence of Zina Ordinance. Even worse, none of the child protection laws in the country protect the male child.

If left unattended, the sexual exploitation of children can destroy their basic potential. Poverty alone cannot justify or explain the commercial sexual exploitation of children. The range of causative factors includes economic disparities, dysfunctioning families, illiteracy, rural-urban migration, irresponsible male sexual behaviour, gender discrimination, and harmful traditional practices."

The social protection schemes for children consist of measures to provide nutritional support, provision of crèches and day care centres, prevention of child labour, protection of street children and socially maladjusted children and promotion of education

There are a variety of schemes to provide nutritional support to young children including the ICDS and the midday meal scheme. These are fairly successful. The Economic Survey 1998-99 says, "For the welfare and development the children, the Integrated Child Development Services scheme aims to provide an integral package of services of health check-up, immunisation, supplementary nutrition referral services, pre-school education, nutrition and health education to children and pregnant women and nursing mothers. The Scheme which started in 1975-76 on an experimental basis in 33 projects has been extended to 5614 centrally sponsored ICDS projects of which 4200 projects are now operational. The programme benefited 3.81 million expectant mothers and 21 million children under six years of age. A sum of Rs. 60 crore has been provided in 1998-99 (B.E.) Apart from ICDS the other programme for child development are day care centres for children below five years belonging to weaker sections of the society, Balwadi Nutrition Programme, Early Childhood Education and National Institute of Public cooperation and Child Development."

Several measures have also been taken to provide crèches and day care centers for looking after the children when their mothers go to work. Their adequacy is open to question

The Ministry of Labour has undertaken a series of measures to eliminate child labour or to reduce its incidence by stepping up enforcement of child labour laws, creating public awareness against it and providing for their education through non-formal and other means. It is doubtful if these measures have made any dent on the problem of child labour and whether the incidence of child labour has been reduced. There is a possibility that the children weaned away from work will go into the streets and pose greater problem by their presence as street children. It is extremely doubtful if a direct attack on child labour through enforcement of the laws will be effective. A better course would appear to be provide monetary incentives to the parents to withdraw the children from labour and to put them in schools. There are such schemes for Scheduled Castes and Tribes. Similar, incentives are being given in respect of girl children. The effectiveness of these measures may be evaluated and if they are found to be successful steps may be taken to replicate them

The governments depend largely on non-governmental organisations for dealing with the problem of street children. There is no information about the number of such children and how many of them are being looked after by the NGOs. It is necessary to collect this information to evaluate the effectiveness of the policy and the programmes being pushed by the government.

Education in India

As per the Annual Status of Education Report (ASER) 2012, 96.5 per cent of all rural children between the ages of 6-14 were enrolled in school. This is the fourth annual survey to report enrolment above 96 per cent. Another report from 2013 stated that there were 22.9 crore students enrolled in different accredited urban and rural schools of India, from Class I to XII, representing an increase of 23 lakh students over 2002 total enrolment, and a 19 per cent increase in girl's enrolment. While quantitatively India is inching closer to universal education, the quality of its education has been questioned particularly in its government run school system.While more than 95 percent of children attend primary school, just 40 percent of Indian adolescents attend secondary school (Grades 9-12). Since 2000, the World Bank has committed over $2 billion to education in India. Some of the reasons for the poor quality include absence of around 25 per cent of teachers every day. States of India have introduced tests and education assessment system to identify and improve such schools.

'Beyond Basics': An overview

ASER has reported on children's schooling status and their ability to do basic reading and arithmetic tasks. Year after year, ASER has highlighted the fact that although almost all children are enrolled in school, many are not acquiring foundational skills like reading and basic arithmetic that can help them progress in school and in life. Since 2006, ASER has focused on the age group 5 to 16. Over this period, a clearly visible trend is that more and more students are completing eight years of elementary school at about age 14. Just four years later, these young people will become adults. So what do these youth do during these four years? Are we ensuring that they acquire the skills and abilities they will need to lead productive lives as adults? To answer this question, ASER 2017 focuses on an older age group: youth who are 14 to 18 years old. The survey looks 'Beyond Basics', exploring a wider set of domains beyond foundational reading and arithmetic in an attempt to throw light on the status and abilities of youth in this age group. For more on why ASER 2017 targets this age group. In what ways is ASER 2017 similar to earlier ASER surveys? The ASER model has several design characteristics that distinguish it from other learning assessments. ASER 2017 retains these key characteristics. First, ASER is a household-based, rather than school-based, survey. This design enables ASER to generate estimates of schooling and basic learning for all children, rather than only those enrolled in government schools and present on the day of the assessment. ASER 2017 is also a household-based survey. Piloting the 'Beyond Basics' package and over ten years of experience of the ASER survey showed that youth in the 14-18 age group are harder to find at home. Thus, in order to take into account the fact that older children are often more difficult to find in rural locations, the usual sample size of 30 villages per district has been doubled to 60 villages per district for ASER 2017. Second, ASER tools and processes are designed to be easy to administer and to understand, so that ordinary people can participate in the survey and understand its findings. ASER 2017 has retained this characteristic, staying away from traditional pen-paper testing and instead using pictorial questions administered in an oral, one-on-one format. Moreover, this format engages the curiosity and interest of family members and others in the community. Third, the survey is conducted each year in partnership with organizations and institutions in the districts where the data is being collected, so that those closest to the villages and children being reported on can take the lead in disseminating the findings and acting to change the situation. ASER 2017 continues this pattern, partnering with 35 local colleges and universities to collect conduct the survey. How is ASER 2017 different from earlier ASER surveys? Because the target age group for ASER comprises children in the elementary school age group, ASER normally collects information only about sampled children's school enrollment and basic learning abilities. But youth in the 14-18 age group are far more varied with respect to what they do, what they know, and what they want. ASER 2017 , therefore, attempts to capture characteristics of the target age group covering a broader set of dimensions, framed here as four components:

- Activity: What are the youth currently doing? Are they enrolled in school or college, working, taking vocational training, preparing for entrance exams? Or some combination of these activities?
- Ability: Can they apply basic reading and arithmetic abilities to everyday situations? Can they do simple financial calculations?
- Awareness and exposure: What do youth report in terms of their exposure to media? Are they familiar with common digital and financial instruments and processes?
- Aspirations: What do youth in this age group report as their educational and career goals?

Nutrition Support

Betterment of nutritional status of the people is one of the prime responsibilities of the State. Article 47 of the Constitution states that the State should regard the raising of the level of nutrition and the standard of living of its people and the improvement of public health as among its primary duties. Despite achieving self-sufficiency in food production, there is widespread malnutrition among the lower strata of the society. Malnutrition is not necessarily a problem of food deficiency but it is a multifaceted problem requiring multi sectoral action.

The per capita calorie intake for the last three deciles of the population in 1983 was 1599 and 1583 in rural and urban areas respectively. These caloric intakes were only 73 per cent of the average calorie intake of all classes. In fact, the per capita daily intake of calories for the lowest expenditure class was 779 calories. The per capita daily intake of protein and fat was also much lower for the poorer expenditure classes.

According to the UNICEF (1995), around 69 per cent of under-five children suffer from moderate and severe malnutrition in India. Again, 27 per cent of under-five children suffer from severe malnutrition. The estimates of the National Nutrition Monitoring Bureau in India show that around 53 per cent of the children aged 1-5 years suffered from moderate to severe malnutrition in1988-89. Thus, the problem of malnutrition or under nutrition among children seem to be severe in India.

According to the Report of Human Development in South Asia, 1998, the daily calorie supply in 1992 was 2395, 113 per cent of the total requirements. Percentage of malnourished children was, however, 53.

The National Commission on Rural Labour says: "The latest per capita average expenditure figures for rural families, available only for the year 1983 show that agricultural labourers, at Rs. 85.28, have the least per capita per month expenditure, the corresponding figures for self-employed and rural labour being Rs. 122.85 and Rs. 89.09, respectively. It is obvious that the impact of rising prices will be most felt by agricultural labourers who are at the bottom of the line and that their consumption of essential food items will decline when their prices rise shortly. This seems to have happened in the case of cereals where the per capita daily consumption went down from 480 g in 1977-78 to 465 g in 1983 for agricultural labourers and from 480 g to 437 g for all rural households in the same period. The per capita availability of protein rich pulses has also been declining and the expenditure on pulses as a percentage of total expenditure on food in rural labour households was 5.24 in 1977-78 and it went down to 4.86 in 1983; milk and milk products went down from 6.30 per cent to 5.78 per cent in the same period.

The NSS data collected in its 27th (1972-73) and 38th (1983) rounds reveal that for rural India the per capita per day average intake of both calorie and protein declined slightly over a decade from 2,266 to 2,221 and 62.7 to 62 g respectively. The per capita intake of 2,221 in 1983 is about 7.5 per cent less compared to the officially accepted normative minimum of 2,400 calories. In 1983, in rural households as a whole, almost one fourth of the households (23.97 per cent) consumed less than 1,800 calories per day whereas the percentage of households whose calorie intake was less than the normative minimum was as high as little over 68 per cent.

The problem of low consumption is related to variables like increase in prices, agricultural production, size of land holdings, extent of unemployment, etc. Under consumption being the severest in the case of agricultural labour, measures to increase their income will increase their level of food consumption. This can be done both by increasing their income directly through enforcing the payment of minimum wages and employment guarantee schemes and by subsidised supply of essential commodities through the Public Distribution System."

The Eighth Five Year Plan recognised malnutrition as a multifaceted problem requiring an inter sectional approach. Consistent with this, the Government adopted a National Nutrition Policy and initiated the National Plan of Action in 1995. NNP recognises the significance of short term measures such as nutrition intervention for special vulnerable groups, fortification of food items, control of micro-nutrient and protein-energy deficiencies through inter-sectional programmes such as universalisation of supplementary feeding for pre-school children and expectant and nursing mothers through ICDS, basic minimum services including midday meals for school-going children, child survival and safe motherhood programme to extend nutritional prophylaxis and universal immunisation.

The major nutritional programmes that currently exist are the following:

1. Supplementary feeding
   (a) Special Nutrition Programme
   (b) Midday Meal Programme
2. Massive dose of vitamin A distribution
3. Iron and folic acid tablet distribution
4. Iodized salt distribution.

The most important nationwide nutrition scheme in India is the ICDS. This programme integrates supplementary nutrition with primary health care and informal education.

In addition to nationwide programmes, there are other nutritional schemes in some States. Tamil Nadu has a large number of nutrition programmes. Its noon meal programme is well known.

The total expenditure on nutrition by the Central as well as the State Governments has been estimated to be about Rs. 762 crore in 1989-90 and as a percentage of the GDP, it was just 0.24 per cent. Central Government expenditure on ICDS increased from Rs. 337.6 million in 1983-84 to Rs. 4,740 million in 1993-94. This programme is reported to have been successful in reducing malnourishment among pre-school children with the result that there has been a decline in the percentage of children afflicted by moderate malnutrition from 62.5 in 1975-79 to 50.9 in 1994 and severe malnutrition from 15 to 7.5. The decline is said to be striking in Kerala and Tamil Nadu.

Integrated Child Development Services Scheme (ICDS) Programme

The Integrated Child Development Services Scheme is one of the flagship programmes of the Government of India. It represents one of the world's largest and unique programmes for early childhood care and development. It is the foremost symbol of the country's commitment to its children and nursing mothers. As a response to the challenge of providing pre-school non-formal education on the one hand and breaking the vicious cycle of malnutrition, morbidity, reduced learning capacity on the other.

The beneficiaries of the scheme are the children in the age group 0-6 years, and pregnant and lactating mothers.

The objectives of the scheme include "to improve the nutritional and health status of the children in the age group 0-6 years"

Nutritional Norms (Revised)

Norms	*Calories*	*Protein*	*Cost in Rs.*
Children age group 6 to 72 months	500	12.15	6
Severely malnourished	800	20.15	9
Pregnant women and lactating mothers	600	18.20	7
Total expenditure on the scheme 2013-14			Rs. 16,267 cr

In spite of such a programme the state of malnutrition among children in India has been deplorable. This fact was recognised by a person no less than the then Prime Minisiter in the these words: Maintaining that the problem of malnutrition is a matter of national shame, former Prime Minister Manmohan Singh, on 11 January 2012, said that the level of under-nutrition in the country was unacceptably high.

While releasing a report on Hunger and Malnutrition (HUNGaMA), Mr. Singh said, "Despite impressive growth in our GDP, the level of under-nutrition in the country is unacceptably high. The problem of malnutrition is a matter of national shame."

He said, "Though the Integrated Child Development Services (ICDS) continues to be our most important tool to fight malnutrition, we can no longer rely solely on it. We need to focus on districts where malnutrition levels are high and where conditions causing malnutrition prevail." India has not succeeded in reducing the levels of malnutrition fast enough, he added.

He further said, "Policy makers and those who implement programmes need to clearly understand many linkages – between education and health, sanitation and hygiene, drinking water and nutrition – and then shape their responses accordingly."

The ICDS scheme is a major national programme that addresses the health and nutrition needs of children under the age of six. The HUNGaMA report states that the prevalence of child underweight has decreased from 53 per cent to 42 per cent, marking a 20.3 per cent fall over a seven year period with an average annual rate of reduction of 2.9 per cent. The survey found that the rates of child malnutrition were still unacceptably high in the 100 focus districts with the poorest child development indicators where over 40 per cent of children were underweight and almost 60 per cent stunted.

Dr Singh pointed out that while the survey reports high levels of malnutrition, it also indicates that one child in five has reached an acceptable healthy weight during the last seven years in 100 focus districts.

"This 20 per cent decline in malnourishment in the last seven years is better than the rate of decline reported in National Family Health Survey-III," he said. "However, what concerns me is that 42 per cent of our children are still underweight. This is an unacceptably high occurrence," he said.

Ladli Scheme

Ladli Scheme is a scheme that aims to alter the position of the girl kid in family/the public. It also aims to help modify the people's mindsets for appropriately taking care of the girl kid and as well to offer the girl child their birth rights as stated in Indian Constitution. Daughters care is extremely deprived in contrast to boys in the current society. The behaviour a girl child takes from the family members is extremely pitiable. To battle all the troubles such as female foeticide, waning females sexratio and to augment the figure of daughters in the families of society government has set up a variety of plans in which a girl child obtains particular profits. Ladli Yojna is among such plans and schemes. On the occasion of birthday of late Prime Minister Rajiv Gandhi, this scheme was started in the year of 2008.

According to the scheme, the daughter child obtains free education and upbringing additionally after eighteen years of age, she will be permitted to acquire one Lakh rupees. This money is given in her name and it can be utilised for the marriage of the girl which is considered by some parents as burden in the society.

New Savings Scheme for Girls Launched

Sukanya Samriddhi Scheme: There is a new entrant in the small savings scheme category. Sukanya Samriddhi Scheme, launched on 22 January 2015, is aimed at encouraging people to save for girl child's education and marriage. It is part of the government's efforts to encourage financial inclusion and increase domestic savings, which have fallen from 36 per cent of gross domestic product in 2008 to 30 per cent in 2013.

Under the scheme, parents and legal guardians can open accounts in the name of two girl children up to 10 years of age. However, as part of the initial offer, one-year grace period is being given. Now, any girl child born between 2 December 2003 and 1 December 2004 can have account opened for her till 1 December 2015.

The account can be opened in post offices or scheduled commercial banks. The minimum investment is Rs. 1,000 a year. Further investments have to be in multiples of Rs. 100. The maximum amount one can deposit is Rs 1.5 lakh, irrespective of the number of accounts. One has to deposit at least Rs. 1,000 every year. An account where the minimum amount has not been deposited can be revived by paying a penalty of Rs. 50 and the minimum amount for each year during which the account holder has not paid.

The scheme is offering an interest rate of 9.1 per cent a year. However, the rate will be revised every year. The interest will be credited in the account every year. The interest rate on Sukanya Samriddhi Scheme will be revised in April every year. However, the government is offering preferential rates. The scheme will continue to get preferential treatment.

While the account can be opened only by natural or legal guardians, the child can operate it after she turns 10. Though the money in the account can be withdrawn only after the girl attains the age of 21, premature withdrawal of 50 per cent of the amount at the end of the previous financial year is allowed for the purpose of the girl's higher education or marriage after she turns 18. If the money is not withdrawn even after the girl is 21, it will continue to earn interest. The account can be transferred anywhere in the country.

The money in the account can be deposited through cash, cheque or draft. "While drafting the rules, the government has kept the fact in mind that many people in rural and semi-urban areas will be depositing money under the scheme and, therefore, has allowed cash deposits," says Anil Rego, CEO, Rights Horizon, a wealth management firm.

Taxation: The amount deposited is proposed to be eligible for tax deduction up to Rs. 1.50 lakh under Section 80C of the Income Tax Act. However, the government has not notified the proposal yet.

Beti Bachao Beti Padhao

The trend of decline in the Child Sex Ratio (CSR), defined as number of girls per 1000 of boys between 0-6 years of age, has been unabated since 1961. The decline from 945 in 1991 to 927 in 2001 and further to 918 in 2011 is alarming. The decline in the CSR is a major indicator of women disempowerment. CSR reflects both, pre-birth discrimination manifested through gender biased sex selection, and post birth discrimination against girls. Social construct discriminating against girls on the one hand, easy availability, affordability and subsequent misuse of diagnostic tools on the other hand, have been critical in increasing Sex Selective Elimination of girls leading to low Child Sex Ratio.

Since coordinated and convergent efforts are needed to ensure survival, protection and empowerment of the girl child, Government has announced Beti Bachao Beti Padhao initiative. This is being implemented through a national campaign and focussed multi sectoral action in 100 selected districts low in CSR, covering all States and UTs. This is a joint initiative of Ministry of Women and Child Development, Ministry of Health and Family Welfare and Ministry of Human Resource Development.

The objectives of this initiative are:

- Prevention of gender biased sex selective elimination
- Ensuring survival and protection of the girl child
- Ensuring education and participation of the girl child

13
Social Protection of the Disabled

The Human Development Report, 1993, has noted that despite the accumulating forces for greater participation, large number of people continue to be excluded from the benefits of development. Disabled persons represent one such excluded group.

The disabled represent at least 10 per cent of the world population. (According to the latest information around 15 per cent of the world's population, or estimated one billion people, live with disabilities. They are the world's largest minority. They include all those who have experienced injury, trauma or disease that results in the long term physical or mental changes.

The NSSO has, however, found that the population of the disabled in India is only about 1.9 per cent of the total population. It needs to be examined whether there is any flaw in the definitions adopted for the purposes or in the statistics.

Census 2001 has revealed that over 21 million people in India are suffering from one or the other kind of disability. (This is equivalent to 2.1 per cent of the population).

Disability even in industrial countries is closely linked with poverty. It is more common in rural areas and among the poor.

The disabled face many barriers to participation in work. Lack of education is one. Discrimination in employment is another.

Some countries have taken measures to give greater opportunities to the disabled. Germany, for instance, has a quota for employment of the disabled of 6 per cent in both government and private businesses. The United States has far-reaching legislation: the 1992 Americans with Disabilities Act sets a large number of standards to be achieved in working life.

National Policy for the Disabled

The government has recently announced the National Policy for the Disabled persons. The salient features of the policy are as follows:

The Constitution of India ensures equality, freedom, justice and dignity of all individuals and implicitly mandates an inclusive society for all including persons with disabilities. In the recent years, there have been vast and positive changes in the perception of the society towards persons with disabilities. It has been realised that a majority of persons with disabilities can lead a better quality of life if they have equal opportunities and effective access to rehabilitation measures.

According to the Census 2001, there are 2.19 crore persons with disabilities in India who constitute 2.13 per cent of the total population. This includes persons with visual, hearing, speech, locomotor and mental disabilities. Seventy five per cent of persons with disabilities live in rural areas, 49 per cent of disabled population is literate and only 34 per cent are employed. The earlier emphasis on medical rehabilitation has now been replaced by an emphasis on social rehabilitation. There has been an increasing recognition of abilities of persons with disabilities and emphasis on mainstreaming them in the society based on their capabilities. The Government of India has enacted three legislations for persons with disabilities, viz.

i. Persons with Disability (Equal Opportunities, Protection of Rights and Full Participation) Act, 1995, which provides for education, employment, creation of barrier free environment, social security, etc.
ii. National Trust for Welfare of Persons with Autism, Cerebral Palsy, Mental Retardation and Multiple Disability Act, 1999 has provisions for legal guardianship of the four categories and creation of enabling environment for as much independent living as possible.
iii. Rehabilitation Council of India Act, 1992 deals with the development of manpower for providing rehabilitation services.

In addition to the legal framework, extensive infrastructure has been developed. Several institutions have been established for implementation of the Policy.

The National Policy recognises that Persons with Disabilities are valuable human resource for the country and seeks to create an environment that provides them equal opportunities, protection of their rights and full participation in society. The focus of the policy shall be on the following:

I. Prevention of Disabilities

Since disability, in a large number of cases, is preventable, there will be strong emphasis on prevention of disabilities. Programme for prevention of diseases, which result in disability and the creation of awareness regarding measures to be taken for prevention of disabilities during the period of pregnancy and thereafter will be intensified and their coverage expanded.

II. Rehabilitation Measures

Rehabilitation measures can be classified into three distinct groups:

i. physical rehabilitation, which includes early detection and intervention, counselling and medical interventions and provision of aids and appliances. It will also include the development of rehabilitation professionals,
ii. educational rehabilitation including vocational education, and
iii. economic rehabilitation for a dignified life in society.

The enactment of the Persons with Disabilities (Protection of Rights and Full Participation) Act, 1995 is a major step taken by the Central Government to ensure equal opportunities for persons with disabilities and their full participation in nation building. Implementation of the Act is left to the State Governments and the measures taken by them can only be described as halting.

A National Programme of Rehabilitation of People with Disabilities is said to have been drawn up. The full details of the programme have not been made public. It is necessary to prepare a comprehensive plan of action covering, inter alia, the following aspects:

Removal of the disabilities, whenever possible, should be the basic objective of any such plan. Where the disabilities cannot be removed, measures should be taken to bring the disabled persons on to the mainstream by providing them appropriate education and skill training.

There is a non-statutory scheme for reservation of 3 per cent of posts in the Central Government for handicapped persons. It should be made statutory and applicable to employment in all Government as well as private establishments as in Germany.

Provision of adequate employment opportunities should be the second priority in any scheme for the welfare of the disabled.

But it may not be possible to provide employment to all the disabled as their capacity to work would not be uniform. In cases of persons who cannot work, the State should undertake a safety net by providing them food, clothing and shelter at its own expense.

There should be proper assessment of the number involved and schemes prepared to cover them.

The Central as well as the State Governments have undoubtedly introduced several schemes for the welfare of the Disabled. On a review of their schemes, one cannot help forming the impression that they are at best ad hoc in nature and do not conform to any overall plan or blueprint. While many of the schemes are laudable, their adequacy and effectiveness are open to quest.

For example, the District Rehabilitation Centres have been set up to provide comprehensive rehabilitation services to the rural disabled in11 districts. Haryana has set up such District Handicapped Welfare Centres, the objective of which is to identify the handicapped, evaluate them and to provide medical, physical and vocational rehabilitation assistance to them. Similar centres should be opened in all the districts and in all the States and UTs. It would be desirable to route the assistance under social safety net provisions also through such centres.

Many States have extended the old age pension schemes to the physically handicapped persons with relaxation of age. Percentage of disability would be a better criterion as in the case of Disablement Benefit under the WC Act and the ESI Act. The quantum of the pension should be such as will be adequate to meet the basic needs.

Disability Pension Scheme (2009)

The Central Government in 2009 has introduced a Disability Pension Scheme. The main features of which are as follows.

Overview

- The government of India plans to offer financial support to people with physical and psychic disabilities.
- The IGNDPS is a relatively new scheme introduced by the government in the month of February 2009.
- It is a component of National Social Assistance program (NSAP)
- Under this initiative, disabled persons will have better living opportunities with financial support from the Indian government.

Eligibility

In order to qualify for the scheme, the applicant has to meet the eligibility criteria. Here are the guidelines:

- The applicant shall belong to Below Poverty Line (BPL) category
- The applicant shall be aged 18 years or above. Age limit for the entry of applicants is 18-79 years
- The applicant's disability level has to be 80 per cent (disability criteria should match with guidelines laid down in the PWD Act 1995)
- Persons with Autism, Cerebral Palsy, Mental Retardation 'may' also be considered 'disable'
- Dwarfs will also be eligible category for this pension
- Applicant shall not have a son above 21 years of age

Benefits

With the introduction of IGNDPS, physically disabled people received the right impetus to live. Through this scheme, the government plans to reduce the disparities in the social structure. The scheme will ensure that physically or mentally unsound persons will have a financial support every month from the Central and State government.

- Eligible age of the pensioner is 18 years and above.
- Rs. 300 per month to the Disable applicant between 18 to 79 years of age,
- Rs. 500 per month to the Disable applicant aged above 80,
- The assistance is paid to the applicant at his home through Money order or credited to their bank or post office account.

How to Apply

Application Forms can be obtained free of cost (also in the local languages) from the designated officer appointed by the respective State governments. At the district level the implementation of the scheme has been entrusted to Zilla Parishad or its equivalent. At the local level, the Gram Panchayat/ Municipality would implement the scheme. On furnishing of the documents listed, the Disable Identity Card is issued by the Social Security Officer. If sanctioned, beneficiary shall be issued a Pension Passbook.

Documents Required

1. Certificate validating the handicap/disability issued by Chief Medical Officer is mandatory when applying
2. Certificate showing the BPL Score issued by competent authority
3. Proof of Age
    - Aadhaar Card or Aadhaar Enrolment ID slip or Copy of his request made for Aadhaar enrolment; and,
    - Any of the following documents, namely:
        1. Voters' ID Card issued by Election Commission of India
        2. Ration Card
        3. Bank Passbook with Photo (Kisan Photo Passbook also valid)
        4. PAN Card issued by Income Tax Department
        5. Passport
        6. Driving Licence
        7. MGNREGA Card
        8. BPL Status Certificate (verifiable through Ration card)

Employment Injury Benefit

According to ILO Social Security (Minimum Standards) Convention, 1952 (No. 102) , every member should ensure that every person protected under it is covered under the employment injury benefit including the following accident-at-work or employment-related diseases:

- sickness,
- temporary incapacity for work resulting from such a condition,
- total or partial loss of earning capacity, likely to be permanent, and
- the loss of support suffered by dependents as the result of the death of the breadwinner.
- The range of benefits required by Convention No. 102 includes
- necessary medical care,
- sickness benefit for the period of incapacity for work,
- disability pension in case of loss of earning capacity, and
- survivors' pension in case of death of a breadwinner.

However, those benefits are only one, if the most visible, of the facets of employment injury protection

Compensation

When an employment injury scheme kicks in, the benefits in kind or in cash that workers suffering from occupational injury and disease can receive are:

- Temporary incapacity cash benefits: Most employment injury social security systems pay cash benefits to injured workers until the latter return to work or have reached maximum medical recovery. Temporary incapacity also includes periods of absence from work because of rehabilitation programmes aimed at minimizing the permanent loss of earning capacity.
- Permanent incapacity and survivorship benefits: Permanent incapacity benefits are paid after the medical condition of the injured person has stabilized and the worker has gone through vocational rehabilitation programmes, whenever these are available. Permanent incapacity can be either total or partial. When a worker dies due to a work-related accident or disease, benefits are paid to the survivors; the surviving spouse and children are always considered.
- Medical expenses and rehabilitation benefits: these benefits can be provided under the workers' compensation legislation or under general programmes not limited to work injuries and diseases. The injured worker is generally entitled to receive the medical attention necessary for a full recovery. The rehabilitation benefits include the expenses incurred for the services that are needed to return workers to their work and day-to-day living.

Rehabilitation and Back to Work

The Employment Injury Benefits Convention, 1964 (No. 121) (article 26) requires member countries to provide rehabilitation services which are designed to prepare a disabled person for the resumption of his/her previous activity, or, if this is not possible, the most suitable alternative works, having regard to his/her aptitudes and capacity; and to take measures to further the placement of disabled persons in suitable employment.

Sustainability of employment injury and occupational diseases schemes can be achieved by allowing implementation of policies to minimize the side effects of the disability through prevention measures, early-stage medical treatments, and rehabilitation.

There are two laws in India under which compensation for employment injuries are provided, namely, the Employees State Insurance Act and the Workmens' Compensation Act since renamed as Employees Compensation Act. These two laws are discussed below:

Temporary Disablement Benefit

(a) TDB is payable to an employee who suffers employment injury (EI) or Occupational Disease and is certified to be temporarily incapable to work.

"Employment Injury" has been defined under Section 2(8) of the Act, as a personal injury to an employee caused by accident or occupational disease arising out of and in the course of his employment, being in insurable employment, whether the accident occurs or the occupational disease is contracted within or outside the territorial limits of India.

(b) Certificates Required for TDB: Accident Report in form 16, Form 8,9,10, 11 and ESIC Med.13.

(c) Eligibility for TDB: The benefit is not subject to any contributory conditions. An IP is eligible from the day he joins the insurable employment.

(d) TDB Rate is 90 per cent of average daily wages.

(e) Duration of TDB: There is no prescribed limit for the duration of TDB. This is payable as long as temporary disablement lasts and significant improvement by treatment is possible. If a Temporary Disablement spell lasts for less than 3 days (excluding day of accident), IP will be paid sickness benefit, if otherwise eligible. A special point for IMOs/IMPs is that some IPs may resist taking a Final Certificate especially before 3 days for fear of loss of TDB.

Permanent Disablement Benefit

(a) PDB is payable to an IP who suffers permanent residual disablement as a result of occupational injury (including Occupational Diseases) and results in loss of earning capacity. The proper authority for assessing loss of earning capacity for injuries is the Medical Board and for Occupational Diseases, Special Medical Board.

(b) The duration of PDB may be for the period given by Medical Board, if assessment is provisional or for entire life if assessment is final.

(c) PDB Rate: The PDB rate is calculated as percentage of loss of earning capacity as assessed by the Medical Board/MAT/EI Court in relation to TDB. List of injuries deemed to result in permanent total disablement and percentage loss of earning capacity has been previewed in 2nd Schedule to ESIC Act, 1948. Hence, the maximum rate of PDB can be equal to the rate of TDB.

PDB amount is revised by the ESIC from time to time to adjust for inflation. The latest enhancement is with effect from 01.08.2009

(d) Commutation of PDB (Regulation 76-B): IP whose PDB has been assessed as final and who has been awarded the same at the rate not exceeding Rs. 1.50 per day may apply for commutation of periodical payments of PDB into a lump-sum. When an application for commutation is made within 6 months of the date of communication of Medical Board decision periodical payments shall be commuted into a lump sum provided the total commuted value does not exceed Rs. 10,000 at the time of commencement of final award. However, where such an application is made after expiry of 6 months, LO/RO will refer the case to MR/PTMR to certify whether the IP has an average expectation of life for his age. Such a certificate is issued by Medical Referee in the relevant place on RO/LO letter.

(e) Age of an IP will have to be proved to the satisfaction of the Corporation in all cases. Medical Boards assess the age of IPs who are not able to produce satisfactory proof of age and opinion of Medical Board shall be final in this regard.

Workmen Compensation Act vs. Employee Compensation Act – Key Differences

The following are the major differences between the Workmen's Compensation Act (1923) and the Employee Compensation Act.

Workmen Compensation Act, 1923	*Employee Compensation Act*
The insured party is called workman or workmen in the act.	The insured party is called employee or employees in the act.
Clerks were not considered to as workmen and thus, not covered by the act.	Clerks are treated as employees and are included in the act.
The minimum payable compensation for death is Rs. 80,000.	The minimum payable compensation for death is revised to Rs. 1,20,000.
The minimum payable compensation for permanent total disability was Rs. 90,000.	The permanent total disability compensation is revised to Rs. 1,40,000.
No medical treatment expense reimbursement (but can be included by paying extra premium).	The employees now can submit their medical expense bills for reimbursement for the injuries caused during the course of employment.
Maximum wage was Rs. 4,000 for computing the death or permanent disability benefits.	Maximum wage is Rs. 8,000 for computing the same.
The maximum funeral expenses payable was Rs. 2,500.	The maximum funeral expenses payable has been revised to Rs. 5,000.
No claim settlement time limit.	The claims must be settled within three months from the intimation.

The differences between the two Acts are highlighted in the following cases:

Case: 1

Due to his family's modest financial condition, he was unable to pursue his education further and therefore, soon after completing his 12th, Mukesh Saran started working in M.K.S Clothing. He was working as a senior machine operator and earning Rs 9,000. Though the salary was not very high; it was sufficient to meet the ends.

Destiny had a different plan for him and one day while working, his hand gloves caught between the machine and he suffered a major injury to his right arm. Some workers around him rushed him to a nearby hospital.

His treatment was started immediately, however, the severity of the accident was so high that his right arm became permanently disabled. When, after ten days, Mukesh was discharged from the hospital, his supervisor came to see him at his house.

As the accident was occurred during the working hours, the supervisor advised him to file a claim under the workmen compensation insurance policy. Mukesh did the same and approached the insurer for claim settlement.

Here the insurer approached M.K.S Clothing and asked for the complete report on the accident. Along with this, the insurer asked Mukesh to submit medical reports as well to know the extent of disability. Upon receiving all the documents and necessary details, the insurer reviewed them and settled the claim accordingly.

As Mukesh was covered under the Workmen Compensation Act, he did not get reimbursement of medical expenses. In this case, Mukesh incurred the medical expenses of Rs 60,000 and nothing was reimbursed by the insurer. The insurer paid compensation only for the permanent disability which was Rs 90,000.

Case: 2

For the last three years, Mr. Amt Shukla was working as a contractor with T.L. Construction Company. His punctuality and dedication towards work were always appreciated by his seniors. Last year, he got married to his long-term girlfriend, Riya. When everything was looking amazing, life's uncertainty turned Amit's world upside down.

One day at the construction site, he was inspecting the work when suddenly some rods, which were kept there for construction purpose, fell on him and he suffered serious injuries to his head and back. Workers at the site rushed him to a nearby hospital where doctors started the treatment immediately.

Though doctors tried their best and saved Amit's life; he got permanently disabled from the lower body due to the accident.

Suddenly, the future of Amit's family came at stake. Amit was discharged after 15 days, and many of its colleagues came to see him. They advised him to file a claim under the Employee Compensation Act. As the accident occurred during working hours, he was entitled to get claim under the act. As T.L Construction Company had the employee compensation insurance policy, they approached the insurer who agreed to settle the claim.

The insurer asked for the salary details of Amit along with medical reports to know the extent of disability. After analysing all the facts, the insurer agreed to settle the claim and paid the compensation of Rs. 1,40,000. In this case, the insurer also settled the medical expenses incurred by Amit which was Rs 2 lakh.

In the above case, both Mukesh and Amit were unfortunately got permanently disabled, however, the compensation received by both were different. While Mukesh was covered under Workmen's Compensation Act, he got Rs 90,000, Amit was covered under Employee's Compensation Act and thus, received Rs 1,40,000.

14

Social Protections Schemes for SCs/STs and OBCs

Scheduled Castes/ Scheduled Tribes and other backward classes of people are called special groups. The annual and five year plans aim at empowering them socially and economically so that they may join the mainstream of national development. In the programmes of development of these groups emphasis is laid on education, health and employment.

Education is regarded as the most effective instrument for empowering these groups. It is, therefore, given high priority in the development programmes. Keeping in view the low level of literacy and high dropout rates amongst them, special efforts are made to provide them hostel facilities, scholarships, supply of books, uniforms, etc. These have paid rich dividends, as is borne out by the fact that Mizoram which is a Tribal State has become the first State in India to attain 100 per cent literacy, beating even Kerala in the race.

Special attention is also given to promote employment among these classes. Several schemes have been introduced to give them vocational training and to encourage them to take up self employment either directly or through the instrumentality of the Scheduled Castes/ Scheduled Tribes, Backward classes Development Finance Corporations at the Central as well as State levels.

Measures taken to implement the Protection of Civil Rights and the Prevention of Atrocities Acts and to provide relief and rehabilitation assistance to victims of atrocities are commendable.

In this connection special mention needs to be made of the National Scheme for Liberation and Rehabilitation of Scavengers.

The Constitution provides for reservation of seats in Parliament and other Legislative bodies and for reservation of posts in Central and State government Services in relaxation of the principles of equality enshrined therein by way of affirmative action for uplifting these classes of people for limited periods which are being extended from time to time. It seems necessary to make an assessment whether, and if so, to what extent these measures have helped them to get into the mainstream and how much longer such protection would be necessary.

The plans and budgets set targets for giving assistance to these groups in terms of number of individuals and families. The reports and accounts show to what extent the targets were met and how much expenditure was incurred. They do not however indicate whether the assistance provided has fulfilled the purpose for which it was given. It is necessary to devise means to establish procedures for verification of the achievement of the ultimate objectives of the Schemes instead of being satisfied with the fulfillment of the performance targets.

> It may be interesting to note how members of Scheduled Castes and Scheduled Tribes are faring in the government hierarchy? At the very top level of the government bureaucracy, out of a total of 149 secretary-level officers, there were no SC officers while there were only four ST officers, as of March 2011.
>
> Actually, even in the most sought after civil services, IAS, IPS and IFS, the proportion of SC, ST and OBC officers was below the mandated quotas. Out of 3,251 directly recruited IAS officers, SC officers made up 13.9 per cent, ST officers 7.3 per cent and OBCs just 12.9 per cent. This information, too, was stated in the Lok Sabha by Shri Narayanasamy in 2011. Clearly, the underprivileged sections are not yet getting the full advantage of affirmative action envisaged by the Constitution makers. This is further confirmed by the huge number of vacancies in government positions reserved for SCs and STs.
>
> According to a statement given in the LS recently by Shri Narayanasamy, former Minister in the UPA cabinet, there were 25,037 'backlog' posts for SC lying vacant in 73 government departments and bodies. These are positions reserved for SC members that have not been filled over the years and thus have accumulated. They include both direct recruitment and promotion-based positions. Out of these, 4,518 positions were vacant because no candidate was available for promotion. Similarly for ST, 28,173 'backlog' posts were vacant, of which 7,416 were meant for filling up by promotion.
>
> If you look at all central government employees, 17 per cent of them were SC while 7.4 per cent were ST. This appears to be fulfilling the mandated norms of 15 per cent SC and 7.5 per cent ST. But there is a catch. There is a deep skew of SC/ST members in the hierarchy of central government jobs — as you move up the ladder, there are less and less employees/ officers from SC/ST. Among Group A officers, only 11.1 per cent were SC and 4.6 per cent ST. In Group B, the shares were 14.3 per cent and 5.5 per cent, respectively. In group C, there were 16 per cent SC and 7.8 per cent ST, slightly more than the quota. And in Group D, there were 19.3 per cent SC and 7 per cent ST.
>
> This high proportion of SC in Group D is because nearly 40 per cent of "safaikaramcharis" are SC. This pushes up the proportions all round. Actually it only denotes the harsh reality that despite all the talk of ending discrimination and socio-economic upliftment, dalits are still forced to do most menial jobs.
>
> Source: E*conomic Times*, 6 September 2012.

The Hindu in an editorial dated 11 May 2015 has commented on the discrimination against Dalits as follows:

Close to seven decades after Independence, in many villages of India the nature of certain social equations has not changed from what they have been for centuries. Such villages continue to remain what Dr. B.R. Ambedkar called "sinks of localism, dens of ignorance and narrow-mindedness". How else could one see certain recent incidents reported from Tumakuru in Karnataka about village barber shops denying haircuts for Dalits, temple festivities remaining out-of-bounds for Dalit families, and other forms of prevalent discrimination? By all accounts these are not isolated incidents. Discrimination against Dalits is widespread and ingrained in the psyche across India, in rural settings in particular. In some places it takes the form of violent oppression, in others it is disguised yet omnipresent. To be fair, when the incidents in Tumkuru came to notice, the administration took corrective steps immediately. This suggests responsiveness on the part of the State to issues of social justice at least in some cases. But recurring acts and persisting practices against the Dalit community beg the question whether State response and Constitutional remedies alone are enough to overcome longstanding social injustice and prejudices in India's villages.

In other words, has political justice — achieved in some respects over time by means of affirmative action — managed to overcome social injustice at all? The alacrity shown by State authorities in the Tumkaru cases reflects to some extent the political power gained by Dalits in India and the efficacy of the rule of law. After all, the Constitution guarantees the right to equality of all citizens and affirmative action for Dalits. Years of following the policy of affirmative action has yielded a high degree of participation and representation of Dalits in politics and governance. But without progressive social consciousness permeating society at large, Constitutionalism, State action and political equation simply do not suffice. It would help if the political actors who have accommodated Dalits among their party and governance structures, due to their sheer weight of number as a representative section, also believed in and worked as conduits for social transformation. Perhaps if Dalits were not merely accommodated but were accorded leadership roles in parties, that could aid this process of social activism. A recent study pointed out that barring exceptions such as the Bahujan Samaj Party, the leadership of major political parties suffered from a clear diversity deficit, with Dalits being severely under-represented in the leadership across parties. Being made part of the political leadership — one way of being among the elite in the country — will not by itself guarantee the eradication of social prejudice, but it will be a step in the right direction.

Manual Scavenging

Manual scavenging is a caste-based occupation involving the removal of untreated human excreta from bucket toilets or pit latrines, that has been officially abolished by law in India as a dehumanising practice. It involves moving the excreta, using brooms and tin plates, into baskets, which the workers carry to disposal locations sometimes several kilometres away. The workers, called scavengers, rarely have any personal protective equipment. The term is mainly used in the Indian context only.

The employment of manual scavengers to empty "dry toilets" (meaning here toilets that require daily manual cleaning) was prohibited in India in 1993 and the law was extended and clarified to include insanitary latrines, ditches and pits in 2013.

According to Socio Economic Caste Census 2011, 180,657 households are engaged in manual scavenging for a livelihood. The 2011 Census of India found 794,000 cases of manual scavenging across India. The State of Maharashtra, with 63,713, tops the list with the largest number of households working as manual scavengers, followed by the States of Madhya Pradesh, Uttar Pradesh, Tripura and Karnataka.

Definition

Manual scavenging refers to the unsafe and manual removal of raw (fresh and untreated) human excreta from buckets or other containers that are used as toilets or from the pits of simple pit latrines. The safe and controlled emptying of pit latrines, on the other hand, is one component of fecal sludge management.

The official definition of a manual scavenger in Indian law from 1993 is as follows:

"Manual scavenger" means a person engaged or employed, at the commencement of this Act or at any time thereafter, by an individual or a local authority or an agency or a contractor, for manually cleaning, carrying, disposing of, or otherwise handling in any manner, human excreta in an insanitary latrine or in an open drain or pit into which the human excreta from the insanitary latrines is disposed of, in railway track or in such other spaces or premises, as the Central Government or a State Government may notify, before the excreta fully decomposes in such manner as may be prescribed, and the expression "manual scavenging" shall be construed accordingly.

Not all forms of dry toilets involve "manual scavenging" to empty them, but only those that require unsafe handling of raw excreta. If on the other hand, the excreta is already treated or pre-treated in the dry toilet itself, as is the case for composting toilets and urine-diverting dry toilets, for example, then emptying these types of toilets is not classified as "manual scavenging". Container-based sanitation is another system that does not require manual scavenging to function even though it does involve the emptying of excreta from containers.

Also, emptying the pits of twin-pit pour-flush toilets is not classified as manual scavenging in India, as the excreta is already partly treated and degraded in those pits.

The International Labour Organization describes three forms of manual scavenging in India:

- Removal of human excrement from public streets and "dry latrines" (meaning simple pit latrines without a water seal, but not dry toilets in general)
- Cleaning septic tanks
- Cleaning gutters and sewers

Manual cleaning of railway lines of excreta dropped from toilets of trains is another form of manual scavenging in India.

Current Prevalence

Manual scavenging still survives in parts of India without proper sewage systems or safe fecal sludge management practices. It is thought to be most prevalent in Gujarat, Madhya Pradesh, Uttar Pradesh, and Rajasthan. Some municipalities in India still run public toilets using simple pit latrines.

The biggest violator of this law in India is the Indian Railways where many train carriages have toilets dropping the excreta from trains on the tracks and who employ scavengers to clean the tracks manually.

Manual scavenging is traditionally a role determined by the outlawed caste system in India for members of the Dalit caste, usually from the Balmiki (or Valmiki) or Hela subcaste.

In March 2014, the Supreme Court of India declared that there were 96 lakhs (9.6 million) dry latrines being manually emptied but the exact number of manual scavengers is disputed — official figures put it at less than 700,000.

Manual scavenging is done with basic tools like thin boards and either buckets or baskets lined with sacking and carried on the head. Due to the nature of the job, many of the workers have related health problems.

Initiatives for Eradication

Legislation

In the late 1950s, freedom fighter G. S. Lakshman Iyer banned manual scavenging when he was the chairman of Gobichettipalayam Municipality, which became the first local body to ban it officially. Sanitation is a State subject as per entry six of the Constitution. Under this, in February, 2013 Delhi announced that they are banning manual scavenging, making them the first State in India to do so. District magistrates are responsible for ensuring that there are no manual scavengers working in their district. Within three years time municipalities, railways and cantonments must make sufficient sanitary latrines available. The government of the State of Maharashtra has planned to abolish the menace of manual scavenging completely from the State soon. But by using Article 252 of the constitution which empowers Parliament to legislate for two or more States by consent and adoption of such legislation by any other State, the Government of India has enacted various laws. The continuance of such discriminatory practice is violation of ILO's Convention 111 (Discrimination in Employment and Occupation)

The Employment of Manual Scavengers and Construction of Dry Latrines (Prohibition) Act, 1993

After six States passed resolutions requesting the Central Government to frame a law, The Employment of Manual Scavengers and Construction of Dry

Latrines (Prohibition) Act, 1993, drafted by the Ministry of Urban Development under the Narasimha Rao government, was passed by Parliament in 1993.

The Employment of Manual Scavengers and Construction of Dry Latrines (Prohibition) Act, 1993 punishes the employment of scavengers or the construction of dry (non-flush) latrines with imprisonment for up to one year and/ or a fine of Rs. 2,000. No convictions were obtained under the law during the 20 years it was in force.

The Prohibition of Employment as Manual Scavengers and their Rehabilitation Act, 2013 or MS Act, 2013

Government has passed the new legislation in September, 2013 and issued Government notification for the same. In December, 2013 Government has also formulated Rules-2013 called as "The Prohibition of Employment as Manual Scavengers and their Rehabilitation Rules 2013" or "MS Rules 2013". The details about Act and Rules are available on the website of Ministry of Social Justice and Empowerment, GOI.

Further, the hearing on 27 March 2014 was held on Manual Scavenging of writ petition number 583 of 2003, and Supreme Court has issued final orders and case is disposed of with various directions to the Government.

The broad objectives of the Act are to eliminate unsanitary latrines, prohibit the employment of manual scavengers and the hazardous manual cleaning of sewer and septic tanks, and to maintain a survey of manual scavengers and their rehabilitation.

Activism

In India, in 1970s, Dr. Bindeshwar Pathak introduced his "Sulabh" concept for building and managing public toilets in India, which has introduced hygienic and well-managed public toilet system. Activist Bezwada Wilson founded a group in 1994, Safai Karmachari Andolan, to campaign for the demolition of then newly illegal 'dry latrines' (pit latrines) and the abolition of manual scavenging. Despite the efforts of Wilson and other activists, the practice persists two decades later. In July, 2008 "MissionSanitation" was a fashion show held by the United Nations as part of its International Year of Sanitation. On the runway were 36 previous workers, called scavengers, and top models to help bring awareness of the issue of manual scavenging.

In a landmark judgement, the Supreme Court ordered the abolition of manual scavenging and asked State governments to provide financial assistance and rehabilitation to those who had lost a family member to the inhuman practice.

The three judge bench of the Supreme Court, led by the Chief Justice P. Sathasivam, said that "the official statistics of the Ministry of Social Justice and Empowerment for the year 2002-2003 put the figure of identified manual scavengers at 6,76,009. Of these, over 95 per cent are Dalits, compelled to undertake this denigrating task."

The court ordered that if the practice of manual scavenging has to be brought to a close, certain measures had to be taken. The court ordered the payment of Rs. 10 lakh to the family of those who died cleaning sewers since 1993. The court also asked for the provision of residential plots or a flat to the deceased's family and scholarship to the children. While also asking all States to implement the new 2013 law, prohibiting manual scavenging entirely.

The big culprit, the Railways was also taken to task with the court saying it must ensure a time-bound strategy to end manual scavenging, prevalent at all railway stations.

The court's decision was based on the writ petition by the Safai Karanchari Andolan, which claimed that the custom not only continues in several States but had also increased. It also claimed that over 95 per cent of those who continue this inhuman practice are Dalits, with majority of them being women. However, the bigger task for States now will be to identify the families of all those who died cleaning sewers since 1993 and make sure that the adequate compensation reaches them in a time-bound manner.

15
Social Security in the Context of Natural Disasters

Natural and man-made disasters in the form of floods, droughts, land shocks, cyclones, super-cyclones, tsunami, railway accidents, etc. have been occurring frequently in one part or the other of the country. Whenever a calamity occurs special measures are taken on ad hoc basis to provide relief and rehabilitation assistance to the affected people. The nature and scale of assistance vary and there is no machinery to monitor the results. It seems necessary to devise a mechanism to keep a watch over the occurrence of such disasters and to provide the relief and rehabilitation assistance in a planned manner.

There are other countries akin to India in terms of the proneness to disasters. We can learn much from their experience in handling disasters.

For example, Australia's climate, geography, geology and vegetation makes it prone to a range of emergencies and disasters resulting from natural hazards such as severe storms, floods, droughts, cyclones earthquakes and bushfires. In that country, a National Disasters Organisation was established in 1974. It was renamed as Emergency Management Australia in 1993. The object of the organisation is to promote and support comprehensive integrated and effective emergency management in Australia. Its functions include:

(a) Enhancing national emergency management capabilities by developing appropriate policies and programmes including national emergency management education and training programmes and delivering emergency management education and training, etc.
(b) Coordinating Commonwealth physical support to the States and territories in times of danger.

This organisation is involved in all types of disasters, natural, human caused, technological or otherwise. Its activities span the aspects of prevention, preparedness response and recovery. They include training, awareness, planning, equipment, and volunteer-unit accommodation subsidies.

In the U.K. the Home Office has drawn up a manual for dealing with Disasters. It provides guidance to all agencies involved in dealing with disasters. It has set out the objectives of a combined response to disasters. They are:

(a) to save life
(b) to prevent escalation of the disaster
(c) to relieve suffering
(d) to safeguard the environment

(e) to protect property
(f) to facilitate criminal investigation and judicial public technical or other inquiries
(g) to inform the public
(h) to promote self help and recovery; and
(i) to restore normality as soon as possible.

The Government of UK has evolved a system of integrated emergency management embracing a number of concepts such as follows:

(a) *Prevention*: This phase encompasses measures which are adopted in advance of an emergency and which seek to prevent it from occurring or to reduce its severity;
(b) *Preparedness*: This is the insurance policy and includes planning, warning, and the preparation of resource registers and stockpiles. An essential part of planning is an assessment of hazard/ risk. Planning needs to be underpinned by training and exercise.
(c) *Response*: The initial response is normally provided by the Statuary emergency services supported as necessary by the appropriate local authorities and voluntary organisations. The basic objectives of the response which will vary according to the circumstances of the event, will be to save life; prevent escalation of the emergency, relieve suffering, protect property, enable criminal and forensic investigations to be undertaken where necessary and facilitate subsequent recovery;
(d) *Recovery*: This phase will encompass those activities necessary to provide a rapid return to normalcy both for those affected by the crisis and those providing the mitigating services.

There is an obvious need for setting up a similar integrated disaster management system in India by institutionalising the existing arrangements.

The Second National Commission on Labour had recommended that an appropriate National Scheme for providing relief and rehabilitation to people affected by economic and social distress including natural disasters may be designed. It had also recommended that a permanent commission for disaster management should be set up on the lines of the Election Commission. It should be responsible for the management of relief and rehabilitation after every drought, loss of crops, floods, cyclones, earthquake and other disasters. This body could study how disasters are managed in other countries and suggest the equipments to be purchased. It should also be empowered to seek help from the army police and other personnel in times of acute crisis due to calamities.

Recently a National Disaster Management Authority (NDMA) has been set up in India. It is an agency under the Ministry of Home Affairs. The primary purpose of the authority is to coordinate response to natural or man-made disasters and for capacity-building in disaster resiliency and crisis response. NDMA was established through the Disaster Management Act enacted by the Government of India in December 2005. The Prime Minister is the ex-officio chairperson of NDMA. The agency is responsible for framing policies, laying down guidelines and best practices and coordinating with the State Disaster Management Authorities (SDMAs) to ensure a holistic and distributed approach to disaster management by a nine member board chaired by the Prime Minister of India. The remainder of the board consists of members nominated based on their expertise in areas such as planning, infrastructure management, communications, meteorology and natural sciences. The day-to-day management of the agency is overseen by the office of the Vice Chair.

The authority is reported to have been ineffective in carrying out most of its functions.

NDMA initiated projects for flood mitigation and landslide mitigation at the national level in 2008. However, those projects have either been abandoned midway or are being redesigned because of poor planning. The projects to prepare national vulnerability atlases of landslides, floods and earthquake are also incomplete. Experts feel if such projects would have been implemented properly, the damage in Uttarakhand could have been much less.

As per the performance audit report of the disaster management mechanism in the country by the Comptroller and Auditor General (CAG) of India, submitted to the Parliament, NDMA has neither information and control over the progress of disaster management work in the States, nor could it successfully implement various projects it had initiated for disaster preparedness and mitigation. What's more, the authority has been functioning without its core advisory committee of experts that advises it on different aspects of disaster management for the past three years.

According to law, NDMA should have an advisory committee of experts in the field of disaster management at the national, State or district level. The first advisory committee of NDMA was constituted in 2007 for two years. Later, the term was extended for one more year. However, since June 2010, NDMA is functioning without the advisory committee. First, the reason for delay that was cited was that several ministries had not sent the proposals of the names of experts to be included in the committee. Now, it is being said that the names are being reviewed by the Prime Minister's Office.

No Major Project Completed

The CAG report also highlighted several other loopholes in the functioning of NDMA. It said none of the major projects taken up by NDMA was complete even after seven years of its functioning. The projects were either abandoned midway or were being redesigned because of initial poor planning. The major projects include producing vulnerability atlases for floods, earthquakes and landslides, national landslide risk mitigation project, national flood risk mitigation project and national disaster management information system.

As per the CAG report, NDMA has also not been performing several functions as prescribed in the Disaster Management Act. These include recommending provision of funds for the purpose of mitigation and recommending relief in repayment of loans or for grant of fresh loans. Besides, several critical posts in NDMA are vacant and consultants were used for day–to-day working.

CAG's 2013 Report Notes

- National Plan for Disaster Management had not been formulated even after six years of the enactment of the Disaster Management Act, 2005.
- National Executive Committee responsible for preparation of the National Plan had not met between May 2008 and December 2012, although the country faced many disasters during this period.
- The national guidelines developed by NDMA were not adopted and applied by the nodal agencies and State governments. NDMA did not take effective measures to ensure the application of its guidelines.
- NDMA's project management capacity was found deficient. No major project taken up by NDMA had seen completion so far. Due to deficient planning, either the projects were abandoned midway or were still incomplete.
- In many cases, audit report found projects with similar objectives being executed by NDMA and also by nodal ministries, indicating lack of coordination.
- The management of the State Disaster Response Fund (SDRF) in the States was poor.
- The States were not regular in sending the details of utilisation and unspent balances under SDRF to MHA. States did not invest the unspent balances under SDRF as in the guidelines.
- National Disaster Response Fund was utilised for various purposes other than those stated in the Governmnt of India guidelines.
- Many communication projects were either incomplete or not operational, despite procurement of expensive equipment years earlier.
- National Database for Emergency Management, to be completed by August 2011, was yet to become operational.
- The satellite-based communication network was also not fully operational even after six years of receipt of the communication equipment. The Doppler Weather Radars for surveillance and monitoring of severe weather systems did not fructify, after spending Rs. 35.64 crore.
- The report noted in National Disaster Response Force had not emerged as a well-equipped, well-trained, specialised force.

Conclusion

The habit of knee-jerk official response to disasters must be broken by public pressure.

The news of building crashes, fires and other accidents in Indian cities and towns are almost always suffered with outrage and an underlying sense of déjà vu and near resignation by most citizens. Almost everything about the so-called accident seems to follow a set pattern: exposure of a series of violations of safety norms and laws aided and abetted by the authorities and promises of swift punitive action by the said authorities, including sympathetic noises. In December 2017, Mumbai witnessed two major fires — one in a swanky pub on the 29th that claimed 14 lives and another in a suburban snack-making unit on the 18th that killed 12 workers. The expected reactions followed in these cases too, accompanied by the familiar knee-jerk one of demolishing illegal structures and extensions all over the city. However, the most significant issue that these two incidents and innumerable others (including the stampede at a railway station in September 2017 that led to 22 deaths) across the country bring home is that of ongoing apathy from citizens and authorities alike. The lack of urban planning is only equalled by the lack of the community's involvement in the process. Such apathy is fuelled by cynicism that things cannot and will not change.

The India Risk Survey 2017 by the Federation of Indian Chambers of Commerce and Industry lists 12 risks to business perception and operations in the country. Fire ranks fifth on the list, having gone up by three places from the 2016 survey. The National Crime Records Bureau says that in 2015 a total of 18,450 cases of fire accidents were reported and 17,700 persons were killed. It further adds that 42.1 per cent of those deaths were due to fire accidents in residential buildings. The majority of fire accidents were reported in Maharashtra, which accounted for 22 per cent of these accidents. Interestingly, the survey put corruption, bribery and corporate frauds at the third position. Perhaps, this is a textbook indicator that the more things change the more they remain the same.

As the municipal authorities and the government point to action taken (post the incidents) and justify lack of accountability before, it is time to point out that nothing has been learnt or remembered from a horrific fire that was greeted with similar official action and public outrage. In 2015, eight college students were charred to death in Mumbai as they sat eating lunch in a hotel that had made several illegal changes in its interiors and stored gas cylinders carelessly. The Uphaar cinema hall fire in which 59 persons died in 1997, trapped due to illegal changes in the layout, and the AMRI Hospital fire in Kolkata in 2011 that led to 89 deaths have become part of public memory. But in terms of change for the better in implementation of safety laws, there has been no effect. Doubtless, this is the situation in an overwhelming majority of eateries, hotels, pubs, cinema halls, hospitals, small "industrial" units, sheds, factories and residential buildings across urban India. Any attempt to enforce safety regulations is seen as "harassment" by the builders and business operators. The snack-making unit had stored gas cylinders and other combustible material haphazardly and the workers, many of them migrants, stayed and slept in the loft of the small structure.

The municipal authorities now claim that the owner of the snack-making business had not taken any of the requisite permissions for running it. Similarly, a number of activists claimed that they had alerted the authorities about illegal constructions in the Kamala Mills complex, which houses a large number of posh eateries and pubs. The pub in question opened after being closed for a fortnight but there was no action. Mumbai's saga of unplanned construction and the use of mill lands to set up businesses and build residential buildings, actively helped and in many cases partnered by politicians is too well known to be repeated here. The situation is not much different in other cities and towns. Across the country, in small or big commercial establishments as well as residential buildings, corrupt and vested interests rule the roost. As is obvious by now, it is not the lack of laws that is the problem but their strict implementation without fear or favour.

It is here that the awareness and vigilance of the community at large play a big role. In most residential buildings, industrial estates as well as so-called illegal settlements, there are residents' associations that look after day-to-day affairs. Tapping these bodies would be a first step in raising awareness of safety issues. On the one hand, there must be greater respect for safety norms (sadly lacking across all sections) and on the other, a pressure lobby of citizens that must ensure that politicians in power and the authorities enforce these norms. For this, civil society must come together and agitate. The costs of apathy and indifference are too dear.

16

Schemes for Protection of Labour against Unemployment

The World Bank expert Samuel Liberman, author of the book "Poverty, Employment and Social Sciences" is reported to have observed:

> "High real wage rates in the eighties, backed by protective labour laws making retrenchment difficult have been forcing employers to economize on labor. As a result, despite higher growth rates of the economy, the rate of growth in employment has remained stagnant. The outward looking aggressive industrial strategy for India should consist of deregulation, reduction in incentives for capital intensive industries, permission to close down sick units and hire and fire of labor".

He has also observed that one reason why the Government has not allowed easy retrenchment could be the absence of social security system. He has recommended that Government should improve the quality of Indian labour by spending more on health and education.

These sentiments had been echoed by Indian economists also. In an "Agenda for Economic Reform" drawn up by the four well-known economists P.N. Dhar, I.G. Patel, Narasimhan and R.N. Malhotra, it was stated as follows:-

> "Movement towards a vibrant and competitive economy calls for a new approach to industrial relations and exit policies....our present policies are biased against the use of labour which is abundant and in favor of use of capital which is scarce. Wage policies and wage negotiations are distorted because of undue and unwarranted intervention by the State. We recognize that relaxation of labour market rigidities will take time but we stress that a discernible movement for lowering such rigidities will lead to larger employment and output benefits for the economy, closure of unviable units with adequate provisions for employment, termination benefits and schemes for worker training are a sine qua non for a strong industrial sector".

These arguments have been carried forward by others and certain specific proposals have also been made. Prem Shankar Jha in his article "Reforms: a long long way to go" which appeared in the *Hindu*, on November 20, 1991 had put forth the following proposals:

> "The country, however, needs an exit policy not only for industry but also for labour and salaried employees. And it needs this even more urgently in the public than the private sector. Not till workers and managers become aware that they can lose their jobs if they do not perform the tasks assigned to them will

they begin to exert themselves fully. And not till the government can hold the threat of dismissal or retrenchment over its employee's heads will it get their full co-operation in making the policy changes or achieving the goals that it has set for itself.

The obstacle to an exit policy, whether for sick enterprises or inefficient or redundant workers is the same: in a country with an already alarming level of unemployment, where will the retrenched worker or government employee go? How long will he take to find another job? Will he find another job? And what will happen to him and his family if he doesn't? Small wonder then those trade unions stops at nothing to prevent retrenchment, and political leaders eternally shy away from closing the 225,000 sick units that litter the industrial landscape. This is not politics, but simple humanity.

The solution to the problem must, therefore, also be a human one. It lies in the creation of a comprehensive system of unemployment insurance. The scheme must first cover the entire organized sector of industry and government and, when its managers have acquired sufficient experience, be extended to cover the self-employed and the unorganized sector. The proposal is by no means new. At the annual meeting of the Federation of Indian Chamber of Commerce and Industry in 1990, the outgoing president urged the V.P. Singh Government to consider setting up an unemployment insurance scheme to which employers and employees would contribute one per cent of their gross salaries. The proposal has also been made to the present Government, and is believed to be under consideration.

Such a scheme is long overdue. Despite every effort of the Government and the trade unions to make retrenchment as difficult as possible, between 25,000 and 40,000 workers do get laid off every year. Officials in the Labour Ministry estimate that up to twice that many get retrenched illegally because their employers simply close down their enterprises and disappear. Lastly, large numbers of temporary workers are retrenched without the employers having to go through the elaborate formalities of sacking permanent workers. It is true that most of the workers who are laid off do manage to get other work. But the harsh fact is that under the present supposedly benign system, no one bothers to find out what happens to them when their severance benefits are exhausted.

A steady steam of reports in the daily papers, of mass suicides by entire families, suggests, however, that a very few among them are left with no choice but death. The despair of many others who are not driven to the point of suicide, and therefore do not impinge upon the consciousness of the elite, can easily be imagined. Thus, in a society where the safety net provided by the joint family system is beginning to break down under the pressures of urbanization and destitution, the creation of a social security system cannot be postponed much longer.

But as has been pointed out, unemployment insurance must not be conceived of in this limited way. It must be seen also as an essential catalyst to modernization,

> and efficiency. If that is the goal, its scope must be extended to cover not only the private sector but all employees of the Central, State and local governments. What is more, while initially the number of employees likely to be retrenched every year will not be much larger than it is today, the numbers will rise as modernization gathers momentum and workers and trade unions lose some of their fear of unemployment. Thus, to be on the safe side, the scheme must be tailored to meet the needs of an annual retrenchment of around 400,000 persons.
>
> If the social security contribution of employers, employees and the government is pegged at two per cent of the salary, instead of the one percent suggested by FICCI, and is paid by all the 19million employees in the public sector in addition to the seven million in the organized private sector, the insurance fund will net around Rs. 2,500 crores a year, enough to pay two thirds of the last salary drawn to half a million workers a year of an average unemployment period of two years and still leave a large balance to meet other essential needs such as post-retirement hospitalization insurance. There might even be enough left over to set up a loan fund for retraining and reeducation.
>
> Social security on these lines should not be considered a substitute for the severance benefits that permanent employees in the organized sector now receive. The purpose is not to make sacking of employees easy: only to make it possible without inflicting an unacceptably high cost in human terms.
>
> The fear, often voiced, that the power to lay people off is likely to be abused is also not completely unfounded but the danger can be greatly reduced if the primary responsibility for deciding who is to be laid off is given to administrative tribunals within the executive branch, if the trade unions are represented on the tribunals, and the procedure is kept free of political intervention to the maximum extent possible. What must be borne in mind is that without it there is no way of enforcing accountability for work done and without accountability India will never become a modern nation."

Dr. A. Vaidyanathan in his Dr. John Mathai Memorial Lecture had pointed out another dimension of the problem:

> "A 'safety net' for workers in the organized sector who may lose their jobs in the process of adjustment is on the agenda. But there is hardly any talk of the far more numerous rural wage labour and workers in urban unorganized activities who are relatively worse off, whose jobs and incomes are also at risk and who have neither legislative nor union protection. It is extremely important, at a minimum, to ensure that the employment and anti-poverty programs and access of the poor to the PDS do not get whittled down in the name of fiscal crisis".

Finally, Dr. Manmohan Singh, the then Union Finance Minister accepted the need for developing credible instruments of social security for the workers in the unorganized sector as well as the workers who may be affected by technical change. Inaugurating the Social Security Association of India on December 31, 1991, he stated inter alia:

> "...The need for social security is an established reality in all civilized societies today.
>
> ....A caring society, and any civilized society must aspire to be a caring society, cannot leave those who suffer from these misfortunes to suffer in silence, that society has a responsibility to its unfortunate members to come to their assistance....
>
> ...We have to recognize that the bulk of Indian labour force is to be found in the unorganized sectors. We have millions of our people who have nothing but two bare hands to offer....They have no social security of any kind....Those are the people whose needs of social security have remained unattended thus far, by and large. While we expand, improve the facilities of social security for our industrial workforce we must not forget those millions of our countrymen and women who simply do not come within the ambit of social security legislation that has been devised....
>
> ....Technical change is a fact of life....we cannot survive in a world in which knowledge is growing at such a fast pace without making conscious efforts to absorb, assimilate and adapt this knowledge for improving our living standards. But the process of technical change, howsoever beneficial it might be, is also in some way disruptive. When you introduce new technologies it hurts those who are using techniques of an earlier vintage. There is the problem or the fear of unemployment, loss of jobs. This cannot be wished away. If we want our society to accept the need for technical change then we need credible instruments of social security to ensure that the process of technical change will not impose undue burden on the working classes. We must work towards a society--- which would be a caring society....a society which would ensure as a whole, then the costs of technical change and the costs of adjustment would not be borne exclusively by the working class and that those who have the least capacity to bear these costs are not asked to bear them".

All these statements point to the need for developing appropriate and credible instruments of social security for the people of this country generally and those who may be affected by the process of technical and other changes in the economy in particular. Introduction of an unemployment insurance scheme has been suggested. We have to consider whether that is the only measure that could be thought of or whether any other measure is also necessary and whether all such measures would be feasible.

A Rational System of Social Security for Protection of Workers and their Families

A rational system of social security for protection of workers and their families against loss or diminution of income due to termination of service by superannuation, retirement, retrenchment for no fault of theirs, disability or death would have the following elements:

- Old age pension,
- Survivors benefit or dependants' benefit
- Disability benefit and invalidity benefit
- Terminal benefit or gratuity
- Unemployment insurance
- And Provident Fund.

In addition, a fund to guarantee the payment due to the workers in the event of the failure of the employers to make them at the time of closure or liquidation of an establishment would also be necessary. Medical Benefit, sickness benefit and maternity benefit will be separate.

We are at present concerned with premature termination of service due to retrenchment or closure of establishments. Under the existing laws, provision exists for Payment of Gratuity, pension and Provident fund. There is no provision for or unemployment insurance. Nor is there a wage guarantee fund.

A Scheme for Unemployment Insurance

The system of unemployment benefit is designed to meet situations where the workers have become unemployed involuntarily and lost their earnings. According to ILO, Income Security Recommendation 1944 the Contingency for which unemployment benefit should be paid is loss of earnings due to the unemployment of an insured person who is ordinarily employed capable of regular employment in some occupation, and searching suitable employment or due to part time unemployment. The principle underlying this scheme is that if a person through no fault of his own is deprived of an income consisting of his earning from employment he has a right to expect income support at least for the necessities of life while he remains available for work.

The Industrial Disputes Act provides that a worker who is retrenched due to closure or lay off is entitled to retrenchment compensation at a rate of 15 days' wages for every year of continuous service in addition to gratuity. This is meant to help the workers who are thrown out of employment to maintain themselves until they are able to secure alternative jobs. Unfortunately, however, the establishments, which close down due to financial stringency, would not be able to pay the retrenchment compensation and the provisions of the law, therefore, become inoperative unless a separate provision is made for compulsory insurance against the risk of closure.

A social insurance scheme transfers the uncertainty of the risk from an individual or individual employer to the community and the transfer enhances the welfare of the community as a whole. It is a form of social security, an organized and systematic form of protection against a defined risk, whereby contributions are pooled in a fund from which benefit is paid tot hose experiencing the risk at any time. Contribution income and benefit expenditure are rationally related, solvency is protected and objectivity in paying the benefit ensured that those receiving it are not blamed for having been affected by circumstances, which they could not control.

For the most part, contingencies covered by social security systems are associated with demographic phenomena, such as fertility, marriage, morbidity and mortality. Although these can to some extent be conditioned by economic factors, the main contingencies such as old age, disability etc. can be predicted to an acceptable degree by the application of actuarial techniques. In this respect unemployment is different. It is a contingency, which in effect is imposed upon workers, at best by recessions, which can affect virtually all sectors of labour or single out specific industries affected by a fall in demand for their products or by inability to supply them. This, in turn, might mean singling out specific areas in which those industries are the predominant employers of labor. The impact can be sudden. Moreover, technological, structural and economic changes are inevitable and will cause some unemployment in market economics. In the result the unemployment contingency being essentially economic in origin is not easily predictable. The almost inevitable response of unemployment benefit schemes, in order to preserve their viability, is to define the contingency under which payments have to be made in precise terms to be explicit and often restrictive about coverage the and to attach to the provisions of benefit a variety of controlling and other conditions of which duration of the maximum period during which the benefit can be paid is currently one of the most important.

In 1967, the Government of India drew up a pilot scheme of unemployment insurance to cover workers in the coal mining industry who were members of the coalmines provident fund. An ILO expert from U.K. was invited to examine the scheme and to make suggestions for improving it in the light of experience in countries in which such schemes have been in operation.

The expert had recommended inter-alia that the legislation to establish an employment insurance scheme should confine itself as far as possible, to the provisions concerning general principles and basic legal framework of the scheme bearing technical details to be governed by regulations and rules with a view to ensuring flexibility so that the scheme may be easily adopted to changing social and economic conditions of the country. This is a valuable suggestion. It is , therefore, proposed that the Government may consider bringing forward an enabling legislation with provisions for introduction of separate schemes of unemployment insurance industry-wise. Thus while the legislation will be in general terms there could be a separate scheme for each industry. It is suggested that to begin with the scheme may be introduced in a few industries such as the textile industry.

Coverage: All establishments in the covered industries employing 20 or more persons may be covered under the Act.

All persons who have been in the employment of an establishment for more than one year and drawing wages not exceeding Rs. 2,500 per month including D.A. may be covered. Those who are employed on casual basis or as badlis may not be covered. Persons who suffer from a permanent disability, total or partial as the case may be, and those who are of age exceeding 50 may also not be covered. They may be given appropriate terminal and old age benefits.

Contingency to be covered: A worker who loses employment because of retrenchment for reduction in the workforce, closure of an establishment as defined in the Industrial Disputes Act or because of liquidation of an establishment as defined in Companies Act shall be entitled to unemployment benefit under the Act.

Qualification for the Benefit: The workers should have been in employment with the employer concerned for a minimum period of one year. This is with a view to limit the benefit only to those who are really in regular employment, continuous service for a period of one year being taken as evidence of the permanency of service.

Duration of the Benefit: The unemployment benefit shall be payable up to a period of two years from the date of termination of employment or till the date of commencement of reemployment whichever is earlier.

Rate of Benefit: To begin with the unemployment benefit may be limited to 50 per cent of the wages drawn immediately before the termination of employment for the first year and 25 per cent of the wages last drawn for the second year.

Financing of the Scheme: The ILO Expert had recommended that in view of the scarcity of statistical data on the basis of which the costs of the new scheme can be estimated it is advisable that the basic legislation should not specify the rate of contributions to be paid by the parties concerned and it should leave the specification to regulations to be issued by Government. If this is not technically possible, the basic legislation should confine itself to indicate the range for the maximum and minimum rates of contributions, within which the administrative authority is empowered to fix and modify the rate of contributions to be paid. The cost of this scheme depends not only upon the rates of duration of the benefit, waiting period and qualifying condition, but also upon the administrative set up of the scheme.

It is felt that in schemes of this kind it is advisable that the workers as well as the employers should make contributions. Workers involved in the scheme through contributions will help to minimize the incidence of unemployment and the benefit payment to be made.

Keeping these facts in view it is proposed that the legislation may provide for payment of contribution by the employers as well as he workers at the rate to be specified by Government by notification in the official gazette but not exceeding

5 per cent of the wages, which may be defined in the Act. The employers will contribute 2 per cent of the wages and the employees will contribute 1.5 per cent of the wages.

As large-scale unemployment may occur due to change of policy on the part of the Government it would be in fitness of things if the Government can also share the cost of the scheme. The Government of India may also, therefore, contribute an amount equal to 1.5 per cent of the wages.

The term 'wages' may be defined for purpose of the scheme in the same way as under the ESI Act.

In addition, the employers may be required to pay to the organization administering the scheme the amount of retrenchment compensation they are liable to pay under the Industrial Disputes Act.

The cost of administration of the scheme may be borne by the Government. Claims arising during the first year after commencement of a scheme pending accumulation of funds by way of contributions may be met by the Government of India out of an earmarked fund such as the National Renewal Fund either on loan or grant basis

Administration: There are two alternatives:

The Government of India may administer the scheme through the EPF organization or the ESIC which has a record of the coverable establishments, a system of collection of contributions under various schemes and a network of offices through which payments can be made. This will be an agency function the cost of which may be borne by the Government.

The Government of India may prepare the schemes but their administration may be entrusted to the appropriate Governments. In that case each State Governments may set up a separate Social Security Authority, which may administer the scheme along with other Social Security type of schemes introduced by it such as old age pension scheme.

Implementation of the Scheme: In order to ensure successful implementation of the schemes it is desirable to hold tripartite consultations before launching the same. It is, therefore, proposed that a separate tripartite committee may be set up for each industry covered under the law for advising the Government on the implementation of the scheme.

Terminal Benefit

The ILO Recommendation No. 119 concerning Termination of employment at the initiative of the employer requires that some form of income protection should be provided for workers whose employment has been terminated and that such protection may include unemployment insurance or other forms of social security or severance allowances or other types of separation benefits paid for by the employer or a combination of benefits.

The Indian laws provide for payment of retrenchment compensation as well as gratuity. There is a further safeguard in cases of establishments employing more than 100 persons that prior permission of the Government should be obtained before retrenchment of any worker. This permission is rarely given and this fact is regarded as an element of rigidity in the labour laws. A proposal has recently been mooted that the requirement of seeking prior permission of Government may be done away with by prescribing a higher rate of gratuity and/or retrenchment compensation.

Index